The Third Sector

The Third Sector

Community Organizations, NGOs, and Nonprofits

MEGHAN ELIZABETH KALLMAN
TERRY NICHOLS CLARK

With assistance from CARY WU
and JEAN YEN-CHUN LIN

University of Illinois Press
URBANA, CHICAGO, AND SPRINGFIELD

Library of Congress Control Number: 2016948563
ISBN 978-0-252-04043-6 (hardcover)
ISBN 978-0-252-09885-7 (e-book)

*This book is dedicated to the activists,
volunteers, and employees that comprise
the third sector worldwide.*

Contents

List of Illustrations   ix

Acknowledgments   xi

Introduction: Democratic Governance and
Institutional Logics within the Third Sector
(or, How Habermas Discovered the Coffee House)   1

1. Civil Society, Social Capital, and the Growth
    of the Third Sector   37

2. The United States   68

3. France   105

4. Japan   124

5. South Korea   141

6. Taiwan   155

7. China   169

8. Looking Forward: Understanding Associations
    and Trust Patterns   191

    Conclusion: Global Themes   213

References   227

Index   249

List of Illustrations

Figures

1. Average years of total schooling for individuals aged 15+ in selected countries, 1950–2010   30
2. Factors contributing to the rise of the New Political Culture   47
3. Source of third sector contribution to GDP vs. other factors in seven countries   48
4. Civil society organization workforce as a share of the economically active population, by country, 1995–2000   49
5. Employment in the nonprofit sector vs. selected industries, 2010   70
6. Nonprofit employment, 45 states and District of Columbia, by field, 2010   70
7. Comparison of attitudes toward capitalism and the market economy in six nations   117
8. Source of civil society organization revenue in South Korea   148
9. Expenditures for Children Are Us Foundation   166
10. Income for Children Are Us Foundation   167
11. Founding year of associations in nine selected regions of China   175
12. The development of associations in China, 2001–2010   177
13. The development of foundations in China, 2001–2010   177
14. National giving levels as percentage of GDP   178
15. Chinese philanthropy development, 2011   178
16. Number of Chinese Internet users and Internet penetration rate, 2004–2011   186

17. Registered governmental Weibos, 2012   187
18. Membership in associations in the six profiled countries,
    as a percentage of total population   201
19. Variations in cultural activities, 1981–2000   202
20. Total organizations by type in France and the United States   203

Tables

1. Contribution to GDP, NPOs vs. other industries, by country   48
2. Civil society sector full-time exempt workforce, by field,
    33 countries   50
3. Third sector sources of support, with and without volunteers,
    34 countries   51
4. Growth in registered public charities over time   80
5. Change in foundation gifts received, 1978–2008   83
6. Financing resources of NGOs in Mainland China, 1998   181
7. Response to the question: Would you join an environmental
    social organization?   185
8. Response to the question: Are you currently a member of a
    social group, club, or other organization?   185
9. National differences in association membership, 2005–2008,
    as a percentage of total population   200
10. Descriptive statistics for key variables used in analysis,
    2005–2008   205
11. Descriptive statistics for six countries (mean), 2005–2008   206
12. Logit models predicting the effect of organization membership
    on trust   208
13. Logit models predicting the effect of organization membership
    on social trust   209
14. Logit models predicting the effect of organization membership
    on political trust   210
15. Response to the question: Having encountered something unfair,
    which department would you want to turn to?   215

Acknowledgments

We gratefully acknowledge assistance from Xia Jianzhong and the Chinese Ministry of Commerce, undergraduate student research assistants Predrag Pandiloski, Andrea Wistuba Behrens, Maxine Frendel, and Samuel Braxton, support from the Scenes Project at the University of Chicago, as well as input from anonymous reviewers.

The Third Sector

Introduction

Democratic Governance and Institutional Logics within the Third Sector (or, How Habermas Discovered the Coffee House)

It would be well to infuse political life into each portion of the
territory, in order to multiply to an infinite extent opportunities
of acting in concert for all the members of the community, and to
make them constantly feel their mutual dependence on each other
. . . if the object be to have the local affairs of a district conducted
by the men who reside there, the same persons are always in
contact, and they are, in a manner, forced to be acquainted, and to
adapt themselves to one another.
—Alexis de Tocqueville

CSOs (civil society organizations), NPOs (nonprofit organizations),
NGOs (nongovernmental organizations), INGOS (international nongovernmental organizations), and formal and informal associations are part of an
important, relatively new sector that is now a world political force. Though
the components of this "third sector" vary by country, their net effect is increasingly important across the globe. This third sector plays a critical role
in creating values worldwide, through its work in service delivery, advocacy,
cultural programs, and social movements. The third sector includes different
types of relief and welfare organizations, innovation organizations, public
service organizations, economic development organizations, grassroots mobilization groups, advocacy groups, and social networks (J. Clark 1991:40–41).

This book is an international comparison of third sectors. It builds on
recent work on the origins, dynamics, and effects of civil society in different
parts of the world; we include the political-historical background and third
sector interactions with state institutions, as well as analysis of how those
dynamics vary by region. We then examine functions, impacts, and composition of the nonprofit sector for six key countries.

Foundational differences in religious and political tradition across these different countries create different types of meanings for third sector organizations. Contexts shift drastically, internationally and over time. A children's art group, for example, means something very different in a wealthy Los Angeles suburb than in a poor Lima neighborhood. Chinese civic organizations, for example, follow the predominantly Asian model of being funded largely by government and are linked to goals of national politics. This contrasts with Western experience of the third sector, which has often explicitly challenged government objectives. Most existing studies are of one or a few countries; moving to a global perspective adds considerable insights in highlighting variations and offers policy options of borrowing across national systems. We hope in this book to encourage others to look more sensitively at different national systems.

This study began at an invitation from the Chinese government in 2009 and was published in Mandarin in 2011. This English version incorporates new material for a more global audience, emphasizing the presence of different institutional logics born of different cultural traditions and historical trajectories. The book's history thus led to a national policy-oriented perspective informing the broader theoretical observations below. As such, it is our hope that it constitutes a useful guide for a wide variety of audiences, ranging from policymakers who may find it useful to locate their work within a broader context, to academics looking for a comparative frame to situate their own scholarship, to third sector practitioners, who may find reflections and insights germane to their careers.

We begin with questions of legitimacy and trust that have affected leadership in recent decades. As the conflicting and conflating forces of neoliberalism, egalitarianism, and globalization have interacted uneasily with traditional models of leadership and citizen participation, leaders around the world have sought to counter negative impacts of such unsettled culture through projects of participation, decentralization, and associationalism. Where and why do these work or fail? There is much to learn by reviewing successes and failures globally.

Our introduction offers new theoretical perspectives on how different types of participation can increase generalized trust and state legitimacy, and more importantly, how the different institutional logics within the third sector articulate globally. We progress through cross-national comparisons to specific elements of these different third sectors. Chapters 2–7 examine the development and infrastructure of the nonprofit sectors in the United States, France, Japan, Korea, Taiwan, and China, respectively.

Chapter 8 examines legitimacy and trust by analyzing membership in different *types* of social organizations. Some of the trust discussion addresses how leaders in different political situations can marshal trust in the name of governance; thus decentralized, associations are a potentially apt policy solution for a place like China, wherein leaders are deeply concerned with legitimacy. Interestingly, certain parts of the third sector in the United States have been moving more toward explicit coordination with (indeed, often via subcontract) the federal or state governments. Such a shift changes the dynamic of the third sector considerably, moving it away from an "independent sector" and more toward a position of third-party governance. Does this enhance or weaken trust among US citizens? We report original data analyses on these points in chapter 8. The conclusion analyzes some of the regional and national differences between third sectors, discussing how the different dynamics of third sectors may lead to different political outcomes more broadly.

Generally speaking, the countries examined fall into one of two categories: those with a strong central state and—we argue, consequently—a weaker involvement of third sector organizations in some regards, and those comparatively "weak" national governments with historically strong third sector organizations. These differences have important implications for current policy debate and changes of the third sector in each country. Countries with historically weak state involvement (like the United States) often have a third sector that began as an independent sector and more recently has moved closer to government. Countries with strong state traditions (like China and Japan) generally have had a government-linked third sector and more recently diversified to include more advocacy-oriented activities. As these two categories move toward one another, participants can learn from one another, if one recognizes these broad policy shifts and looks for cross-national lessons.

Often referred to as the "nonprofit" sector, the third sector is ironically characterized by a relative failure to settle on a common definition of what, precisely, it is, and where its boundaries lie. Technically and philosophically, the third sector itself has undergone variations in nomenclature worldwide. Five crucial features of third sector organizations have been widely identified in the literature (see Salamon, Hems, and Chinnock 2000:8). Fundamentally, the third sector can be conceptualized as a set of entities that is composed of *organizations that are self-governing, do not distribute profit, are primarily private and nongovernmental* in basic structure, and are *meaningfully voluntary*, thus likely to engage constituents on the basis of shared interest. This definition we follow throughout the book.[1]

Case Selection

We selected as our cases the United States, France, Korea, Taiwan, Japan, and China. Korea, Taiwan, China, and Japan were chosen for their regional and cultural similarities; what Przeworski and Teune (2001) might call "most similar systems." The United States was included because it has the most comprehensive body of nonprofit tax law in the world, and one of the better-supported third sectors in terms of infrastructure. It also stands in sharp contrast to some of the other cases, given its notoriously weak state and its long history of using associations to augment services in the face of state shortcomings. We selected France as a comparison both because of its strong third sector—similar to the United States—but also because of its marked difference from the United States in questions of state power and centralization. Where the United States has a famously difficult time accomplishing anything on a national level, the French Napoleonic tradition and highly effective, hierarchical centralized state history provides an interesting contrast.

We also follow Przeworski and Teune's (2001 [1970]) method of selecting variables that are thought to be similar across various social and political systems. That is, we examine some key common processes (like fundraising) but probe how they shift across national boundaries. Our comparisons thus include, for each country, an overview of background and political and institutional context, an outline of formal and legal design of third sector organizations, a series of case studies that serve to illustrate some of these dynamics, and a brief discussion on the challenges and future paths for each of these third sectors.

These questions—of how the state interacts with other, nonstate actors in the third sector, of how social movements become institutionalized into NGOs, and how governments use associations either to bolster their own images or to accomplish goals—are very new animals in most of the world. They are classically undertheorized by political philosophers. The third sector as it is commonly known has its roots in an Anglo-Saxon tradition that only arrived on the general theoretical map with the publication of Alexis de Tocqueville's seminal *Democracy in America*.

Some recent work, however, has taken up these relationships between third sector organizations and the state. Da Silva's (2010) book on the rise of the welfare state theorized the United States as normatively "behind" the rest of the Western world because it lacked a welfare state—in the United States, the third sector has always been an excuse to neither more fully develop nor continue centralized welfare policies, particularly since the decline of Keynesianism. The political right has classically invoked civic groups as a reason *not* to fund state agencies. The end of communism in 1989 brought out a drastic drop in the hierarchy of the state, and neoliberalization processes have brought about a new political emphasis on third sector organizations as the central state shrinks, and policy work is "rescaled" (Brenner 2009) to municipal governments and civil society organizations (Castree 2008, 2010).

And these transformations have been powerful. Jürgen Habermas himself, a political philosopher most famous for his work on the public sphere, went from being a Frankfort Marxist to a student of civil society in the late twentieth century. He began to theorize how the potential of this sort of discursive, "coffee house model" of associationalism could serve as the basis for extra-state democratic engagement and participation in general. His work on the public sphere expanded to include theories of a "post-national constellation" (Habermas 2001)—a public sphere for the globalized world, or an international civil society. For both Habermas and da Silva, Mead's influence is visible: participation is necessarily constituted *in communication with another*. It cannot be done alone. Mead's well-known distinction between the "I" and the "me" only becomes possible in the context of another person, which suggests communicative action. That is, this type of participation is generated through horizontal *inter*action, rather than from the Horkheimer/Adorno model of hierarchy. Habermas joins Horkheimer and Adorno's model of hierarchical interaction with the US egalitarian tradition, illustrating this civic mix with the example of the English coffee house. Here begins a more contemporary version of thinking on the building of citizenship through participatory organizations, a tradition with which we engage through the remainder of this book.

Deep Structures of the Third Sector: Religious Traditions, Organizational Impulses

The classic starting point for discussions of organizations and associations is Alexis de Tocqueville's *Democracy in America*, first published in 1835. He and other French leaders were then fearful of what the impending French democracy might entail, and a leading French advisory group sent Tocqueville to investigate crime in the United States, which broadened into a study of how democracy functioned. The United States was chosen as a young society wherein democracy had started recently after colonization, and where there was minimal tradition associated with older Western economic and political arrangements. Tocqueville spent several months traveling around the United States talking to citizens about their society and civic activities, seeking commentary on a broad range of social, economic, and political practices. The result was *Democracy in America*, a project that intended to find lessons on associationalism and democracy in general to bring back to Europe and France.

Tocqueville's original conclusion was that local organized groups were one of the most critical building blocks of the entire US society. These organizations were one of the most distinctively non-European aspects of America, important primarily because they and their participants were separate and autonomous from the state and from higher-level political officials. Tocqueville stressed how, in the United States, the "engaged citizen" was really quite an average person in most instances. In the process of participating in these small civic groups, average citizens created new services, new social arrangements, and during that process, *they themselves were transformed*. As they planned the construction of churches or worked together on projects, citizens learned to trust their neighbors more; they learned to serve as leaders themselves, temporarily or for long periods of time. Neighborhood groups brought together average persons, fostering feelings of pride and commitment for having completed a specific task jointly and successfully. Consider this passage from *Democracy in America*:

> The legislators of America did not suppose that a general representation of the whole nation would suffice to ward off a disaster [despotism] at once so natural to the frame of democratic society, and so fatal: they also thought that it would be well to infuse political life into each portion of the territory, in order to multiply to an infinite extent opportunities of acting in concert for all the members of the community, and to make them constantly feel their mutual dependence on each other . . . if the object be to have the local affairs of a district conducted by the men who reside there, the same persons are always in contact, and they are, in a manner, forced to be acquainted, and to adapt themselves to one another. (1969:126)

Importantly, in the United States, some of the most salient of these original third sector groups were small churches, representative of the many branches of Protestantism that split apart during the early years of US history as a formally independent nation. Protestantism's influence on poverty and civic life generally emerged in both Europe and the United States in local-level organizations (Kahl 2005), with their focus on providing food, clothing, and basic necessities, rather than with systemic political advocacy or agitation. The little churches were highly competitive with one another, and their independence was an especially important point in New England (a region that had been founded primarily on concerns for religious freedom and was highly politically participatory). By contrast, the southern United States had a comparatively hierarchical social structure, and its civic groups were much less visible.

In addition to Protestantism, there are several fundamental traditions that have helped structure the development of organizational life (and consequently the third sector) in the United States and in Western Europe. These traditions come from the European context and deserve separate consideration; these religious roots affect the third sector across the globe today.

One tradition is Lutheranism (the sect following the sixteenth-century German Protestant reformer Martin Luther). Luther broke with the Roman Catholic Church in the early sixteenth century but nevertheless managed to find converts in many of the central European countries that had been Roman Catholic for centuries. Under Luther, the idea of the "undeserving" poor emerged—those who were able-bodied but unwilling to work—and notions of individual responsibility took hold (Kahl 2005:103). Despite his radically different perspective, Luther succeeded in part because he was a good compromiser; he involved political leaders in choosing many of the church leaders, and he did not approve the appointment of church leaders that were critical of the state. That is, he trod a delicate line between dissent and cooperation—one could see parallels between this approach and contemporary third sector organizations working in a close and politically cooperative relationship with strong state leaders. Many of these current third sector organizations are highly attuned to the (sometimes conflicting) demands of their governing bodies, the state, and their constituents; they embody an institutional logic of activism, operate within certain domains, and choose their political battles carefully. The success of Martin Luther is certainly worth attending to, as Lutheranism's spread had tremendous subsequent impacts not only on religious, but also on cultural development throughout both Western Europe and North America.

Calvinism is the other major European religious tradition that has had powerful effects on traditions of associationalism. John Calvin broke with the overwhelmingly hierarchical tradition of French Roman Catholicism as a young priest. He migrated to Switzerland, where he found many followers, who in turn spread Calvinism to the Netherlands, Scotland, parts of Scandinavia, and New England. Calvinists were critically different from the Lutherans and the Roman Catholics in their organizational structure; they employed a bottom-up rather than a top-down principle of organization and governance, captured in the principle of "sovereignty in one's own social circles" (Cox 1993:64), and the role of the state in this sort of framework was to encourage spontaneity in private life by affording private groups sufficient space in which to operate. According to Calvin, poor relief should be part of the Church's purview rather than the state's, and therefore Calvinism encouraged a great deal of private charity (Kahl 2005). The average Calvinist church member was a direct participant in church leadership, because congregations selected church leaders. The "aldermen"—as they were termed in the Netherlands, for instance, and as they are known in the United States today—were responsible to their parishioners in a manner that is much more like contemporary democracy than like the vertical relationship between a Roman Catholic priest and his "flock."[2] Indeed, contemporary democracy has strong Calvinist components, which have increased in visibility and salience in the last years of the twentieth century.[3] The Calvinist Church was the classic bottom-up model of the organized group in Western society, that of the active citizen, and many activist third sector organizations.

This Calvinist tendency toward bottom-up organization manifested itself in many ways, (dramatically so in Switzerland, which did not develop a national government but rather remained a federation of highly autonomous communes). For instance, in the unequal society of Europe from the Middle Ages onward, it was generally expected that the poor would steal from the rich. The general answer to such a problem was to deal with the poor as criminals, locking them into prisons or poorhouses. The Calvinist Dutch, by contrast, consistent with their principles of sovereignty, dealt with their poor differently: each was assigned a family and adopted as an extended family member. The ethic of predestination within Calvinism held that the poor are sinners and the rich are not; it implied that the poor needed to be punished and corrected (Kahl 2005). These communities felt religiously and morally compelled to help the person who had sinned against society either by formal crime or by the crime of poverty (see also Weber 2008), and through their counsel, the sinner returned to obedience to the rules of God and to upstanding church membership. Bracketing for a moment the problematic conflation of poverty and deviance, we can nonetheless see that this approach had widespread impact: the rates of crime were minimal in the Netherlands in the sixteenth century such that it was possible for women to walk alone at night in cities like Amsterdam.

In the eighteenth and early nineteenth centuries in regions of England, the churches and associated civic groups, similarly to the Dutch, sought to address the problems confronting the poor and new industrial workers who had recently left their farms. Farmers had driven peasants off the land in an era when selling wool brought a better return, and vast farm areas of Scotland and England were thus transformed into market-oriented industrial farming regions. This in turn drove peasants to the new manufacturing towns of Manchester and Glasgow. There was great concern, of course, about crime and possible revolution in these newly industrializing areas. But serious uprisings were minimal, in part due to this tradition of civic and political participation. By contrast, similar social and economic problems were found in continental Europe, including in Germany, Italy, and France; in those cases peasants revolted, crime was rampant, and there was more commonly talk of class warfare. The patterns of conflict and accommodation that were reached by these groups are interesting to briefly consider: these examples suggest that local-level associations can potentially serve as integrating mechanisms for dangerous or dislocated individuals.

Even today we can see the impact of this sort of Calvinist approach to governance and participation. This story of bottom-up accountability and associational structure is essentially what Tocqueville observed with respect to New England civic life. Associationalism has been labeled American; however, later work has shown that it was more fundamentally Calvinist and not uniquely or even most powerfully American (Gorski 2003)—Tocqueville could have found a more pure version of his democracy story if he had gone to parts of Switzerland and the Netherlands and probed the workings of Calvinist institutions and churches there. We would do well to consider the reverberations that continue from these traditions until today.

Neoliberalism and the New Political Culture

The conservative turn in the West took hold in the early 1970s and spurred the transformation of centralized state social services to an intersectoral social service design such as that which we know today. There are two components of liberalism: the fiscal and the social. For many scholars of political economy, the past four decades have been characterized by "neoliberalism": a theoretical treatment that handles the effects of fiscal conservatism and relates it to social outcomes. Theorists of neoliberalism have provided compelling accounts of the ways that neoliberal fiscal policies have created reverberating social policies, particularly in questions of scale (Brenner 2001, 2009; Brenner, Peck, and Theodore 2010), and regarding the relationship of the state to the market and to polity.

The term "neoliberalism" was originally developed by the German scholar Alexander Rüstow at the Colloque Walter Lippmann (Boas and Gans-Morse 2009). Originally, neoliberalism was defined as "the priority of the price mechanism, the free enterprise, the system of competition and a strong and impartial state" (Mirowski and Plehwe 2009:13–14). The term has been popular in discussing areas like Eastern Europe and Latin America; for example, Chile's military rule under Augusto Pinochet (1973–90).

Neoliberalism refers broadly to the set of policies originally enacted in the United States and the UK (and subsequently adopted throughout the world) since the late 1970s and the decline of Keynesianism. It is characterized by the widespread subordination of productive sectors to financial concerns; by a massive reduction of the role of the national state, including increasing privatization of formerly state-run directives (such as welfare; state intervention and regulation is seen as distorting the market) and devolution from the national level to the state or municipal levels; by the lifting of capital barriers between countries to facilitate transnational transactions; and by increasing concern for property rights, a key factor in the market logic of deregulation. In the last two decades neoliberalism has come to suggest a market fundamentalism that embodies laissez-faire principles. The term "neoliberalism" has been used by scholars as a means of denaturalizing globalization processes and simultaneously calling attention to their associated ideological and political implications (Peck, Theodore, and Brenner 2010:97).

But the left-right distinction, upon which such analyses of neoliberalism depend, works less well for the social dimension of liberalism, which is driven more by education than by markets. And while some policies—like interest rates—are more "purely fiscal," there is meaningful social content in most public policies, and within neoliberalism, there is room to analyze differences of approach. Our point is simply that the conservative ideologies summoned by the image of "neoliberalism" as a term are too one-dimensional. If we introduce the social content of such policies within the neoliberal economic paradigm—ranging from women's rights to abortion to class solidarity—we can analyze these social transformations more precisely.

In particular, we stress the ways that classic fiscal conservatives (like Reagan or Thatcher) differ profoundly from Bill Clinton or Tony Blair. Both Clinton and Blair were more socially liberal, even though their fiscal policies were conservative compared to those advocated by the left. Clinton and Blair illustrate the unique blend of fiscal conservatism and social liberalism, sometimes dubbed the "New Political Culture" (T. Clark and Hoffmann-Martinot 1998). We explore the explicit ideological conflicts among proponents of these two new dimensions (previously labeled "liberal" and "conservative") and multiple ways of joining them, below. We note here simply that when one shifts from government to third sector organizations, the "purity" of ideology and distinctive types of institutional logics can grow more salient and differentiated as there are far more organizations than governments. Third sector organizations, like local governments, can thus contribute to deeper understandings of national and global processes by virtue of the greater range and diversity they illustrate. Third sector analysis can correspondingly build on related insights about political and cultural transformations, national and especially local. This New Political Culture created a new set of social and economic conditions that helped spark the global rise of nonprofits, which has been analyzed with data for thousands of local governments and neighborhoods (Silver and Clark 2016; T. Clark et al. 2014) in related work to date.

The nonprofit sector across the world grew rapidly after the 1980s, and inevitably, it bears the markings of a combination of factors that have helped engender that growth. Some are shared globally. But there are also important national institutional components that shifted how the third sector took shape. A variety of pressures stemming from government, civil, and other kinds of social configurations all act on the third sector. A major theme of this book is to identify and explore the dynamics of some of these pressures, and how they shape third sector organizations cross-nationally.

Institutional Logics in the Third Sector

We think about these pressures in terms of institutional logics. Institutional logics (Alford and Friedland 1985; Friedland and Alford 1991; Fligstein 1987) are an organizational-sociological concept that illustrates how socially constructed belief systems shape people's cognition and behavior in a given environment. Thornton and Ocasio (1999:804) define them as "the socially constructed, historical patterns of practices, assumptions, values, beliefs, and rules by which individuals produce and reproduce their material subsistence, organize time and space, and provide meaning to their social reality." They are important organizational characteristics, defining the "desirable," setting up norms and values, and mediating meaning within an organization. Institutional logics are intertwined with the construction of social identities; those identities then reinforce participants' positions as stakeholders and their associated discourse (Creed, Scully, and Austin 2002).

Our approach—using institutional logics to study the third sector—is distinct from Jeffery C. Alexander's (1997, 2006) neo-Hegelianism, which emphasizes solidarity and a deterministic collective mechanism across the entire third sector; our study suggests that such solidarity is less common than a fragmented, pluralistic, and semi-professionalized industry. We instead show multicausality, different cases of countries, and organizations within them that follow different and conflicting rules. This shifts the focus to interpret these differences, for which our institutional logics are key.

We are distinct as well from one-country studies, which dominate the research and writing on third sector organizations (see Ljubownikow and

Crotty 2014; Stride and Higgs 2014). Similarly, our analytical approach is distinct from the empiricism of Almond and Verba (1989) and Putnam (2000), as well as from those who deny cultural interpretations, and most importantly, from the general descriptive perspective in much of the nonprofit literature that does not ask why the third sector exists at all, but rather focuses on its specifics (see Salamon, Hems, and Chinnock 2000; Salamon 2002).

The omission of culture specifically can lead scholars to think and write as if the morality of the Old Testament and Calvin, and the moral ground on which the activists stand and critique capitalism and the foundation managers, do not exist (or if they exist, are false consciousness). Yet many activists are informed by moralistic concerns (Gross 1997; Kallman 2015), and we and others have used that moralism to interpret the core tensions among third sector volunteers, managers, funders, and others (T. Clark and Hoffmann-Martinot 1998). This perspective, which privileges the cultural underpinnings of nonprofit organization, shows how this moralism is an ethical battleground over legitimacy throughout the third sector.

Our approach stresses the sources of cross-national and cross-organizational variation, and we develop distinctive tools to join past and present via the concept of institutional logics and, more broadly, the historical roots of current policy discussion, including key conflicts.

This project has unearthed five basic institutional logics operating simultaneously within the third sector. Their combined presences create tensions, synergies, and unevenness that can be seen in different proportions in civil societies across the globe. These logics are present to different degrees in different places, but are present in all the countries we have studied here. The five institutional logics are:

- Clientelism
- Paternalism
- Bureaucracy
- Activism
- Professionalism

At times, some of these logics emerge into a hybrid sort of approach that we examine on a case-by-case basis. Here we take each logic one by one to outline its components and its theoretical contours.

Clientelism

The first institutional logic present within the third sector is *clientelism*. Clientelism and patronage refer to the "trade of votes and other types of partisan support in exchange for public decisions with divisible benefits" (Piattoni 2001:4). Clientelist polities are those in which particular interests are promoted at the expense of the general interest. Political clientelism and patronage are typically understood as cultural phenomena: a reflection within the political sphere of a certain way of understanding interpersonal relationships between those with power and those without it. In other words, clientelism is a strategy for acquiring or increasing political power on the part of the patrons and for protecting and promoting interests on the part of the clients; the incentives and disincentives to engage in clientelism are structural. In other words, clientelism is a structural feature of a given political setup, shaped by political institutions and historical circumstances (Piattoni 2001:2).

Clientelism emerges in the third sector primarily in terms of financial support that is exchanged for political favors. As a Chicago alderman, for example, one might give money to an influential person's pet charity, thereby hoping to win that person's support, especially for reelection. Clientelism has long been the foundation of most politics globally, but it has come under attack in recent decades as globalization processes and social movements have brought about new emphases on transparency. Critics have used the media and international organizations to bring out scandals and variously seek to change the clientelist rules of the game that have long governed political relationships across the world.

Paternalism

The second institutional logic that is widely identifiable within the third sector we term *paternalism*. Paternalism is behavior that limits the autonomy or decision-making power of individuals or entities for their own good; it describes a relationship in which one entity's choice is insufficiently voluntary to be genuinely considered her own. Paternalism, unlike clientelism, is not a relationship that is meant to produce material or power benefits for a certain group, but rather an approach that emphasizes the condescending nature of interactions between the powerful and the powerless.

Dynamics of paternalism are deeply implicated in charity historically. Indeed, the very notion of noblesse oblige suggests that privilege entails responsibility; those who are fortunate are required to aid those who are understood as less so. Individual paternalistic support could be leveraged though charitable organizations. And it was often upper-status persons, especially women, who showed their personal kindness on a one-to-one basis with the poor by volunteering in hospitals, churches, and social agencies. Interestingly, Tocqueville characterized the organizations providing such services as distinctly democratic when he saw them in America in the 1830s, but not in his native France.

The nineteenth- and early twentieth-century British and American models of such paternalism spread globally in the late twentieth century. Paternalism moved beyond the individual, expanded though benevolent or charity organizations, and gave distinctive character to locations where they were more widespread, like British and American cities in the late nineteenth century. This sort of benevolent voluntarism included conceptual ideals and pointed to role models that responded to the Protestant call to do "good works": "voluntarism was the social currency which bound antebellum communities together, nurturing a sense of communal spirit and constantly renewing public commitment to community wellbeing" (McCarthy 1982:4). Volunteers work, and society praises them for reaching out beyond their own spheres. In other words, charity was attached to social prestige, but the self-defined driver was not prestige but "doing good." Critics have long pointed out that more is involved in charity than simply "doing good," building on ideas such as the classic Marxist concept of "false consciousness" (extended by Adorno, Gramsci, Foucault, Bourdieu, and others).

The institutional logic of paternalism appears contemporarily in private practices of philanthropy, particularly in small family foundations that are managed by individuals or family members of wealthy individuals who create and manage the foundations themselves. In many cases these foundations continue to be administered by people with no expertise other than their own wealth. The accountability structures for this kind of third sector work were historically few, and family foundations in the United States served as both tax havens and as sites of social prestige among wealthy individuals.

Bureaucracy

The third institutional logic that we identify is *bureaucracy*. Especially in the European and Asian contexts, the national state incarnates centralized bureaucratic power. The central state in many places traditionally resisted the "private" initiatives of the third sector, as it often sought monopolistic control of fundamental social policies. Some trace this emphasis on a unified central state to the desire for military preparedness. However, in the globally important French case, the monopolistic state bureaucracy was legitimated by a combination of principles of liberty, equality, and fraternity after the 1789 Revolution. Its republican logic drove the state to impose limits against its classic enemies (in this case the Church and the royal/aristocratic legacy). This fraternal impulse that created the state, ironically, left no space for a third sector, which was legally prohibited in much of nineteenth-century France and was similarly weak in Asia. But as education and incomes have risen, unskilled labor declined, and media and travel increased, the hierarchy of the central state in France has come under attack. After the political uprisings of 1968, demands for more democracy by average citizens rose, leading to the subsequent logic of activism.

An institutional logic of bureaucracy continues to articulate within the third sector as these organizations learn to negotiate power sharing and responsibilities in conjunction with local or national arms of government around the world.

Activism

A fourth institutional logic in the third sector we call *activism*, primarily seen among the grassroots organizations and volunteers who are impatient with the bureaucratic constraints of their institutional contexts and who are more open to using contentious practices to further their goals. Those operating under this kind of institutional logic often call on the language and tactics of social movements to make sense of their own participation. The activist frame of many social movement and collective action discourses strongly values qualities of individual charisma, leadership, and flexibility. These are "informal networks based on shared beliefs and solidarity which mobilize around conflictual issues and deploy frequent and varying forms of protest" (Della Porta and Diani 1999:16). If clientelism and paternalism are centuries old, activism enters seriously after the 1968 student uprisings in the West, which subsequently spread globally.

This activist logic typically shows up in smaller or more grassroots organizations, formal and informal. Take the experience of one employee, who works for a small social justice organization:

> I had this "conversion experience" [. . .] and it was clear from that moment forward that I needed to be doing something with my life, which was bringing more justice to the world. I didn't know what that meant at the time, but as I explored that and this and that organization, I came to be hooked up with [my social justice organization] pretty shortly after that. (Kallman 2013:59)

The institutional logic of activism matches easily with a small, fluid organization of volunteers, where the entire organization feels itself to be part of an ongoing social movement, rather than organizational employees. But it can also penetrate the staff and programs of churches, foundations, big social agencies, and even some government agencies where some staff may be appointed—or understand themselves—as trying to make traditional institutions less bureaucratic and more activist. They may seek allies with others outside the organization. For example in China after 2000, some Beijing ministry staff encouraged local protests, even if these were opposed by other national ministries.

Amateurs' activism is often contrasted with a professional side of management. The activists are often more amateur in the sense that they may be volunteers, working without pay. What, then, drives them? It is often their commitment to values, particularly egalitarianism, manifesting through such specific concerns as human rights, feminism, environmentalism, and anti-poverty efforts. They are often driven to advance these values in opposition to those who resist them (Capital, The State, The Man, The Establishment, or Neoliberalism). The distinction between amateurs and professionals has been used to interpret many past political battles (see, for example, *The Amateur Democrat* [Wilson 1962] or Trounstine [2008] on professional political monopolies). We stress the critical role of volunteers in responding to natural disasters in our chapters on China, Korea, and Taiwan, where there has been a huge increase in voluntarism since the end of the twentieth century. Voluntarism in Asian countries has often been less explicitly linked to movements than in the West, but it does share a broad and strong commitment to humanistic values and helping those most in need.

These volunteers illustrate the distinct characteristics shared by many activists within the third sector. They are by-and-large youthful, well-educated, idealistic, and value-driven liberal/left persons who bring a serious commitment to third sector issues. This demographic group takes on more importance as democracy, education, human rights, individualism, and related social and political values are codified internationally (T. Clark and Hoffmann-Martinot 1998). The new technologies widely available in the last sixty years, ranging from television to cell phones to social media and Internet calls, have helped this kind of activist organize more quickly and fluidly and evade some of the constraints that states imposed.

Professionalization

The fifth and most novel institutional logic that appears within the third sector is *professionalization*. The process of professionalization involves transforming a job into a skilled profession, typically implying the establishment of accepted qualifications, professional norms, industry standards, professional bodies, and training programs. Professionalization as a term, first explored in depth by Carr-Saunders and Parsons in the 1930s, later Wilensky (1964), refers to a technical, systematic knowledge of something, as well as the presence of professional norms within any given occupation. These norms are defined by professional associations, not the state or the foundation leadership. This professionalization, within the field of foundations and funding, is a relatively new phenomenon and has increased dramatically in recent decades, generating a "program professional," who is an expert in a particular field of social policy, moving between government agencies, community organizations, foundations, and universities (McCarthy and Zald 1977b; Wilensky 1964). The development of the foundation "program professional" has been encouraged by the institutionalization of dissent within mainstream US society: "as a result of the massive growth in funding, it has become possible for a larger number of professionals to earn a respectable income committing themselves full-time to activities related to social movements" (McCarthy and Zald 1977b:15). Two different dynamics, both rooted in bureaucracy, can be credited with its emergence.

First, professionalization can be a reaction against both central state control and the clientelist approach that earlier characterized philanthropy in places as diverse as Chicago and Japan. Ostensibly meritocratic structures, clear programmatic goals and designations, bureaucratic organizational structures, progress indicators, evaluative terms, and an infrastructure supporting philanthropy can provide common standards against which to measure organizational behavior. Professionalization suggests that philanthropic programs and their supporters need to justify their behavior using more "universalistic," accepted standards of the third sector, seeking to reduce the subjectivity associated with paternalistic or clientelist charity.

The second reason for the emergence of professionalization is structural and pertains to the increasingly important role that the central state has played in funding the third sector worldwide in the last forty years—ironically in some ways, given the difficulties that the third sector had in breaking free of that very state in places like France. When private organizations accept money from state entities, particularly in places like the United States and France, they become accountable for its use. These questions of accountability have engendered the growth of whole industries devoted to monitoring, compliance, and program evaluation. Yet, as organizational forms and public values merge, the traditional boundaries of governance that have relied on legal and organizational measures of answerability are no longer adequate for measuring public accountability. With the growing involvement of third sector organizations in governance, accountability takes on new meanings (Choudhury and Ahmed 2002). This can be seen in the emergence and rapid growth of nonprofit MBA programs within well-esteemed universities such as Harvard, Yale, and Stanford in the United States, and in a host of other institutions worldwide.

Professionalization can have both normatively positive and negative impacts for the organizations that sustain it. Clearly, transparency has a plethora of benefits for a democratic society, and the benefits of systems of accountability in the third sector have been widely documented by academics and policymakers (DeHoog and Salamon 2002; Salamon 2003).

But professionalization has shortcomings too; many nonprofit workers and activists complain that it creates yet another instantiation of Weber's iron cage, at worst ensnaring participants in endless red tape, and at best functioning as a short-sighted approach to nonprofit programming (see Ebrahim 2005). A program officer from a large nonprofit offers her perspective on how standard evaluative practices within philanthropy fail to serve their purpose fully:

> A lot of places that we work are places where USAID goes. USAID, and World Bank [. . .] so the norm in philanthropy, the norm in the evaluation thinking [. . .] is more logframe,[4] compliance, and bean counting, in my perspective. And questions of utility and credibility get lost in that. It's kind of this top-down show of—you know, "we've got to report to Uncle Sam and the American People that you're using your money right!" (Kallman 2013:56)

Professionalization, like the other institutional logics that we explore in this book, creates social patterns within the third sector that produce both normatively positive and negative effects. Like clientelism, patriarchy, and activism, professionalization is not unique to the third sector. There are similar dynamics, critiques, and conflicts within corporations, government agencies, and foundations. Participants can thus learn by talking or reading about parallels elsewhere. But how these general processes play out to generate more concrete institutional rules of the game, and how they vary from agency to country, are central themes we explore below.

In the United States and throughout the world, these multiple institutional logics have led to some mini culture wars within individual organizations, organizational fields, and third sectors in general. While this diversity is by no means a new theme, our project has sought to identify the major components of this diversity and to show how the broader context has specifically contributed to its development. In each country we explain the emergence/ presence of the institutional logics, illustrate their presences and combinations based on the development of their activities and legal structure, and offer brief distinctive examples.

A major story that emerges throughout the book is how these institutional logics have acted on the third sector as a whole. In the West, including in our case study countries of the United States and France, political and social dynamics have created conditions under which nonprofit organizations continue to become highly institutionalized: professionalization reigns, coming into periodic conflict with dynamics of clientelism and paternalism, and is occasionally criticized for subduing activism. In recent decades, third sector actors have become noticeably less independent from the government agencies that increased their funding. In the East, in our case study countries of China, South Korea, Japan, and Taiwan, third sector organizations are spinning off of state agencies and have often, through that very professionalization, become *more* independent than the state agencies that birthed them. The transition from authoritarian clientelism in the East to respect for associational autonomy is an important dimension of democratization, unfolding unevenly through iterative cycles of conflict among authoritarian rulers, reformist elites, and autonomous social movements (Fox 1994). The high degrees of professionalization and institutionalization in the United States, by contrast, make the historically fractious third sector start to look much less radical. This movement toward "joining the establishment" is a central theme of self-criticism by more activist commentators on third sector developments in, for example, France and the United States. Yet simultaneously, some national governments have explicitly opposed or limited activities of third sector activists in areas like China and Japan, as illustrated in the two cases below. Themes of openness and closure, as they stand in relation to each other, become salient as third sector participants jockey for position and, in the process, create new rules among the competing institutional logics within the field. Two illustrations from different parts of the world elucidate these points.

Susan G. Komen for the Cure and Planned Parenthood

In late December 2011, the world's largest breast cancer foundation, Susan G. Komen for the Cure, announced that it would be halting its funding to health and education programs run by Planned Parenthood and its affiliates, who also perform abortion services. The move stopped a flow of nearly $700,000 in healthcare support to low-income women. Though a spokeswoman for the Komen foundation claimed that the main factor in the decision was a new rule that prohibits grants to organizations being investigated by local, state, or federal authorities, the Komen foundation's decision was widely understood as yielding to longstanding pressure from anti-abortion groups.

Cecile Richards, Planned Parenthood's leader, said that the decision "came so abruptly in the face of a long, good, working relationship with Komen" and that the change in financing criteria "was written specifically to address the political pressure that they've been under[. . . .] Until really recently, the Komen foundation had been praising [Planned Parenthood's] breast health programs as essential," Richards said. "This really abrupt about-face was very surprising. I think that the Komen foundation has been bullied by right-wing groups" (Belluck 2012).

A barrage of popular support for Planned Parenthood—including more than $3 million for its breast cancer program from private donations in the space of a week (Khan 2012)—led the Komen foundation to reverse its course. The organization apologized, stating that only those organizations under "criminal" investigation will be barred from receiving funding. Planned Parenthood was once again deemed eligible to apply for support. Several days later, in February 2012, Karen Handel, a Susan G. Komen executive, resigned from her post. Popular donations to the Komen foundation dropped in 2012.

Upper-Level Japanese Officials Fired in Wake of Political Brawl

Makiko Tanaka, foreign minister, was relieved of her post in 2002 in the wake of a battle over who caused two NGOs to be barred from an Afghanistan Reconstruction conference. Tanaka's arch-rival in the NGO dispute, Administrative Vice Foreign Minister Yoshiji Nogami, was also fired, and a chairman of the lower house steering committee, Muneo Suzuki, voluntarily resigned.

The clash erupted over the issue of whether political pressure played a role in the ministry's decision to bar two Japanese nongovernmental organizations—Peace Winds Japan and Japan Platform—from the conference. The groups attended the second day of the conference as observers after Tanaka intervened. Prime Minister Koizumi hastily called a news conference early Wednesday morning and explained that the ousters were necessary to have the budget enacted as swiftly as possible amid the stalling economy (*Japan Times* 2002). Tanaka and Vice Foreign Minister Yoshiji Nogami gave contradictory testimonies at the Diet on whether Muneo Suzuki, a senior Liberal Democratic Party lawmaker with strong influence at the Foreign Ministry, was involved in the Foreign Ministry decision to bar the two NGOs from participation.

Tanaka quoted Nogami as telling her that influential LDP lawmaker Muneo Suzuki had pressured the ministry to bar the groups from the event. Nogami later flatly denied making any such statement, and still later Chief Cabinet Secretary Yasuo Fukuda told reporters he believed the vice minister had said nothing of this nature to Tanaka. Suzuki denied the allegation, telling reporters, "The foreign minister lied. I am quite displeased." Suzuki had considerable influence over foreign policy decisions despite the fact he did not hold any administrative post within the ministry.

Tanaka's dismissal was the culmination of a turbulent nine-month alliance in which two of Japan's most popular politicians tried to balance their reformist tactics within the same government. Tanaka, Japan's first female foreign minister and highly activist by standards of the Foreign Ministry, had won followers by criticizing Japan's conservative old guard and their clientelist political policies. But her constant feuding with bureaucrats made her a liability for an administration burdened by a poor economy and economic challenges. Both political analysts and voters saw her dismissal as a sign that Koizumi was giving in to the conservative old guard in an effort to stabilize his weakening government (Brooke 2002a, 2002b).

In both these vignettes, popular support stood in tension with administrative decisions made within the organizations themselves, and ex post facto mobilization of the organizations' supporters led to a reconfiguration of the organization's administrative boards, as well as a reversal of the contentious decisions themselves.

In the Japanese case, political pressures and clientelism backfired when an activist (and female) minister challenged entrenched power; the state bureaucracy then clamped down on both parties, causing all involved to lose their positions. Similarly, the Komen case illustrates the ways that activists organized to challenge what they perceived as clientelist funding decisions, calling on both Planned Parenthood's professional comportment and legions of individual donors and activists to contest and repeal a decision. In the Komen case particularly, the activism in support of Planned Parenthood largely sidestepped the polarized fight about abortion access—the service for which Planned Parenthood is best known—transcending the classic left-right distinctions surrounding the organization and focusing instead on breast cancer.

These similar cases illustrate some of the ways that these five logics interarticulate within the third sector. They show the importance of articulating the separate institutional logics that drove specific conflicts. In subsequent chapters we explore such dynamics more thoroughly with respect to the United States, France, Japan, Korea, and China.

Social Movements within the Third Sector: From Radical to Establishment

The New Social Movements that are most commonly discussed today are those that emerged in the 1970s. They were labeled "New" because they differed from earlier interest groups, such as unions and churches. New Social Movements generally emerged around issues of environmentalism, human rights, women's issues, peace, antinuclear protest, and the like—they were nonmaterial movements focusing on more abstract ideas and postmaterialist values. As close studies of these have shown, many of them did not seek to be anti-establishment; for example, the Italian and German environmental movements approached the communist and socialist political parties in Germany and Italy and asked if they could collaborate to add environmental issues to the party programs. They were seeking to become engaged in an establishment-oriented, traditional manner. But the political parties in both countries refused, as environmental issues were not seen as part of the classic working-class socialist program.

So the environmental movements pressed on independently of party affiliation, but they were so small and had so little visible impact on elected officials that they became frustrated. There were no means of effective communication with elected officials, and the media marginalized them. They then embraced a dramatically new style of activism: they became terrorists. They dynamited railroad trains, they took hostages and kidnapped high-level political officials, and they assassinated professors and engaged in many highly visible, media-oriented activities that clearly brought them to public attention. This continued for several years in both Italy and Germany.

In the next decades, however, it became clear that environmental issues were popular with a wide part of the general public. The leading political parties, especially those on the left, began to engage with environmental issues. There were also efforts to create Green political parties, and these have had a significant competitive impact on the large established parties, especially in Europe. This change has been termed "reframing" (Snow 2007); it has transformed the political opportunity structure within which the environmental movement could operate, creating a far more hospitable environment for issues of environmentalism. As the opportunity structure opened up and they were welcomed into the established political parties, the radical terrorist groups suddenly became quite conventional in their style of operation. Environmentalism was added to the socialist program, and many cities and regions elected combinations of candidates who became labeled "Red-Green," referring to this new combination of socialism and environmentalism. Cities like Freiburg, Germany, were governed by Red-Green coalitions for many years and implemented some of the most active and comprehensive environmental socialists plans and programs (see Sellers 2002).

Many related issues (those of women, moralism, etc.), which were launched in the 1970s as New Social Movements, have since been incorporated into various political party programs. As the numbers of citizens who support these issues have risen, especially for questions of issues like human rights, the notion of the social movement organization as the "extreme outsider" is much less relevant. The social movements have been institutionalized and, in many cases, professionalized.

These drastic transformations of social movement styles have led many interpreters to change their conceptualization of how these New Social Movements work. In the beginning, they were analyzed in terms of the people who joined them, why they did so, what their social backgrounds were, and the like. But as the context changed, the political opportunity structure opened, and the movements themselves changed as well; analysis shifted away from the internal dynamics of these groups and instead focused on the rules of the game under which the organizations were permitted to operate.

For a country such as China, whose third sector is tightly regulated, these concepts of the political opportunity structure and the transformation of social movements, (termed "framing" in social movement language), are quite illuminating. Framing has to do with the language in which an idea is discussed—it can be considered as the process of attaching meaning to something and situating it within a relevant cultural discourse. In the example of European environmental movements, the same issue (environmentalism) was framed several ways—first as an outside movement, then as a terrorist movement, and finally as a standard part of the governmental and party fare.

Another perspective would label this transition of the environmental movement "cooptation"; that is, the leaders of the European environmental movement were brought into the establishment, and some critics accuse them of abandoning their earlier perspectives and constituents. This type of critique would see the radical quasi-terrorist style as having been "sold out" or abandoned in favor of joining "the establishment." The establishment, by definition, implies more established rules of the game, which includes formalized guidance on everything from seeking members to fundraising.

The irony of this example is that one begins with an effort that seemed very anti-Tocquevillian and yet ended with a model wherein the formerly "outsider" group, once it entered the public policy arena, was transformed in a manner that seems to resemble the classic participatory organization.

Nevertheless, these examples are mainly from Western Europe and the United States, as we do not have as clear, detailed data on other countries. There are, of course, important variations across countries, especially in countries that have an established, antagonistic, nonlegitimate subculture. In parts of Korea and Eastern Europe, more participation may lead to less trust, in a manner that refutes the classic Tocquevillian model (see chapter 8, this volume).

Internet Organizing and Critical Mass: Highly Decentralized Activism— "New New Social Movements"?

Many movements increasingly emerge with minimal coordination or leadership. One case, international in its scope, is that of Critical Mass. Critical Mass is a "spontaneous" community bike ride held in over three hundred cities worldwide on the last Friday of every month, in all weathers. It purports to be a leaderless, structureless bike gathering and can include thousands of participants. While originally established with the idea of "taking back the streets" (drawing attention to the safety issues posed between bikes and motorists) in San Francisco, different riders have different political agendas—some participate just for fun, while some see it as an explicitly political act. Because it has no stated goals, Critical Mass can occur without notifying the police in advance of its presence and has neither organized hierarchical structure nor organized membership, though frequent riders are sometimes called "massers." Critical Mass rides vary greatly in numbers, ranging from several thousand participants in large cities to only twenty or so in small ones. Because of its structure (or lack thereof), Critical Mass is free of the costs associated with a centralized program or a formal "organization." The only requirement for the event to function is a "critical mass" of riders, dense enough to occupy a piece of road to the exclusion of motorized vehicles. Indeed, cars seem to be more supportive than one might think: the Halloween Critical Mass ride in Chicago in 2008, consisting of nearly two thousand cyclists, flowed through the city to the cheers, enthusiastic honks, and supportive whooping from drivers whose commutes had been interrupted.

In another example of decentralized activism, when Proposition 8 passed on November 4, 2008, and effectively banned marriage equality for gay and lesbian people in the state of California, a group of community organizers took immediate action online. Coordinating via email, these protesters created the website JointheImpact.com to combat the California decision. The site launched overnight and within days had built a base of hundreds of thousands of supporters. On Saturday, November 14, only ten days after the marriage ban, people who had connected on the site staged rallies in eight countries, all fifty states, and over three hundred cities in support of gay rights. The *New York Times*' Claire Cain Miller wrote of this action, "the Internet played an unprecedented role in rallying voters during this year's election. In the aftermath of the election, Web 2.0 tools are continuing to play a role in other causes, astonishing long-time activists with the power and speed with which it gets their message out" (Cain Miller 2008).

A similar instance of electronic activism unfolded around the same time in Seoul, South Korea. In June 2008, President Lee Myung Bak reversed a 2003 decision to ban the import of US beef, and protesters fearing the spread of mad cow disease used a decidedly high-tech tactic. As the dissent battle began, it was waged via text message, blogs, and personal websites. When a high school student called for Lee's impeachment in April via text messaging, the petition garnered 1.3 million signatures within a week. Other online communities in Korea, heretofore brought together by a common interest for fashion or a certain musician, banded together during the protests to make their presence known and spread the message against US beef (Jack Kim 2008; Sang-hun 2008).

These examples of protests reveal a new and decentralized political actor in that of high-tech organizing. The Internet has markedly changed the sphere of influence in which activists operate. When even social mechanisms such as Facebook, Twitter, and MySpace act as players in larger-scale movements, from the Korean beef ban to the 2009 Green Revolt in Iran, it is obvious that action via technology is rapidly expanding. In the words of Kim Joo Hyung, a fifteen-year-old involved in the Korean protests: "What we do is faster and more real than the ordinary news media" (Sang-hun 2008, n.p.).

These are important illustrative examples of the independent, unorganized nature of an emerging set of social movement tactics (of which social media and information technologies are inarguably a large part). These events seek to portray themselves as spontaneous and independent of any centralized organization, and each one is interpreted individually by individual actors, absent a centralized organizational discourse.

Online organizing that occurs within more restrictive political contexts represents an important new move in social movements. While it is necessary not to confuse Internet-facilitated activism with "slacktivism" (a disparaging term coined to describe political acts done over the Internet, but requiring little time, involvement, or investment), we must also be sensitive to the potential of new organizing tools. In Kiev in 2014, for instance, masses of protestors were coordinated via text message and Twitter, a type of social organization that in other times would have been done with flyers and posters. Though writers such as Gladwell (2010) express skepticism about the role of the Internet, we see its potential as a tool to be dramatically reshaping how organizing is conducted.

This Internet-oriented, "invisible" style of public engagement has spread worldwide since 2000 and can be a very powerful force. We could interpret this as illustrating a new form of New New Social Movement (NNSM) political engagement. The difference between New Social Movements (NSMs) and NNSMs is that the NNSMs do not have any formal organization—they lack a president, a board, a budget, formalized membership cards, a fundraising program, or other similar activities. Rather, they permit individuals to be much more anonymously engaged and only to the degree that they choose. Larger activities and meetings have been described in these terms as well, such as the protests against the World Trade Organization and international financial agencies that occurred in cities where these organizations meet. People travel, individually or through organizational coordination, to places like Seattle or Genoa, making substantial commitments of time and money to fly often halfway around the world in order to participate in street-like activities.[5] The Occupy movement included protests in 951 cities across 82 countries in just 2011 (Thompson 2011). Quite unlike earlier protests over race or the environment or human rights, many of these NNSMs have been highly disorganized, dispersed, uncoordinated, and filled with dozens and dozens of individual small organizations and many individuals who do not identify with any organization.

Further, in an age where professionalization within third sector organizations is prevalent and people are inundated by a great deal of news—much of it bad—from at home and abroad, social movement activity has been seeking to incorporate actions and activities that engage the participants and audience in an explicitly emotional manner. For instance, they may use makeup, costuming, dancing, or other symbols designed to attract a television camera or photographer that can in turn show some drama to others who were not present at the event. The preparations for these demonstrations are a focal point for recruitment of new members, although in many cases there is no organization; it is more of a diffuse movement of people who come together as they feel justified and interested in participating. The demonstrations increasingly involve music, art, or dancing in part as these seem to engage more emotion among the participants—who may lack any official structure—and they communicate powerfully to others via mass media. They help create what we have analyzed as "scenes," which energize associations (see Scenes Overview n.d.; Scenes Project n.d.).

Just as the new social movements in the 1970s were seen as external, non-institutionally engaged, improper organizations by the established political parties as well as the social scientists and journalists writing about them, so these New New Social Movements have not even been recognized as political movements or social movements by many of the participants, organizers, or analysts. NNSMs are seen as too individualized or fragmented to really "count," but more recent global analyses show that they can be powerfully impactful.

Looking Forward:
Associational Politics and Political Life

We lay out three ways of looking at the role of associational politics and how they might fit into the large picture of political life. The first is the Tocquevillian discourse, which is often seen as linking citizens to government through civic participation. Although the goals and activities of the citizens—and associations that they create and energize—are not independent of government, they nevertheless keep citizens engaged in part of a legitimating process. This participation incorporates citizens and their groups into public decision making in important ways.

We can see the impacts of associationalism when contrasting associational politics with the second, highly individualized approach to participation that relies on preexisting networks, kinship groups, and the like. We see this, for example, in places like southern Italy, where voluntary associations are either absent or mistrusted.

A third approach is to consider organizations as quite explicitly opposed to the "establishment," openly critical, seeking sometimes to consciously undermine the legitimacy and the stability of government. The extreme version would be terrorist organizations, but such organizations are not generally included in the broader conversation about the third sector. However, it may be worth considering them in such context—they are organizations sometimes explicitly linked to the Calvinist tradition of being bottom-up, engaging citizens in issues that are important to them, but also overtly challenging general authority and leadership. This is discussed below in the context of new social movements.

As will become clear, this book considers all three perspectives. For us, the point is not so much which is the correct interpretation, but rather that all three interpretations have offered important insights into associative life and the third sector generally at different times and in different places.

Even if traditions of these sorts help explain the background against which third sector organizations have developed around the world, we should not assume them to be unchanging. The dramatic transformations in China in the last few decades, for instance, are one of the most powerful testimonies as to how rapidly change can occur. From the strong political model of egalitarianism to the spread of market principles, and then the global integration with other economies, China has shown the world how forcefully a nation can craft such a change. With other transformations underway around the globe, increasingly since the fall of the Berlin wall in 1989, the concepts of capitalism and socialism as competing worldviews are no longer such helpful guides to interpret many specific policies. More specific elements, like those debated around Tocqueville or Calvinism, grow more salient.

These sorts of civic traditions have since been institutionalized in the political (and economic) fabric of the societies in which they began. The US nonprofit sector, for example, was composed of 1.5 million formal third sector organizations in 2013 (National Center 2013). As far back as 1998, it employed 11 million paid workers (over 7 percent of the country's workforce) and the equivalent of 5.7 million full-time volunteers. These numbers indicate that paid employment in third sector organizations is three times greater than agriculture, and almost 50 percent greater than that in construction and finance (not counting volunteers). Most of this work is in the fields of education, health, and the social services (Salamon 2003:9); that is to say, this institutionalization has been both civic and economic in nature and is far-reaching. And this impulse has been spreading; one of the most common ways to increase confidence in governments and leadership worldwide is to engage citizens in organized or decentralized groups, whether or not they are entirely nongovernmental (Baiocchi 2006).

A clear shift in the contemporary iteration of this third sector development, however, is that it is no longer solely Calvinist, nor even religious. Many of these social organizations are secular; many have no concern with religion, explicitly or otherwise, and yet they bear the markings of the political and social dynamics that birthed them. Some of the participants and members still carry on a fervent moralistic concern to make the world a better place, to improve the lot of the disadvantaged, to help the poor, or to help women or endangered species; they are identifiable as activists and working within an institutional logic of activism. Clearly, not all nonprofit organizations are moralistic even in this sense; many are technical, non-ideological, and highly professionalized. Nevertheless it would be shortsighted to ignore the moral agenda driving many of these nonprofits, especially those with Western roots and affiliations—Amnesty International, the Sierra Club, Doctors Without Borders, and others—all organizations with no formal religious affiliation, but with a strong sense of social commitment regardless.

This moralistic agenda is visible—increasingly so—throughout third sectors globally, although it remains secular in its terminology, reflecting, perhaps, the sense that moralism is an effective motivator of social change, even when not explicitly linked to a faith tradition. Recent movements seeking to combat climate change, for instance, have explicitly charged their adversaries with the responsibility to be on the morally "right" side of history. Former editor-in-chief of the *Guardian* Alan Rusbridger decided to dedicate his last year of editorial work to climate change, writing that, over his career, he had few regrets except "this one: that we had not done justice to this huge, overshadowing, overwhelming issue of how climate change will probably, within the lifetime of our children, cause untold havoc and stress to our species. So, in the time left to me as editor, I thought I would try to harness the Guardian's best resources to describe what is happening and what—if we do nothing—is almost certain to occur" (Rusbridger 2015). Similarly, Russian punk band Pussy Riot attracted attention in 2012 for staging a guerilla performance in Moscow's Cathedral of Christ the Savior protesting Vladimir Putin, whom the group considers a dictator. The performance sparked charges, imprisonment for several group members, and international condemnation, but the real point for us is that the group's message—which advocates for feminism and LGBT rights, and which criticizes Putin—is as powerfully moralistic as that of other faith-based groups.

A third factor that may be contributing to the reconfiguration of third sector activities is educational achievement. Worldwide, educational levels have been rising, helping to create a new group of people who have high school diplomas or some college education, making potential supporters (literate, informed citizens) of NNSMs much larger. For instance, in all our case study countries the percent of the workforce with tertiary education

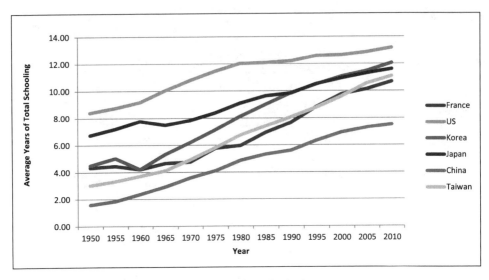

Figure 1. Average years of total schooling for individuals aged 15+ in selected countries, 1950–2010.

Source: Barro and Lee 2013:190.

increased dramatically over the last few decades. Similarly, the size of the blue collar sector has dropped by half since the 1950s in nineteen of twenty countries studied by Clark and Hoffmann-Martinot (1998:128), undermining the traditional left parties and encouraging their adoption of new issues such as human rights, women's rights, and environmentalism. But there are substantial (often national) differences in political parties in these regards, complicating their relations with the third sector across the world. This rise of moralism, especially egalitarianism, is widely shared among citizens even if unevenly pursued by political parties and civic leaders.

Such participants are able to challenge the establishment in new and specific ways. For instance, the "Twitter revolutions" everywhere from Moldova in 2009 to Tunisia in 2010–2011 (and across the world) are dependent not only on technology but also on literacy: increasing numbers of literate, informed people, coupled with increasing availability of technology, create a new class of potential participants in civic and social movement behavior.

Likewise, there has been a mushrooming of third sector organizations internationally within the last several decades. Some suggest this is because citizens and their economic systems have performed so well that they can now "afford" to pay attention to these new kinds of issues, such as environmentalism and women's movements—the pressing concerns in their hierarchy of needs are met, and citizens now have "time" to devote to such causes. The ongoing international crisis of the financial system certainly suggests that such arguments are debatable, and in any case, they do not account for the healthy development of the third sector in, say, Bolivia, which as of 2015 still retains the dubious honor of being the second-poorest country in the Western Hemisphere. In any case, it is clear that the world has experienced profound political changes in recent decades. The role of the third sector remains controversial and central to these changing priorities.

Social challenges, taking contemporary forms in the likes of air pollution, traffic, crime, theft, family conflicts, and so forth, become more visible and challenging as the traditional family structure weakens in the context of a metropolis, particularly a modern metropolis. Whereas grandmothers and neighbors may have assisted young families in a traditional village, a city (especially a globalized city) ruptures accommodations previously made on the basis of kinship ties and spatial proximity. In this new context, the third sector is seen as providing an assertive new version of such social cohesion and community; community organizations can move in to replace the neighbor who enforced sidewalk etiquette among the children in the village, and the after-school youth groups can be a good proxy for the grandmother who used to supervise homework.

From Tocqueville through Putnam, analysts did not stress differences in *types* of organizations: churches, Lions Clubs, and charities were treated as variations of a common theme. Putnam's *Bowling Alone* stressed the decline of membership in civic groups generally. But looking more closely, we shall see in later chapters that membership in different *types* of organizations has changed. This chapter introduces foundational differences in such patterns. Historically many of the political developments from Calvinism in Switzerland and the Netherlands continued in the so-called nonconformist regions of England and Scotland. These regions had few aristocratic or Church of England leaders, but more often nonconformists like Baptists or Methodists who were essentially Calvinist. The major difference between continental Europe in general and the Calvinist areas of the Netherlands, Switzerland, and parts of England was that there was a greater open concern to help the disadvantaged, to act charitably, to found hospitals, to set up schools for the illiterate—following the Bible *but using participation and civic acts as a mechanism*. Thus, nonconformist Calvinists brought new members into their churches, teaching them about participation through religion. They developed the rhetoric of helping and assistance that one still finds today, inside and outside churches.

By contrast, most of continental Europe has strong central states that took responsibility for the poor and the criminals and sought to provide welfare through the major state institutions. They either prohibited or discouraged the development of separate charitable civic groups such as emerged in the Calvinist regions of Europe and later in New England. Recently, similar developments have been more visible in Asia, Africa, and Latin America: strong control followed by a recent rise in third sector activities.

All this is to say that the role of activism has been changing, and in some cases taking on more symbolic, emotional, and theatrical elements in conversing with this new constituency. Contemporary Chinese leaders, for example, have made direct linkages to the traditional Chinese past, referencing clothing, history, religion, art, and music that both enhance these past traditions and join them definitively with ongoing cultural, artistic, and political concerns. The French Ministry of Culture has employed this approach as well: it has taken as an objective the enhancement of the "national patrimony" by investing in museums, statues, national theaters, and so on, but has linked that initiative with an ongoing effort to support innovation and artistic creativity in new forms.

The arts are an increasingly important policy arena and, as Silver, Clark, and Graziul (2011) show, are driving job growth and innovation, especially in cities like Chicago and Toronto, as well as nationally in the United States and other countries (see Grodach and Silver 2012). Third sector organizations are important incubators of these processes, serving as "greenhouses" in which these young artistic and cultural groups can grow.[6]

Performance and entertainment is a forum that political leaders can readily join, in both subtle and direct manners. Political campaigners in Austria would regularly attend traditional folk festivals in small towns, using them as a means to keep in touch with their constituencies. Antanas Mockus, mayor of Bogotá, Colombia, for two terms, used creative symbolic policies to reinforce his leadership and achieve even difficult policy goals. He did so by joining humor and performance with empathy and concern for the average citizen. For example, he would walk the streets dressed in spandex and a cape as "Supercitizen," and when the city faced a water shortage, he went on television to demonstrate the "modern shower" (turning water on to get wet, turning it off to apply soap, and turning it on again to rinse). The "modern shower" led to a dramatic reduction in water consumption within a few weeks and solved a crisis in an unusually creative manner. Here, the rise of arts and of citizens as political drivers joins New Social Movements. Chapter 8 is dedicated explicitly to a deeper analysis of these dynamics.

Conclusion

Internationally, the third sector is widely celebrated (Salamon 2003, 1995), sometimes uncritically. It is also growing. Such a form of political participation resonates deeply with advocates of and for democracy in development, policy, and international relations fields. Watching leaders throughout the world grapple with political legitimacy through decentralization and associationalism is instructive. This leads us to a central question of this book: can organized third sector groups help governance? If so, where, why, and in what contexts?

The following are some general points to consider on organizational life and guide our analysis of the development of associational life and the institutional logics that contour it:

- The rapid rise of third sector organizations has been particularly dramatic and sometimes disruptive in more traditional and more isolated societies. International communication between these organizations has brought newer issues, such as gender equality, into the spotlight.
- The third sector has become a major economic force in the past twenty years, and is currently the seventh largest economy in the world, responsible for $1.3 trillion in expenditures in the late 1990s (Salamon and Sokolowski 2004:15).

  Many political systems, in areas like Eastern Europe and the former Soviet Union, as well as much of Latin America and parts of Asia and Africa, previously had strong hierarchical political systems that either closely contained or prohibited many organized groups from becoming politically engaged. This is changing, but often with doubts, complex adaptations, and challenges. We examine several cases to try to understand some of these dynamics.
- In areas such as continental Europe, civic and third sector organization work has been traditionally weak. Political parties were generally much stronger than third sector organizations and tended to subordinate them. Countries like France, Germany, and Italy, as well as Japan and China, have changed profoundly in this regard in recent years, having created new legal and administrative provisions that provide more autonomy for organized groups. The main point here is that this transformation is not an issue of one country, but a global occurrence. Worldwide, countries' embrace of the third sector is often so rapid, and conflictual, that it is useful to look comparatively to see what mechanisms can yield solutions among the emerging third sector groups.
- Increased income and wider diversity of citizen preferences makes it harder for governments and their agencies to satisfy all citizens. That is, demand is

diversifying. The variability and volatility of citizen/consumer preferences is especially challenging for leaders of large organizations and high-level political officials. A common solution has been decentralization: to delegate responsibilities to third sector organizations, families, or citizens. This same sort of decentralization holds for everything from choosing and producing clothing styles, types of coffee, designing a sensitive retirement facility, or providing health services.

- The challenge of providing services or products to a diverse population has been heightened by the fact that the types and qualities of services and products have changed. Notably, these new products or services may involve average citizens in more of their provision. The term "coproduction" has been introduced to describe such activities as citizens engaged in recycling efforts. The term is meant to designate a transformation among citizens from passive subject to more active, engaged participant.

- These new sectoral projects are international, creating new kinds of relationships, flows of resources, and discourses that can generate both development and pathologies. They are participating in a kind of international linkage that the world has never seen before. (Santos 2002) suggests that transnational NGOs (TNGOS) are civil society's answer to multinational corporations, and that the third sector can answer to neoliberal globalization in kind. Others disagree, claiming that the very nature of the current political economy necessitates a rethinking of civil society as we know it.

With these dynamics in mind, we now briefly turn to general background on social capital before moving into country-by-country analyses of third sectors and civic associations.

Notes

1. The idea of a "tax-exempt organization" does not capture the huge array of informal organizations that comprises the nonprofit sector. The third sector continues to this day in its search for identity; today, the term "nongovernmental organization" (NGO) remains popular around the world. An interesting element of the term "nongovernmental" is that it defines these independent organizations in opposition to the government, rather than in opposition to private sector firms; the sector is thus defined as that which is not part of the state, rather than that which is not oriented toward profit making (Frumkin 2005:11–12). The internationally popular term "independent sector" has its roots in the Independent Sector, the US trade association of grant makers and grant receivers, formed in an effort to bring some streamlined communication to the scattered world of foundations and nonprofit organizations. The notion of a "third sector" is beneficial in that it can refer to both the formal and informal organizations that constitute it. Popular in Europe has been the "charitable sector," a term that has encountered criticism for summoning forth images of alms and charity; while encompassing the essential philanthropic element of nonprofit

work, it ignores the discourses of community building, self-help, and empowerment that have been a fundamental part of the sector in some locations. Defourny (2001) suggests that third sector activities can be classified along two lines: legal-institutional definitions would entail grouping associations by the characteristics of their formal organizational structures (such as by tax-exempt or legal status, by 501(c) designation, etc.), and a normative or ethical definition of the third sector would group organizations by the principles that they have in common (such as the aim of serving members of the community rather than generating profit, etc.). We often refer to the "third sector," as the term reflects both the institutional and ethical components of the kind of work that the sector performs.

2. The Catholic Church in the early post-Reformation period was highly isolationist, but still highly hierarchical. Historical events, including the Schism of Utrecht, helped reinforce the introverted nature of the Dutch Catholic Church. Though it operated in some ways independently of Rome, its clergy still "maintained a high degree of control over their flocks" (Bakvis 1981:23).

3. A "moralism" was added to the public culture/media discussion of many continental European and some Asian countries in these years. This is part of the general rise of the New Political Culture, especially the populist egalitarianism wherein political leaders were increasingly treated as if the morality of the average citizen should apply to them as well. The most dramatic historical shift was after the 1968 student disturbances, from Paris to California, compounded by the rise of "advocacy journalism," i.e., the critical style of younger journalists in interviewing and commenting on established leaders. See T. Clark and Hoffmann-Martinot (1998:2–3).

4. The Logical Framework Approach, or "logframe," is a management tool mainly used in the design, monitoring, and evaluation of international development projects.

5. Clark (2004) has explored these themes.

6. See one related Chinese discussion in Zheng (2010).

1. Civil Society, Social Capital, and the Growth of the Third Sector

Scholarly literature in North America and Western Europe commonly equates the third sector and associationalism with the concept of *civil society*. We find this concept useful for the purposes of thinking about citizen participation and, further, because civil society has shown itself to be deeply entwined with the formal development of the third sector worldwide. This section thus starts with a brief overview on civil society and social capital and then shows how it helps understand workings of the institutional logics from the introduction.

By Walzer's (1998:9) definition, civil society is "an area where citizens and organizations are not restricted by the government and are able to form groups and networks without interference." In this sense, it is by no means limited to voluntary or not-for-profit organizations but includes the entire universe of extra-statal organizations (including everything from business organizations to unions to book clubs to dance companies to congregations) that interface, cooperate, liaise, and compete with each other to supplement the political, economic, and cultural life of the state. This definition reflects conceptual roots in the work of Hobbes, Montesquieu, and Hegel, among others, and has been famously theorized by Habermas; all of these scholars employed it to refer to the broad and multifaceted realm outside the state (Frumkin 2005:13). The value of the third sector specifically, within civil society, is that it acts as a mechanism by which people are drawn out of individual concern for themselves and into concern for society as a whole; the third sector is thus a vehicle for community involvement.

Civil society in general, and the third sector in particular, varies widely in its relationship with the state throughout the world. The US third sector, for example, developed for many years without an explicit relationship to the government and was tasked with either filling in the "holes" in service provision that the government missed or with advocating specific social policies, at times positioning itself against prevailing state policy. China, on the other hand, has a third sector that developed almost exclusively in conjunction with the government, the third sector organizations therein acting largely as service providers.

There are tensions between both practitioners and scholars about the relationship of the third sector to the central government, a theme that this book examines in detail throughout, characterized under the institutional logics of both bureaucracy and professionalization. Government-nonprofit relationships are often typologized as either supplementary, complementary, or adversarial (Young 2000). A relationship is *supplementary* when nonprofits are seen as fulfilling the demand for public goods left unsatisfied by government; therefore, as government takes more responsibility for provision, less needs to be raised through voluntary collective means. This is the Tocquevillian discourse, which is often seen as linking citizens to government. Although the goals and activities of the citizens—and associations that they create and energize—are not independent of government, they nevertheless keep citizens engaged in part of a legitimating process within political life.

In the *complementary* view, nonprofits are seen as partners to government, helping to carry out the delivery of public goods largely financed by government itself. In this perspective, nonprofit and government expenditures have a direct relationship with one another: as government expenditures increase, they help finance increasing levels of activity by nonprofits. This perspective would understand the voluntary sector as a sort of "third-party" governance, supplementing the state's initiatives and sometimes directly funded by them.

The *adversarial* view sees nonprofits as instigators, encouraging government to alter public policy and maintain accountability to the public, while the government attempts to influence the behavior of nonprofit organizations by regulating their services and responding to advocacy initiatives. This perspective considers organizations as quite explicitly opposed to the "establishment," openly critical, seeking sometimes to consciously undermine the legitimacy and the stability of government.

These themes are larger than definitions; they bear heavily on how we understand the meanings and success of the third sector and civic participation. Scholars who value the adversarial component of the third sector see it as a sphere of action that is independent of the state and that is capable—precisely for this reason—of energizing resistance to a tyrannical regime (Foley and Edwards 1996). The supplementary and complimentary formulations of the third sector postulate the positive effects of association for governance (albeit democratic governance), while the latter emphasizes the importance of civil association as a counterweight to the state. A third view comes from some economists who interpret the "dense webs of association" praised by civil society scholars as "raising transaction costs" to markets reaching citizens and thus undermining the smooth and equitable functioning of modern states and markets (Olson 1982).

As the discussion below highlights, for us, the issue is not so much to ask if one interpretation is correct, but rather to include all three interpretations for insights into associative life and the third sector generally at different times and in different places. We consider how civil society works as a dynamic force within the entirety of a political and social experience; we variously invoke multiple analytical perspectives. Third sector organizations in the United States, for instance, can be supplementary, complimentary, *and* adversarial, sometimes simultaneously. (Planned Parenthood is a good example of such an organization. It provides healthcare services for low-income individuals, it fulfills state healthcare contracts, and it advocates healthcare policies.) Edward Shils writes, "Although autonomy vis-à-vis the state is one of the features of a civil society, the autonomy is far from complete. Civil society operates within the framework set by laws. . . . Laws require that rights within the civil society be respected and that duties be performed" (quoted in Chamberlain 1993: 208). Chamberlain expands: "Civil society, then, is a community in constant tension, its members pulled in several directions simultaneously: toward one another and apart, both toward their individual private worlds and the more public realm of state authority. Tension is a defining feature of civil society and a major source of both its strength and weakness" (208). For us, these tensions emerge in the broader conceptual format of institutional logics.

Tensions among institutional rules come most clearly into relief among states and civil societies without a history of democratic engagement. For example, Napoleon outlawed civic associations, and so dissenters found a creative outlet for their conversations in sometimes huge dinners throughout the nineteenth century (thus termed the "banquet years" in Roger Shattuck's [1958] book on the French avant-garde). Similarly, some attempts to frame Chinese institutions and practices in terms of Western notions of civil society appeared in the mid-1980s in histories of the late Qing Dynasty and engendered a discussion on if and how the idea is relevant to China's concepts of state-society relations. The notion of civil society as such has enjoyed widespread intellectual currency in comparative communist studies and was used to analyze opposition groups in the Soviet bloc. By the end of the 1980s, the civil society concept was employed to think about pluralistic group formation and autonomy in the era of reform (Ma 2002b:314–16).

We begin with the first and most obvious—associations as integrative mechanisms in social life. Associational life and civil society has been positively linked in the literature with themes of social integration, social capital, and generalized trust, with correspondingly positive economic impacts. In this section we review these linkages briefly, to set the stage for country-specific analyses of the third sector.

Organizations as Integrative Mechanisms: Social Capital, Trust, Development

In a description of Korean immigrants to the United States, Choi (2012) shows that Koreans who have worked in the United States for thirty to forty years often, even in retirement, continue to participate in book clubs and sing in church choirs. His point is simple: that such collective activities engender a persistent sense of community, linking people to each other and to places, and firmly integrating individuals into participatory society. Nonprofit and voluntary organizations worldwide understand this kind of linkage as valuable and regularly rely on this very sort of exchange.

The influence of this Putnam-Tocqueville model of participation in political sociology has been substantial: "participation," "trust," and "social capital" became buzzwords of early twenty-first-century social science and defined the approaches of many nonprofit and third sector organizations. In the late twentieth century, social scientists began to employ the term "social capital" to describe the tools and training that enhance productive human social life, and this notion has been increasingly linked with the idea of the third sector.

The basic theory of social capital is that social networks have value, and that healthy ones can affect the "social production" of individuals and groups; therefore, the existence of social capital has important consequences for the quality of civic engagement and politics. Trust built through civic associations and community projects extends into the political realm and creates enthusiasm for public life, which is in turn linked to more active political engagement and participation (Frumkin 2005:40). Social capital "calls attention to the fact that civic virtue is most powerful when embedded in a dense network of reciprocal social relations. A society of many virtuous but isolated individuals is not necessarily rich in social capital" (Putnam 2000:61). As Putnam demonstrates for the United States, a well-connected individual in a poorly connected society is not as productive as a well-connected individual in a well-connected society—you are better off if everyone around you is connected as well. Though debates rage about whether online platforms such as Facebook truly engender social capital (rather than simply weak ties—see Gladwell [2010]), social media do try to capitalize on and facilitate this type of reciprocal social exchange.

Nevertheless, social capital in every country develops against each country's own backdrop of political, social, and cultural reality. For example, in France, the *economie social* came to prominence as part of the government's strategy to decentralize public administration and social service delivery (Salamon and Anheier 1996:84); it evolved within a long French tradition of hostility toward voluntary organizations, rooted in the French Revolution's prevailing concept of the "general will" and its suspicion of any institution that purported to mediate between the citizen and this general will. Between 1791 and 1901 nonprofit organizations were actually illegal in France. Thus a long tradition of state-provided services developed. As another example, in some Asian countries, interest groups are built through interpersonal and familial relationships (called *guanxi* in China and Taiwan), often related to market functions (T. Lin 2005:23), and are an equally important function in civil society, though we have not found a study of *guanxi* that includes sufficient detail and international comparisons to indicate how distinct *guanxi* are from various Western civic groups. The general impression most studies convey is that *guanxi* are more personalistic and familialist and are intended for private (often material) benefit of the participants—rather than seeking the ideal of "elevating" an individual's conception of self-interest to incorporate "the public interest," or "commonwealth," in the manner philosophized in (part of) the Western tradition.

Framed positively, social capital can transform associations into mediating agents between individuals and deviant behavior. Associational relationships, rich in social capital, can bring trust into the minds of individuals and encourage socially responsive action toward others. Trust is an important social mediator, helping ensure accountability and decrease the cost of economic and social transactions. (You wouldn't cheat your neighbor in the sale of a used car because you see her on a regular basis around your neighborhood; you are therefore spared the cost of hiring a lawyer to mediate the sale of the car, and in this case, your trust acts as a lubricant for a transaction.) Fukuyama (1996:29) characterizes such scenarios as having a "high degree of generalized social trust and, consequently, a strong propensity for spontaneous sociability." Generalized trust and "weak ties" (Granovetter 1973) can facilitate innovation and adaptation through information exchange and networks. This idea, in Tocqueville and elsewhere, is most powerfully illustrated by looking at the edges of civility and civic activity to see where and how the *lack of* organizational and civic engagement can permit development of deviant subcultures and activities.

One such example is political life in southern Italy, the region's history with the mafia, and the dramatic regional differences that Italy experienced with respect to it. The mafia dominated most aspects of political and social life in Sicily and other parts of southern Italy, beginning with the painful transition from feudalism to capitalism. The organized crime ring, whose initial racket was in "protections" and which subsequently expanded into the drug trade and other forms of trafficking in its two hundred years of operation (Chubb 1982; Gambetta 1996), dominated nearly every facet of social and political life, including representation, institutions, and access to material and social resources. It had strong claims to the public dominion (Paoli 2004) and often effectively shut the state out of administration; its own monopoly over the use of force precluded any such monopoly on the state's part (a monopoly over the legitimate use of force is classically considered the definition of a state).

During the mafia crackdown in the 1990s and early twenty-first century, Italian television would regularly broadcast trials of mafia leaders, as the Italian state sought to publicize and document its punishment of deviance. This publicity presented a difficulty for the courts and judges involved in the trials; there were threats of violence against them from mafia members in the southern part of the country, and some judges and uncooperative public figures were killed in Palermo and elsewhere. The tensions, threats, and fears in the courtroom between the mafia and the prosecution were publicly palpable. This dynamic came to light as the trials were televised across Italy—citizens and national leaders were shocked at the retaliations and felt that something should be done to protect their judges. Meanwhile, no such retributions were taken against law enforcement in the north of the country.

Why were there such dramatic regional differences in political culture, even within one country? The leading book discussing this question and offering an interpretation is by Robert Putnam (1993), entitled *Making Democracy Work: Civic Traditions in Modern Italy*. Putnam begins by showing that such violence as was encountered during the mafia trials is part of a more general sense of strong individualism in southern Italy, wherein there is minimal trust for other persons. Putnam draws in turn on the monograph of Edward Banfield (1958), dramatically entitled *The Moral Basis of a Backward Society*. Banfield spent a year in a village in southern Italy, his wife's hometown, studying this so-called backward approach to politics: among others, he notes that there were no civic organizations that were active or engaging citizens in the town. There were a few business associations; though there were churches and some merchant organizations, they did not engage citizens actively. The peasants did not even trust God, and certainly not the Pope or Catholic priests. Neighbors did not trust neighbors. Husbands did not trust their wives, who did not trust their husbands.

In this context, wherein nobody trusted anyone else, the provider of order was the mafia. It "sold protection"; average persons and small businesspeople paid fees to avoid being attacked by the mafia itself or by anyone else. The mafia was important because there was virtually no other institution between the individual and the state mediating social relationships. By contrast, towns in northern Italy are styled relatively more like the participatory Massachusetts that Tocqueville documented. Citizens voted more, participated more in organizations, trusted each other more, and local governments were much more responsive to their constituencies.

Putnam probed the quality of public institutions by testing public services: he mailed a simple request for a form to local governments in regions across all of Italy. In many regions of the north, the forms came back within a few days. In many regions in the south, however, after repeated mailed requests and personal visits to the administrative agencies, the form was still never provided (while this proxy is in some ways problematic, the general point persists). Putnam concluded from this experiment that northern Italy was able to draw on the experience of several hundred years of democracy at a local level in city-states such as Venice and Florence, which in turn increased the quality of the public institutions. Northern Italian city-states were autonomous; they developed locally, with leaders who were active and negotiated with one another in a locally democratic context. It had a comparatively more vibrant civil society and mechanisms of participation that mediated state functions, and those civil society organizations were able to mediate antisocial impulses (such as the retribution taken against judges during the mafia trials), as well as to be responsive to the needs of its constituents (the ability to return a written request for a form).

Additionally, Putnam analyzed data that suggested that the civic organizations present in early nineteenth-century Italy stimulated much more economic growth—via cooperation—than in other regions that lacked such cooperation. Small towns in parts of the north would specialize in fabric, pottery, machinery, and other products; small artisans would collaborate and help one another. The economic growth rate was so dramatic that this phenomenon has been the subject of much study and speculation. By contrast, many areas in southern Italy have been economically stagnant. Putnam argues through his statistical analysis that the distrust and lack of civic/organizational engagement has suppressed economic development for centuries.

The mafia story provides an anti-model—what can happen in a case *without* civil society—and other studies demonstrate the effect of civil society organizations on both trust and economic development. Francis Fukuyama, in his book on trust (1996), shows that countries that experience or have experienced authoritarian political leadership have citizens who report less civic activity and trust in World Values Surveys. He predicts that the most successful nations in the new free-market world will be those with religious and cultural underpinnings that promote voluntary associations and help prepare people to work cooperatively in large organizations: "Social capital and the proclivity of spontaneous sociability have important economic consequences [. . .] there is a relationship between high-trust societies with plentiful social capital—Germany, Japan, and the United States—and the ability to create large, private business organizations" (Fukuyama 1996:29–30). This perspective reinforces the idea that third sector organizations can culturally and institutionally predispose citizens toward certain behaviors.

There are often dramatic age differences at play in this question of trust—younger people around the world tend to be more open to change than their parents and grandparents. Indeed, the work of Ronald Inglehart (1997) and others suggests that most citizens form their views about political participation, ideology, their identities, and related general conceptions of civic, political, and social engagement as young adults, somewhere between ages eighteen and twenty-five. After this, the fundamental political and social commitments seldom are deeply transformed. Such a finding implies, for instance, that societies that have been drastically changed within a brief period of time by war or an economic shock may differ by age cohort in their serious value commitments due to the area's specific history. This seems to be the case in China, and more explicitly the case in South Korea, where the younger generation has grown up in a fairly open democratic political system that is deeply in conflict with older people's ideas. South Korea had military dictators for many years after the Korean War, who were replaced by elected leaders only in the 1980s, when local elections introduced popularly elected mayors and council members. In the World Values Survey, Korean adults answered that the most desirable traits in children include "obedience to parents," a response that very seldom appears in the answers of European or US surveys, or in other Asian countries like Japan (results from unpublished analyses by Terry Clark, Daniel Elazar, and Jerzy Bartkowski).

This sort of generational rift has obvious implications for participation in associational life and can moderate the institutional logics present within third sectors. Where families are stronger social units (such as in China or Korea), this participation can be more family-oriented and consensual, enacted as a family group (think of neighborhood festivals) that discourages more extreme or ideological activities; where societies are more individualistic, participation is more individual, allowing for more demanding participation (Jang, Clark, and Byun 2011). Whereas organizations in Western Europe or North America are composed of people working face-to-face to bring about changes in environmental policy or to run services for the unemployed, young persons in Korea are more active in individualized or invisible associations; scholars have suggested that this sort of involvement is more common because young Koreans fear sanctions from their parents and grandparents for other kinds of political participation. That is, Koreans take action more often through blogs, Internet sites, flash mobs, and other associations wherein the individual can remain relatively anonymous. This has been interpreted as related to a fear of reprisal, combined with an age conflict, and a conflict over parental power and authority. This pattern has also been linked to a religious tradition of Buddhism and Confucianism, which encourages deference to elders and seeks to avoid personal confrontation; it contrasts with the western Protestant tradition, especially Calvinism, which in some ways explicitly encourages more confrontation.

But whatever their format—public or invisible, formal or informal—these associations become important elements of people's lives. A volunteer with World Relief in Spokane, Washington, put it nicely: "being a volunteer isn't a one way relationship and continues to surprise me with unexpected life lessons" (2011). As Putnam's and Banfield's studies suggest, the mere presence of these organizations can help mediate between citizens and their political lives, tempering some of the more deviant tendencies and providing coherence and integration in a complicated world.

1980s and 1990s: Institutionalization of NGOs and the Proliferation of the Third Sector

Worldwide, a veritable explosion of nonprofit organizations and activities began in the late 1980s and continued well into the first decade of the twenty-first century. In the United States alone, the number of nonprofits went from 1.20 million in 1999 to 1.39 million in 2004, to 1.43 million in 2009 (Roeger, Blackwood, and Pettijohn 2011). This was simultaneous with the spread of the unique blend of fiscal conservatism and social liberalism called the New Political Culture, to which we referred above.

Major socioeconomic changes in developed societies around the world encouraged both the rise the New Political Culture (NPC) and the third sector. While the NPC blend of social liberalism and fiscal conservatism was first identified in the 1970s in urban America, it has spread to many parts of the world in the twenty-first century. The NPC includes several general elements:

- The classic left–right dimension has been transformed.
- Social and fiscal/economic issues are explicitly distinguished from one another.
- Social issues have risen in salience relative to fiscal/economic issues.
- Market individualism and social individualism have grown.
- Issue politics and broader citizen participation have risen, while hierarchical political organizations have declined.
- These NPC views are more pervasive among younger, more educated, and affluent individuals and societies.

Consider the NPC and the role of associations and organizations; there are two main points of particular concern. First, in a New Political Culture analysis, we see citizen concerns becoming less about production and more about consumption. This transformation is heightened by higher income and more education, as citizens and consumers want and expect more subtlety in how they are addressed by employers and salespersons seeking to market to them. In China, the production of large quantities of standardized products at low cost was seen as increasing the economic well-being of most citizens in a powerful way, for decades. As higher levels of income, education, media exposure, Internet penetration, and the like are reached, citizens and consumers grow more sophisticated in their demands for products and services. Income alone no longer dictates specific consumer practices ipso facto. That is, the consumer has become more critical and distinct from the producer. Suddenly the citizen is more than his or her work; *participation, lifestyle, and consumption practices take on increasing importance and merge with identity.* This in turn leads to the development of what we have termed "issue specificity." Citizens do not become engaged by a single factor (like a Left Party program often stressing class cleavages, as was common for many socialist and communist parties in Europe in the twentieth century, and the New Deal Democratic Party tradition in the United States). Instead, different sets of citizens may be engaged by different issues or factors (like the environment or public health).

As class politics has morphed into this New Political Culture, many local and national political leaders later came to adopt an agenda that contained all or parts of it. Some use terms like "neoliberalism" to describe this interlinking of consumption and identity. Multiple patterns can be seen in Europe, Asia, and Latin America. In the 1990s, with the acceleration of economic globalization and the digital revolution (encompassing technological innovations

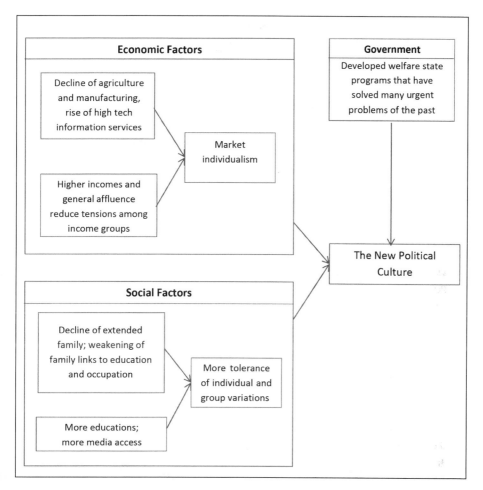

Figure 2. Factors contributing to the rise of the New Political Culture.
Source: Clark and Hoffman-Martinot 1998:37.

such as the Internet, mobile phones, and personal computers), the shift from production to consumption provided fertile territory within which a rapid growth of third sector organizations has occurred.

Within this context, the expansion of the third sector has publically linked a sense of moralism and concern for the disadvantaged to the prevalent political discourse of consumption. Third sector organizations are active in this in-between space. Additionally, governments across the world began to outsource services to the third sector as a way of bringing policies "closer" to their recipients. Such a shift was driven by concern for traditional economic issues (that previously had been more the purview of technical administrators), as well as a sense that they were often more agile than government agencies, and nearly always cheaper. In many instances international NGOs filled the gaps in countries where central administrations were particularly bureaucratic or otherwise dysfunctional.

Unsurprisingly, this "nonprofit explosion" has brought with it a new academic and policy concern with the third sector. The Johns Hopkins University (JHU) Comparative Nonprofit Sector Project has demonstrated that nonprofit institutions constitute a significant economic force; the project has since produced a more comprehensive "Handbook on Non-Profit Institutions in the System of National Accounts" to provide a fuller picture of the

Table 1. Contribution to GDP, NPOs vs. other industries, by country

	France	Japan	United States
Third sector, including volunteers	4.2%	5.2%	7.2%
Electricity, gas, and water supply	1.5%	2.5%	2.0%
Construction	4.7%	6.5%	4.4%
Financial intermediation	4.2%	6.7%	7.7%
Transport, storage, and communication	5.7%	6.8%	5.9%

Source: Adapted from the Johns Hopkins University Center for Civil Society Studies 2004.

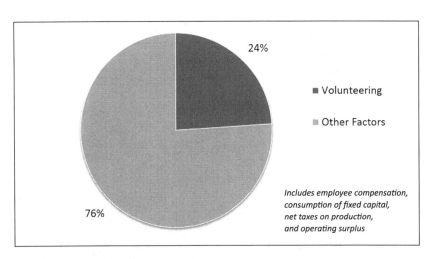

Figure 3. Source of third sector contribution
to GDP vs. other factors in seven countries.

Source: Salmon, Haddock, Solokowski, and Tice 2007:7.

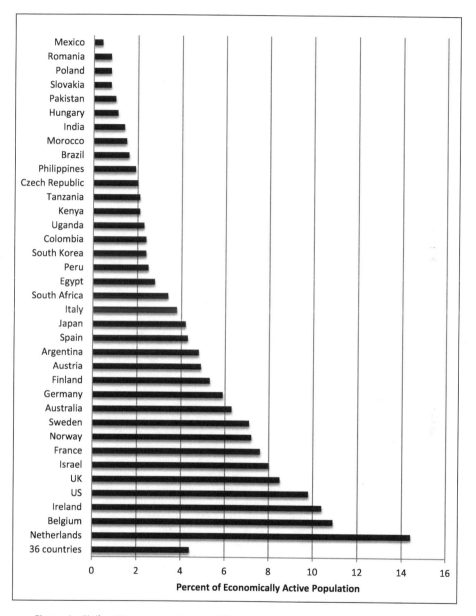

Figure 4. Civil society organization workforce as a share of the economically active population, by country, 1995–2000.

Source: Johns Hopkins Center for Civil Society Studies 2004:1.

Table 2. Civil society sector full-time exempt workforce, by field, 33 countries

Country	Culture	Education	Health	Social Services	Environment	Development	Civic	Foundations	International	Professional	n.e.c.	Total (thousands)
Argentina	13.8	31.5	9.8	13.5	1.6	15.7	1.8	0.1	0.8	8.2	3.2	659.4
Australia	22.7	17.9	14.9	23.6	1.4	10.4	2.9	0.2	0.4	3.3	2.4	579.7
Belgium	11.1	30.5	23.9	22.9	0.5	8.3	0.5	0.3	0.4	1.5	0.0	456.9
Brazil	15.1	35.1	17.5	19.2	0.2	3.0	0.7	0.0	0.4	8.6	0.3	1173.8
Colombia	7.5	20.2	15.3	18.7	0.8	18.5	1.6	1.5	0.1	14.9	0.9	377.6
Czech Re.	35.8	10.6	11.9	13.1	6.1	6.7	3.5	2.2	1.4	8.6	0.0	155.1
Finland	32.6	12.4	13.1	15.5	0.7	1.6	16.8	0.2	0.4	6.2	0.4	137.6
France	30.0	14.6	9.2	27.4	5.0	4.7	1.9	0.6	2.4	4.3	0.0	1981.5
Germany	19.7	7.6	21.8	27.2	2.8	4.4	3.3	1.0	1.6	4.2	6.4	2418.9
Hungary	36.8	8.9	4.7	15.1	2.2	11.3	2.3	3.7	1.0	14.0	0.0	54.8
India	12.2	39.3	12.0	31.6	0.0	0.0	0.0	0.0	0.0	0.0	5.0	6035.0
Ireland	10.5	43.0	23.3	13.0	0.9	5.7	0.5	0.7	0.4	1.7	0.3	150.3
Israel	8.6	41.4	27.2	16.0	0.6	0.8	2.0	1.6	0.1	1.6	0.0	176.7
Italy	23.9	14.8	18.0	26.1	1.2	3.6	3.0	0.8	0.6	6.7	1.2	950.1
Japan	5.5	18.5	37.3	17.3	0.7	1.9	0.5	1.1	1.6	5.0	10.7	2835.2
Kenya	4.7	10.8	10.1	18.6	4.0	20.2	5.3	0.3	0.0	1.5	24.5	287.3
Mexico	6.4	30.7	8.4	16.3	1.8	1.2	0.8	0.8	0.0	33.6	0.0	141.0
Netherlands	17.2	23.1	29.5	20.3	2.0	1.7	2.9	0.2	1.2	1.8	0.0	1051.8
Norway	41.2	11.2	6.0	14.0	0.6	4.3	6.3	0.2	2.9	13.1	0.3	163.0
Pakistan	5.2	56.6	10.4	8.0	0.3	7.8	10.0	0.0	0.0	1.7	0.0	442.7
Peru	2.5	45.2	2.6	38.3	0.4	8.8	0.5	0.9	0.0	0.9	0.0	210.0
Philippines	5.6	30.5	2.0	6.2	2.1	21.3	1.7	1.0	0.4	29.3	0.0	5717.6
Poland	32.7	22.2	6.7	19.5	1.7	1.0	1.0	0.4	1.0	10.8	0.3	154.6
Romania	28.6	15.1	8.5	32.2	2.2	2.4	3.8	1.0	4.0	2.4	0.0	83.9
Slovakia	37.0	20.4	1.9	10.1	9.0	1.1	3.8	5.6	0.9	9.1	1.1	23.0
South Africa	17.6	5.5	10.0	25.6	5.9	17.9	15.9	0.4	0.0	1.1	0.0	562.4
South Korea	4.9	40.5	25.8	15.5	0.0	0.0	9.9	0.0	0.0	3.4	0.0	535.4
Spain	15.2	20.6	10.5	30.8	3.0	9.2	5.9	0.1	2.6	1.8	0.2	728.8
Sweden	45.5	6.8	0.9	10.5	2.1	4.4	10.2	0.2	2.3	15.4	1.7	342.9
Tanzania	10.3	11.7	10.5	16.4	10.6	12.8	7.1	7.8	3.9	3.2	5.8	330.9
Uganda	22.7	12.8	6.7	28.8	1.0	20.2	0.5	1.0	0.2	3.3	2.6	228.6
U.K.	27.5	25.4	8.0	16.0	2.4	12.5	1.8	1.3	2.4	1.5	1.2	2536.0
U.S.	9.0	18.5	34.2	22.1	1.0	4.0	4.9	1.0	0.3	3.9	1.1	13549.1
Developing	16.6	24.9	9.7	19.3	2.8	9.4	3.9	1.5	0.8	8.6	2.6	12720.2
Developed	21.4	20.4	18.5	20.2	1.7	5.2	4.2	0.6	1.3	4.8	1.7	28242.7
33 Countries	18.8	22.9	13.7	19.7	2.3	7.5	4.0	1.1	1.0	6.9	2.2	40149.3

* Percent of total civil society workforce. Percentages add to 100% across fields.
Source: Johns Hopkins Center for Civil Society Studies 2004:5.

Table 3. Third sector sources of support, with and without volunteers, 34 countries

Country	Excluding volunteers				Including volunteers			
	Government (% of total)	Philanthropy (% of total)	Fees (% of total)	Total (US$)	Government (% of total)	Philanthropy (% of total)	Fees (% of total)	Total (US$)
Argentina	19.5%	7.5%	73.1%	$13,321	16.2%	23.0%	60.8%	$16,014
Australia	31.2%	6.3%	62.5%	$19,810	25.4%	23.6%	51.0%	$24,295
Austria	50.4%	6.1%	43.5%	$6,262	41.3%	23.1%	35.6%	$7,643
Belgium	76.8%	4.7%	18.6%	$25,576	65.9%	18.1%	16.0%	$29,773
Brazil	15.5%	10.7%	73.8%	$11,390	14.5%	16.3%	69.2%	$12,144
Colombia	14.9%	14.9%	70.2%	$1,719	13.1%	24.9%	62.0%	$1,948
Czech Re.	39.4%	14.0%	46.6%	$860	32.1%	30.0%	37.9%	$1,056
Finland	36.2%	5.9%	57.9%	$6,064	25.2%	34.6%	40.3%	$8,722
France	57.8%	7.5%	34.6%	$57,304	33.4%	46.6%	20.0%	$99,234
Germany	64.3%	3.4%	32.3%	$94,454	42.5%	36.2%	21.3%	$142,877
Hungary	27.1%	18.4%	54.6%	$1,433	26.2%	21.1%	52.7%	$1,483
India	36.1%	12.9%	51.0%	$3,026	24.9%	39.9%	35.2%	$4,382
Ireland	77.2%	7.0%	15.8%	$5,017	67.6%	18.6%	13.8%	$5,732
Israel	63.9%	10.2%	25.8%	$10,947	59.1%	17.0%	23.9%	$11,842
Italy	36.6%	2.8%	60.6%	$39,356	30.2%	19.7%	50.1%	$47,647
Japan	45.2%	2.6%	52.1%	$258,959	41.5%	10.7%	47.8%	$282,314
Kenya	4.8%	14.2%	81.0%	$404	4.3%	23.9%	71.8%	$456
Mexico	8.5%	6.3%	85.2%	$1,554	7.5%	17.9%	74.7%	$1,774
Netherlands	59.0%	2.4%	38.6%	$60,399	46.1%	23.9%	30.1%	$77,391
Norway	35.0%	6.9%	58.1%	$5,640	20.0%	46.9%	33.1%	$9,895
Pakistan	6.0%	42.9%	51.1%	$310	4.9%	53.1%	41.9%	$378
Peru	18.1%	12.2%	69.8%	$1,272	17.5%	14.7%	67.7%	$1,310
Philippines	5.2%	3.2%	91.6%	$1,103	3.1%	43.2%	53.7%	$1,878
Poland	24.1%	15.5%	60.4%	$2,620	22.8%	20.1%	57.1%	$2,771
Romania	45.0%	26.5%	28.5%	$130	20.5%	66.5%	13.0%	$285
Slovakia	21.9%	23.5%	54.9%	$295	21.3%	25.1%	53.5%	$302
South Africa	44.2%	24.2%	31.7%	$2,386	31.5%	56.9%	22.6%	$3,346
South Korea	24.3%	4.4%	71.4%	$19,753	21.6%	14.9%	63.5%	$22,186
Spain	32.1%	18.8%	49.0%	$25,778	25.2%	36.3%	38.5%	$32,833
Sweden	28.7%	9.1%	62.3%	$10,599	14.6%	53.7%	31.7%	$20,805
Tanzania	27.0%	20.0%	53.1%	$263	12.8%	61.9%	25.3%	$552
Uganda	7.1%	38.2%	54.7%	$108	5.5%	51.8%	42.7%	$139
U.K.	46.7%	8.8%	44.6%	$78,220	36.4%	28.8%	34.8%	$100,196
U.S.	30.5%	12.9%	56.6%	$566,960	25.6%	26.9%	47.4%	$675,973
Developing/ transitional	21.6%	17.2%	61.3%	—	16.7%	33.0%	50.3%	—
Developed	48.2%	7.2%	44.6%	—	37.5%	39.0%	33.5%	—
34 Countries	34.1%	12.5%	53.4%	—	26.5%	31.1%	42.4%	—

Source: Johns Hopkins Center for Civil Society Studies 2004:6.

economic contributions of these organizations (for more information on this project, see Salamon et al. 2007). We draw on these data in the several preceding and following tables and figures, as listed in their notes. The data come from the JHU project on nonprofits and serve to illustrate the growing significance of the third sector globally.

During this time, the world also saw a massive increase in explicitly *transnational* third sector organizations, which were often (though not always) associated with international development projects and humanitarian assistance. In Africa, their influence was such that the 1980s were known as the "NGO Decade" in African development discourse. For instance, the number of transnational NGOs working in the area of human rights went from less than 40 in the 1960s to nearly 180 in the early 1990s (Frumkin 2005:29).

As we have explained, much of the literature sees this development of NGOs as a bottom-up phenomenon, emphasizing the logic of activism, particularly given its Calvinist roots. However, Reimann argues that top-down initiatives have also had a good deal to do with the burgeoning of this sector, especially in terms of transnational organizations, demonstrating that the institutional logics of bureaucracy and professionalization have been powerfully present as the sector developed. This more structuralist perspective recognizes the contributions of states and international organizations that have actively stimulated and promoted the sector from "above." This involvement, she argues, can be seen as a part of an ever-increasing political globalization (Reimann 2006:46). Several UN agencies have supported the development of NGO activities, especially following World War II. Since then, UN support for third sector organizations mushroomed to include funding for programs and activities well outside the original purview of funding development projects. For instance, the UN Children's Fund (UNICEF), since 1989, has worked with NGOs regarding child protection, child labor, and children in armed conflicts; the World Food Program uses nonprofit organizations as its main implementing partners; the UN Commission on Human Rights provides funds to enable NGO participation at meetings and human rights projects; the United Nations Populations Fund has funded NGOs as program implementors since 1969; and the World Bank uses civil society partners in many of its projects (including in its special grant program) for capacity development (Reimann 2006:50–51).

The European Union (EU), for example, began financing nongovernmental organizations in the middle of the 1970s, beginning with a small annual co-financing budget of approximately $3.2 million. That amount increased rapidly to $1 billion by 1995. Similarly, the EU humanitarian aid program also rose dramatically during this time.

Effectiveness and Evaluation

As the third sector formalized in the United States and the institutional logic of professionalization became more deeply entrenched, practitioners, funders, and community groups have had to contend with the question of effectiveness in civil society organizations. This question becomes particularly salient as more and more organizations receive outside funding—private or public—and are consequently asked for indicators that can quantify their progress for those who support them materially. As briefly illustrated here, within the question of evaluation and in the United States especially, a tension emerges between the logic of professionalization and other institutional logics, particularly activism.

Because the third sector encompasses such a broad range of organizations, effectiveness can vary by field, and scholars rightly point out that different observers may vary in the weights that they attach to different impacts, and that impacts will invariably be different among organizations and countries (Salamon, Hems, and Chinnock 2000:5). For example, nonprofit colleges and universities are generally considered to be highly effective entities, whereas international nonprofit organizations doing development work may be less so (additionally, social change as such is notoriously difficult to measure). Generally speaking, most organizations try to measure some combination of the following, broadly recognized benefits of the third sector:

- Service: the nonprofit sector generally provides services that are, to some degree, public. These services may be difficult to supply through the private market because they must be available regardless of ability to pay (e.g., housing and food), or because the services require some special element of trust (e.g., battered women's shelters).
- Innovation: Because they are not driven by the "bottom line," nonprofit organizations are also potentially more flexible and adaptable than other types of organizations and more able to take risks. This point has been debated, as some other scholars contend that because they are bound by certain outcome measurements and external financing, nonprofit organizations may be less innovative than their for-profit counterparts.
- Advocacy: Because they are not beholden to the market, and are not part of the governmental apparatus, nonprofit organizations have the ability to advocate changes in policy or social conditions. This role is also consistent with the voluntary character of nonprofit organizations and the availability of these organizations as mechanisms to rally people who share a particular concern, serving as a link between individuals and the broader political process.

- Expressiveness: These organizations also potentially perform a broader role as vehicles for individual and group self-expression.
- Community building: third sector organizations can build community, by encouraging social interaction and helping to create habits of trust and reciprocity, which in turn support political participation (Salamon, Hems, and Chinnock 2000).

Similarly, and like any sector, the third sector has its drawbacks, which vary by field, location, and social context. Evaluations are also intended to flag the presence of negative dynamics, which can often include the following:

- Particularism: third sector organizations can be inflexible as regards the broad public interest, since they are especially responsive to the concerns of a particular group. They can discriminate in operations on the basis of religious, ethnic, or cultural values. Where groups vary in their resources, this phenomenon can reinforce inequalities at a broader level.
- Paternalism: nonprofits can reinforce dependence on the part of those who rely on their services. In extreme cases, this dependency can be used to force those without an alternative to accept certain religious or moral convictions because they lack other options.
- "Mission creep": because nonprofits depend on outside funding for survival, their mission can "drift" or "creep" away from original intent toward promising sources of support.
- Extreme amateurism or professionalism: though nonprofits can cut overhead considerably by relying on volunteer and private support, organizations can subsequently be unable or unwilling to staff themselves with competitive, qualified personnel. This is known as amateurism. Nonprofits "can also fall prey to excessive professional control and professionalization of problem solving. This happens when professional staff gain too complete control over agency operations and limit the involvement of members, clients, or other nonprofessionals" (Salamon, Hems, and Chinnock 2000)— what we have termed *professionalization*.

However, evaluation particularly can be fraught with differences in opinion and competing priorities. A 2013 paper compares two contrasting institutional logics operating simultaneously within the nonprofit funding relationship. In a study looking at the funding relationships between nonprofit grantees and foundation grantors, Kallman (2013) found evidence of a tension between institutional logics that acted particularly powerfully on issues of evaluation and outcomes. The first logic encompasses both bureaucracy and professionalization, and is generally found among foundation grant makers. The other logic is of social change, relies heavily on the language of social movements, and is generally found among NGO grantees.

The paper demonstrates how foundation staff operate within the logic of professionalization. These foundation program officers are accountable for large sums of money and must allocate it responsibly among a host of compelling projects in a methodical and meritocratic fashion. The third sector, still combating doubts about its legitimacy, has had to answer to recent civil society and government emphases on transparency (Ospina, Diaz, and O'Sullivan 2002; Ylvisaker 1987) that push questions of replicability, reproducibility, accountability, and efficiency to the forefront. Through a process of mimetic isomorphism (DiMaggio and Powell 1983), the third sector thus adopts practices of measurability and transparency that reference the private sector. These practices are intended to strengthen its legitimacy, though they are sometimes seen as "colonizing" philanthropy through inappropriate frames (Wirgau, Farley, and Jensen 2010).

Many foundation staff, however, come from an activist background and are charged with combining the passion and charisma of grassroots organizations—the institutional logic of activism, to which many owe ideological allegiances and professional development—with the bureaucratic ideals of professional grant making organizations and the accompanying political pressures.

NGO workers, on the other hand, use issue framing tactics (Snow 2007), respond to political opportunities, and deploy a language of resource mobilization (McCarthy and Zald 1977a) when discussing their searches for funding and their work generally. The activist logic of social movement discourses values individual charisma and collective activist identity, and contains a strong critique of the power distribution in society; these concerns are apparent in the practices and language of NGO staff members. Formalized NGOs count social movements as important predecessors to both their identities and their approaches to their work; nongovernmental organizations ranging from the Southern Poverty Law Center to Greenpeace were born of specific activist and social movement traditions and LAGI, discussed below, was formalized after years of activism in communities ravaged by the Salvadorian civil war. The logic of social movements turns heavily upon the individual identity of an activist, a concept that helps "captur[e] better the pleasures and obligations that actually persuade people to mobilize" (Polletta and Jasper 2001:284).

The logic of social movements also depends on specific leadership qualities (Barker, Johnson, and Lavalette 2001), especially charisma. Many movements and movement organizations count such leaders among their most transformative assets (Burns 2012; Conger and Kanungo 1987, 1998). Tasked with being both "mobilizers," who inspire participants, and "articulators," who link the movement to larger society (Gusfield 1966; Morris and Staggenborg 2007), these charismatic leaders, by virtue of their exceptionalism, are highly attractive to funders and supporters. Charisma is an individual characteristic in the funding relationship that helps shape funding decisions. In its pure form, charisma "has a character specifically foreign to everyday routine structures" (Weber 1947:363)—that is, it is specifically unbureaucratic and unsystematic.

Funding relationships embody strain between these two institutional logics, which becomes particularly present in questions on evaluation and outcome. In many cases, grant-making or foundation staff feel caught between dichotomous views on what evaluation *should actually be* and what it should be used for, and the technical and legal requirements involved with giving money; this tension is reflected in a lack of field-wide best practices or general expectations. Foundation staff report ongoing conversations about the differences between *informational* and *learning* evaluation, as the following quote from a foundation staff member demonstrates:

> There are those of us who believe that evaluation is most effectively used for learning: "How do you learn in order to make your work more effective?" As opposed to a strictly evaluational perspective: "Did you do what you said you were going to do?" And they're not particularly compatible . . . if you put the emphasis on accountability, and doing what you said you were going to do—in most cases we are dealing with support for complex social phenomena. . . . And if you're locked into doing what you said you were going to do . . . You've become a lot less innovative and creative, and are tied into reporting on ideas that . . . have become locked in time. (Quoted in Kallman 2012:17)

She continues,

> We're in a transition time where things are becoming increasingly centralized and bureaucratic, and that makes everything very, very hard, because we're not staffed to deal with the increasing complexity of the requirements that are put on us. . . . When you're staffed this way, it's very hard to be a learning organization . . . And now we're being asked for the product of that without the conditions or having put in place the systems . . . it's a lot easier to assume responsibilities for outcomes if you become more informational. And these strategies become more specific, in which case you're basically looking for people on the ground to carry out the work that you think needs to be done.

Similarly, another foundation director says:

> There is a difference between *outcome* and *output*. Output should be clearly quantifiable, the results of what the money has done. Outcome is hard to measure . . . and has to do more with other changes in society. That's one of the weaknesses of the program. Grantees have a responsibility to the donor

community, but there is also . . . a need to create structure for the grantees themselves. Isaacson staff has a responsibility to its Board, and must show them what has been done with the Board's money. (Kallman 2012:18)

Nonprofit grantees in this study were less enthusiastic about such distinctions. A grantee discussed his program evaluation in this way: "[It was] eighteen questions or so, all sort of essay short answer type things, all fragmented. Nothing that says 'explain what this grant is about' but rather 'explain this little portion of it'" (quoted in Kallman 2012:17). A grantee from Central America says:

[In the US] they want to know: what is the objective, what are the results. The emphasis is much more on results that you can measure, and for that reason it is much more difficult to seek funding, for example, for peace. With an economic project you can say, "these chickens will lay twenty eggs a week," but the question of peace is a question of values, of change, of mentalities, of activities, and it's difficult to subject it to a measure.

Grantors in this study acknowledged that reporting requirements can be a significant time commitment for their grantees, and though no foundation reported having a fully efficient system for tracking grantee progress, many mentioned the burden that reporting constitutes for NGOs. One program officer meets with a group of other conservation donors biweekly to develop common systems for conservation outcomes so "that we don't keep bugging grant recipients with different measurements." This structured, systematic process of reporting outcome is considered a critical part of transparency and professional responsibility within grant making, but it stands in tension with both some of the structures of nonprofit grant making in general, and the institutional logic of activism.

Further, there remains some debate about where, when, and how a formal nonprofit model benefits the ultimate delivery of services. DeMars claims that "the tendency by scholars to create utopian promises based on mundane practices reflects the self-understanding of NGOs themselves" (DeMars 2005). Others see prevalent institutional contexts favoring the "formalization of movements into NGOs through rules related to fundraising, access to representation within decision-making, and enhanced social legitimacy. In these settings, formal NGO formation mitigates important obstacles to the sustenance of collective action" (Teegan, Doh, and Vachani 2004:465), clearly recognizing the model's capacity for resource mobilization and institutional legitimacy in social movement language. Dichter's (2003) searing critique provides an example:

To survive, today's NGO has been forced to be more corporation-like . . . its primary concern, though rhetorically still to actualize social visions, is also to cater to a marketplace (of ideas, funders, backers, supporters). Therefore, internally the idea of product and service and customer satisfaction has taken hold . . . More and more, NGOs take the pulse of their organizational health by checking with their fund-raisers first. The key question for many has become not "Are we doing a good job?" but "Are we continuing to grow our donor base?" Money has become a driving force, whereas once it was merely assumed as a fairly readily available means to an end . . . As a consequence of the subtle cultural shift to private sector commercial values, large numbers of NGOs now exist in what one might call a global marketplace of altruism. (54–55)

This reaction against the corporatization and commodification of activist organizations is present, though not extensively documented. Adjoa Florência Jones de Almeida writes, in "The Revolution Will Not Be Funded,"

We are too busy being told to market ourselves by pimping our communities' poverty in proposals, selling "results" in reports and accounting for our finances in financial reviews. In essence, our organizations have become mini-corporations, because on some level, we have internalized the idea that power—the ability to create change—equals money . . . our activism is held hostage to our jobs . . . many of us spend over half of our staff hours struggling to raise salaries instead of creating real . . . alternatives to the institutional oppression . . . Meanwhile, the imaginative and spiritual perspective that would allow us to question the "givens" dictated by neoliberalism begins to erode. (Jones de Almeida 2009, n.p.)

Competition for funding among nonprofit organizations also brings the same kinds of new values that competition in the for-profit sector implies, including efficiency, customer (donor) satisfaction, and privatization (specialization, in the NGO context): "But although the rhetoric of the reinvented corporation is taken on, the issue of actual performance remains the dilemma for NGOs it always was. In the end poverty alleviation is not a product, and this fact remains the fundamental flaw in these seemingly benign cultural transfers" (Dichter 1999:53). This emphasis on outcomes and corporation rhetoric can place strain on original NGO mission and strategy, diverting energies away from a principal objective to the new, important goal of pleasing a funder.

This section has explored some of the complexities around evaluation for the nonprofit sector as it relates to funding sources. As this case study took place in the United States, one might look to the Western Calvinist values we have described above as root sources of this type of criticism, which does not, in the same fashion, exist in Asia. While there are too many facets of this conversation to cover exhaustively here, this section is intended to alert the reader to some of the main issues at play.

As we enter the second decade of the twenty-first century, it is clear that the third sector constitutes an important part of the economy in many countries. Its presence as a legitimate sector, doing measurable work, has increased dramatically in the last thirty years. The third sector still varies widely in its relationship to funders and to the state and in its organizational form from country to country; these differences are discussed in detail in the subsequent chapters. Next, we provide a brief overview of the relationship of third sector associations with the state and discuss several ways of thinking about the quality and character of those relationships.

Non-Western Traditions and Sharp Contrasts

When Terry Clark presented some observations on associations and democracy to a meeting of the Japanese Political Science Association soon after 2000, several political scientists commented, "We have no democratic tradition in Japan." They recounted a story of Japanese peasants who circulated a petition requesting a small reform, which one person would then place in the carriage of the emperor when he passed through the village. The petitioner was executed, following the tradition that a courier who challenges must be dispensed with; it was considered improper for a peasant to request change from higher authorities. In many instances the administrative staff implemented those very reforms regardless. However, it was considered the responsibility of the administrators to make this judgment, based on *administrative review*, not on the *process* of citizen consultation. Of course, this is the opposite of the Tocqueville/Calvinist story. Max Weber's books on ancient Judaism and China (Weber 1967, 1968) as contrasted with Calvinism and the Protestant ethic are classic sources codifying these background contexts. They point to the core elements of culture and subcultures as explanations for the development of different kinds of political systems and processes of political involvement.

Still, even if traditions of these sorts help explain the background against which third sector organizations have developed around the world, they are neither homogeneous nor unchanging. The dramatic transformations in China in the last few decades are one of the most powerful testimonies as to how rapidly change can occur. In recent years, China has embraced market principles in addition to its strong political egalitarianism, reshaping political and economic life with astounding speed. With other transformations underway around the globe, increasingly since the fall of the Berlin wall in 1989, strong class-based political ideologies as competing worldviews are no longer such helpful guides to interpret many specific policies. The widespread political and economic crises of the early years of the twenty-first century point to problems in how citizens feel they are represented, while specific community organization mechanisms—like those debated in Tocqueville—have grown more salient.

The third sector organizations that in many Asian contexts are linked tightly with the national government often have service provision as a principal concern. That is, the service *recipient* is the main focus: the poor person, the elderly, children. Many organizations, such as small clinics, have been seen as a useful alternative and more efficient mode for providing services than the national government. These are smaller and more nimble (and often less expensive and more efficient) agencies. In some cases, citizens even "coproduce" the service (i.e., citizen volunteers tutor at-risk children after school). Having citizens more actively engaged is thought to generate a higher-quality and lower-cost service. In some cases, private groups are more easily prepared to handle these delicate social projects than the bigger state agencies. The Hungarian-American George Soros funded a large number of studies of this process, and Soros himself wrote books (Soros 2004) on how important the third sector was to the economic and political systems in authoritarian areas like East Europe and Russia.

More generally, there has been a move away from an emphasis on the more technical or the production of service for a single type of recipient. Rather, we have seen an increased emphasis on the participants themselves (the providers of services) working with and within organizations and associations. These questions are central: What is the impact of these associations on participating citizens? Do they trust one another more? Do they trust the state more? Does the quality of life improve when citizen participation improves? Does this vary across the United States, Europe, and Asia? What are the regional differences?

Social Enterprise

The country comparisons we undertake in the remainder of this book are intended to explore the various forms that third sectors take across the globe. In almost all cases we see tensions—and sometimes open conflicts—between governing institutional logics (particular tensions emerge worldwide between bureaucracy and activism, professionalization and activism, and paternalism and professionalization).

And nonprofit practitioners are in no way blind to these tensions. Some, in fact, have been exploring alternatives to the traditional format of the NGO. One type of organization has been broadly termed "social enterprise," which we consider here. A relatively new project that has strong conceptual and practical roots in the third sector, social enterprise has emerged most forcefully in Europe. "Social enterprise," as a term, describes the nonconventional entrepreneurial dynamics of these organizations, which are also meaningfully different from the largely donor-dependent NGO. This sort of organization involves a type of program or activity wherein the business activities and the social interventions are synonymous in that "the work performed by clients is both rehabilitative and revenue generating" (Cooney 2010:1–2).

In other words, social enterprises are organizations that try to do good while also financially supporting themselves through their activities, rendering them less dependent on the whims of outside donors and thus theoretically more able to sustain their own visions. Such organizations include, for example, a home for battered women in Bolivia that serves lunch in its attached restaurant; the proceeds from the restaurant go to support other types or rehabilitative therapies for the program's residents. Social enterprise organizations are "a kind of encompassing set of strategic responses to many of the varieties of environmental turbulence and situational challenges that nonprofit organizations face today" (Dart 2004:413), ranging from financial insecurity to missions that become compromised in the process of trying to please too many stakeholders. The logic of such groups is, in some ways fundamentally similar to that of third sector organizations, to respond to the needs that have not been met by the public or private sectors. Social enterprise is appealing in large part because it has managed to construct a high degree of moral legitimacy for itself, that connects its own emergence to "neoconservative, pro-business, and pro-market political and ideological values" (411) that are central under neoliberalism for many OECD (Organization for Economic Cooperation and Development) countries; it is not antibusiness. And still, social enterprise's motives are similar to those of traditional charitable organizations. In this way, it manages to capitalize on the most powerful institutional and moral components of the third sector.

Social enterprise organizations developed in Europe against a backdrop of persistent unemployment. Along with the shrinking of the social safety nets under neoliberal economics and the fiscal crisis have come factors that accentuate the entrepreneurial character of third sector organizations (in that they have increasing commonalities with traditional companies). A number of new factors have created the political opportunity for the development of social enterprises (Defourny 2001:16):

- Existing associations find themselves competing with each other and some-times with for-profit companies. They are thus obliged to create or reinforce internal management structures very much modeled (isomorphic) on those of the commercial sector.
- Ending certain public monopolies (in Sweden, for example) or larger wel-fare organizations' monopolies (in Germany, for example) encouraged the emergence of new private initiatives (for-profit or nonprofit organizations) structured from the outset to reflect a plurality of organizations in the field.
- For old as well as new associations, the economic risk is greater since their financing henceforward depends on their ability to win these quasi-markets and to satisfy users.

The emergence of social enterprise was linked philosophically with the cooperative movement (Nyssens, Adam, and Johnson 2006:4), and legally spearheaded by the Italian government, whose Parliament first introduced a "social cooperative" status as a legal form. In 1995, Belgium provided for "companies with social purposes," Portugal the "social solidarity coopera-tives" in 1998, and Greece the "social cooperatives with limited liability" in 1999 (Borzaga and Defourny 2004). In 2002 the UK formed the Social En-terprise Coalition and created an attendant unit to improve understanding of social enterprises and promote them throughout Great Britain (Nyssens, Adam, and Johnson 2006). In the United States, the legal form for such enterprises is a benefit corporation, specifically designed for private entities that want to consider social and environmental well-being in their decision making. This kind of legislation is intended to encourage the entrepreneurial and commercial dynamics, while formalizing the multistakeholder decision-making format of this kind of project. It represents the first legal status outside of the 501(c) designations in the United States designed to meet the needs of social enterprise organizations. The accountability provisions in a benefit corporation (also called a B-Corp, for the nonprofit that initially proposed the idea) require a company's director and officials to take environmental and social concerns into consideration in the planning process; in return the company gets some tax breaks. Maryland was the first US state to pass benefit corporation legislation in 2010, but as of this writing California, Hawaii, Il-linois, Louisiana, Massachusetts, New Jersey, New York, Pennsylvania, South Carolina, Vermont, and Virginia had all followed suit.

These new legal frameworks consider *both* the entrepreneurial and com-mercial dynamics an integral part of a social project and are accordingly designed to encourage them. Such frameworks also provide a way of for-malizing a state of multistakeholders by involving the interested parties in decision-making processes (Defourny 2001). European analysis has been split over the concept of social enterprise, with one school of thought stressing the dynamics of entrepreneurship. They cite as examples for-profit firms that seek to "enhance the social impact of their productive activities approach to tackling social needs that is taken by individuals in fostering business, mainly through non-profit organizations, but also in the for-profit sector" (Nyssens, Adam, and Johnson 2006:4). This conceptualization is not unrelated to ideas on corporate responsibility generally.

A second school of thought uses the idea of social enterprise to refer to the organizations that belong to the third sector; in this view, the social impact on the community is not only a consequence or a side effect of economic activity, but its motivation in itself (Nyssens, Adam, and Johnson 2006:5). This perspective sees social enterprise organizations as new entities that, while being a subdivision of the third sector, set out a process: a new (social) enterprise spirit intended to refashion the classic third sector experience (Borzaga and Defourny 2004:1). The primary distinguishing factors in such organizations are their entrepreneurial, and to a degree profit-making, natures.

Social enterprise can be understood as a tool for connecting different parts of the admittedly disparate third sector (organizations that offer "market" services, such as education, and organizations that offer "nonmarket" services, such as youth groups, whose resources, generally speaking, are far less secure). Certainly, if we define both the nonprofit sector and the social economy in terms of their basic structure and organizational rules (rather than in terms of their sources of revenue), social enterprise fits conceptually. The principal difference between social enterprise and traditional associations is that social enterprises place a higher value on economic risk taking, as related to an ongoing productive activity (Nyssens, Adam, and Johnson 2006). Depending on the organization, this profit may go to support other activities within that enterprise, or go to pay workers. As an example, in Buffalo, New York, Buffalo ReUse does green demolition as a part of a work program employing at-risk youth (see Buffalo ReUse n.d.). Moreover,

> Social enterprises are said to combine different types of stakeholders in their membership, whereas traditional co-operatives have generally been set up as single-stakeholder organizations. These contrasting elements, however, should not be overestimated: while social enterprises as we have defined them are in some cases new organizations, which may be regarded as constituting a new subdivision of the third sector, in other cases, they result from a process at work in older experiences within the third sector. In other words, it can be said that the generic term "social enterprise" does not represent a conceptual

break with institutions of the third sector but, rather, a new dynamic within it—encompassing both newly created organizations and older ones that have undergone an evolution (Nyssens, Adam, and Johnson 2006:8–9).

These social enterprises also differ substantively from the general associative character of much of the third sector. Generally speaking, they are not involved in advocacy as a major goal, nor do they concern themselves with the redistribution of money through granting programs (but rather through paid programs). Unlike most public institutions and even third sector organizations, their financial viability depends on the efforts of their members and workers. Like most third sector organizations, decision-making power is not allocated on the basis of ownership (Borzaga and Defourny 2004:17–18). Skeptics might interpret several of these elements as simply internalization of elements often criticized as "corporate," especially the profit focus, lack of redistribution, and minimal outside financing.

Traditional third sectors are often seen as sitting "between" public and private activities, while mobilizing resources from each. The current generation of social enterprises, however, turns on the involvement of different, even diverse partners or categories thereof: "salaried employees, voluntary workers, users, supporting organizations and local authorities are often partners in the same project, whereas the traditional social economy organizations have generally been set up by more homogeneous social groups. If that does not necessarily revolutionize the production process strictly speaking, it often transforms the way in which the activity is organized" (Defourny 2001:14). This cooperation, in some cases, is an alliance of interested parties participating in the coproduction of local services (cooperative, parent-run childcare centers in France and Sweden, for example). In other cases, this kind of a multistakeholder structure may lead social enterprises to compete more effectively with for-profit enterprises within existing market niches.

In the United States the idea of social enterprise is rather vague and refers often to market-oriented economic activities that serve a social goal. The development of social enterprise in the United States has been credited with welfare reform and the Workforce Investment Act of 1998 (Cooney 2010:1–2). Social enterprise is then viewed as both a mechanism to fulfill social goals and an innovative response to the funding problems of third sector organizations (which find it difficult to sustain themselves with private donations and government grants). Social enterprise differs from nonprofit work in that it implies a high degree of innovation, including a not insignificant amount of financial risk taking. Organizations under this broad category can include everything from for-profit businesses engaged in socially beneficial activities to third sector organizations working to support their missions through economic activity. US social enterprise organizations work in a wide range of industries, including construction, manufacturing, and retail. Cooney's (2010) study found that social enterprises in the United States were involved in a vast array of activities, including low-income housing, publishing, horticulture and agriculture (both emerging niches in the United States), retail, construction, manufacturing, restaurant, and maintenance. The work generally targeted at-risk populations, including people with multiple vulnerabilities such as homelessness, mental illness, and substance abuse history, but it is important to note that many of these organizations simply target unemployed or underemployed individuals, suggesting these organizations could emerge as a force in the workforce development arena more generally. With such broad definitions, counting members and distinguishing them from similar organizations is semi-arbitrary.

Funding Social Enterprise

Most social enterprises, similar to both the nonprofit sector and to the social economy, are funded both by market resources (earned income) and noncommercial resources allocated by the public authorities (such as state grants or contracts). These organizations typically also received a substantial amount of nonmonetary resources, such as voluntary labor and in-kind donations (Defourny 2001:17). A 2010 study finds that organizations using earned income as a part of their funding sources sometimes conceptualize the project of social enterprise as part of a move from dependency (on philanthropy, grants, subsidies, etc.) to a position of self-sufficiency:

> Although much of the rhetoric on social entrepreneurship describes a steady march toward self-sufficiency, many scholars and practitioners are coming to recognize that for [social enterprises] the high risk of small business failure combined with the high costs of their job training/work integration social mission require that [. . . they] remain somewhere along the continuum juggling mixed sources of revenues rather than in a state of total self-sufficiency. (Cooney 2010:1–2)

These organizations face something of a difficult balancing act between creating productive and profitable businesses while remaining true to their missions of being client-centered. Social enterprises consequently take different approaches to managing those priorities, including slow growth, cross-subsidization, and diversification. Cooney's study found that many social enterprises subsidize their business ventures, at least in the beginning, with other organizational revenue streams. In other words, the "parent organization" under which the enterprise is established (such as a foundation or social service nonprofit organization) expends money on the for-profit enterprise until the enterprise is able to support itself; theoretically, the pattern then reverses. Social enterprises also often diversify their products and services, and occasionally establish multiple ventures (e.g., an organization running an organic farm can also run a café).

This model, however, frequently meets with problems in attaining self-sufficiency; about 50 percent of the social enterprise businesses continued to require subsidies to remain afloat (Cooney 2010:9). This may occur in part because for-profit and nonprofit organizations require different administrative skill sets, and practitioners meet challenges in managing both things well.

Case Study: YAYA (Young Artists/Young Aspirations)

"Given the right tools and a fertile environment, creative young people can do extraordinary things" (YAYA 2012). So says Jana Napoli, a New Orleans artist and the founder of YAYA (Young Artists/Young Aspirations), Inc., a nonprofit arts and social service organization in Louisiana. Created in 1988, YAYA unites the inner-city youth and business people of NOLA (New Orleans, Louisiana) by empowering young people to create and sell art, all while improving their community. Napoli was spurred into action after witnessing the tensions that arose between local merchants and students from the high school around the corner from her downtown studio. "When I looked at the kids, I saw an enormous amount of creative energy," said Napoli. She noticed, however, that this energy had few outlets. "I thought, 'I bet there are some artists out there. I bet if they had a studio, they could do some great things,'" she continued. Napoli opened her studio doors to the teenagers, and they began to produce art under her guidance. Soon after, she brought in the local businesspeople to see what the kids had been up to. Much of the student art was purchased, and YAYA was quickly off the ground. YAYA's newness, volatility, and recent rise illustrate the rapid emergence of arts-related organizations of all sorts.

The organization has been inspiring students artistically, educationally, and financially ever since. YAYA's stated mission is to "provide educational experiences and opportunities that empower artistically talented inner-city youth to be professionally self-sufficient through creative self-expression." The organization currently operates as a studio-gallery and gives students a chance to apprentice with professional artists, create public artworks, design merchandise, serve as cultural ambassadors, work as project managers, and mentor others in the arts. Indeed, YAYA students are held to high standards: they are expected to maintain good grades and contribute to their community in addition to the work that they do artistically.

This hard work and responsibility pays off in many ways. Through the organization, half of the profits earned from the sale of artwork go directly to the artists (the young people themselves), and the other half is set aside for their college tuition. YAYA participants have higher rates of high school graduation and college matriculation relative to their peers, not to mention professional success in the arts. This student effort has also earned YAYA clients such as Swatch, MTV, the United Nations, Burger King, Whoopi Goldberg, and Spike Lee. By linking youth, art, and business, YAYA brings beauty and empowerment to the local community and has inspired the creation of more than twenty similar organizations across the United States. As Napoli said, "It's incredible to be there for the process of watching greatness unfold."

2. The United States

In the United States, with its history of weak central government, the third sector is seen as playing an essential role in providing services, as well as in organizing and generating political diversity and engendering social capital. In general, understanding individuals as "legitimate and rational social actors, with interests having collective standing, facilitates the creation of a great deal of formal organization" (Jepperson and Meyer 1991:220); the political organization of the United States has provided a fertile breeding ground for civic associations since the country's inception. Because of this, three institutional logics are widely visible in the US third sector: the institutional logics of activism, bureaucracy, and professionalization.

The US third sector is one of the oldest formally acknowledged in so many words, and conceptually it is closely related to democratic values, having developed parallel to a democratic central state. This "weak state" theory has been elevated as a virtue for nonprofit organizations and resonates deeply with American individualism and antistatist tendencies: the idea is basically that when individuals have alternative, nonstate and nongovernmental ways of accomplishing social ends, they are "freer because their destiny is more closely linked to their own will" (Frumkin 2005:31). The US third sector and its nonprofit component have their philosophical roots in associationalism. Alexis de Tocqueville's well-known observations that Americans are prone to forming associations has generated a common (albeit erroneous) tendency to view philanthropy as rather distinctively American:

The free institutions which the inhabitants of the United States possess, and the political rights of which they make so much use, remind every citizen, and in a thousand ways, that he lives in society. They every instant impress upon his mind the notion that it is the duty as well as the interest of men to make themselves useful to their fellow creatures. (1969:112)

The US central state has been famously fragmented since its inception; Tocqueville (1835) noted how the lack of an aristocracy in the colonies fostered the emergence of a township model of governance that diffused authority throughout the country. This diffuse governance structure has been accompanied by a great degree of skepticism about central government throughout the history of the country. The US government constructed itself by borrowing organizational capacity from existing civic groups—for instance, as early as 1904, some 80 percent of private charitable organizations in places like California received some public funding. A full quarter of government payments went to "other institutions" (referring to independent civic groups) in 1915, increasing to just past 50 percent in 1930 (Clemens 2006:197). This history generated durable habits of indirect governance in the United States (in other words, habits of contracting out state business to private organizations). Even researchers that dispute the weak state theory explicitly (e.g., Dobbin and Sutton 1998) acknowledge the powerful effects of indirect governance and borrowed organizational capacity.

Related, political pluralism in the United States was far more a question of political theory than tax policy and has been closely coupled with a mistrust of government. This pluralism is expressed contemporarily in US nonprofit tax law, which provides legal foundations for the array of political organizations that exist. But even John Stuart Mill framed pluralism as beneficial to individual citizens particularly; it was seen as keeping them astute and engaged. He wrote in 1859:

> In many cases, though individuals may not do the particular thing so well, on the average, as officers of government, it is nevertheless desirable that it should be done by them, rather than by the government, as a means to their own mental education—a mode of strengthening their active faculties, exercising their judgment, and giving them a familiar knowledge of the subjects with which they are thus left to deal. This is a principal . . . recommendation of . . . the conduct of industrial and philanthropic enterprises by voluntary associations. (Quoted in Hopkins 2011, n.p.)

As of 2012, there were 1.5 million tax-exempt organizations in the United States, including 956,738 public charities, 97,435 private foundations, and 370,745 other types of nonprofit organizations, including chambers of commerce, fraternal organizations and civic leagues (Roeger, Blackwood, and Pettijohn 2012). Employment in the sector outstripped that of construction,

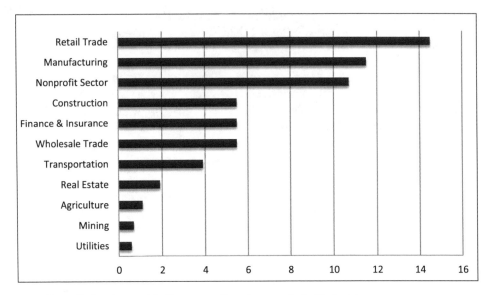

Figure 5. Employment in the nonprofit sector vs. selected industries, 2010 (in millions of persons).

Source: Salamon, Sokolowski, and Geller 2012:2.

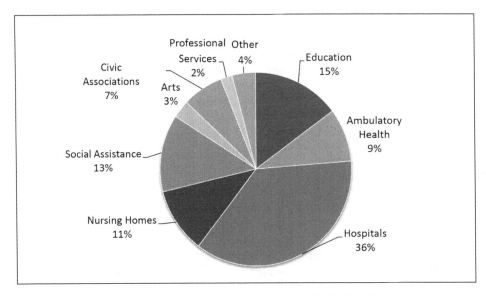

Figure 6. Nonprofit employment, 45 states and District of Columbia, by field, 2010.

Source: Salamon, Sokolowski, and Geller 2012:4.

finance, real estate, and agriculture, among others, making it a substantial economic force.

These organizations work in a mind-boggling array of areas ranging from environmental advocacy to healthcare to youth development. (See appendix for taxonomy of US nonprofit classifications.) For tax year 2008, over 315,000 charities exempt under section 501(c)(3) filed Forms 990 with the US Internal Revenue Service. These organizations reported nearly $2.5 trillion in assets and over $1.4 billion in revenue for 2008 (US IRS Statistics 2008). Additionally, there were about 140,000 social welfare organizations, 65,000 labor and agricultural organizations, 90,000 business leagues, 68,000 social clubs, 82,000 fraternal beneficiary societies, 13,000 political organizations, and 127,000 homeowners' associations (Hopkins 2011).

As in many other countries, a good deal of the nonprofit sector in the United States is dedicated to service provision, ranging from the volunteer (driving the elderly to appointments and tutoring) to the fully staffed, professional facility (the nonprofit teaching hospital). More than half of the nonprofit jobs in the United States are in healthcare (hospitals alone make up 37 percent of nonprofit employment). Health clinics and nursing homes comprise the remaining 20 percent. Similarly, 15 percent of nonprofit jobs in the United States are in education, and 13 percent are in social services, including community services, housing services, and daycare (Salamon, Sokolowski, and Geller 2012:3). Nonprofit service provision in the United States is often linked with the central government through purchase-of-service (POS) contracting. Long a central feature of the US human service delivery system, POS practices expanded dramatically in the 1960s and 1970s (DeHoog and Salamon 2002:320). POSs typically involve the enlistment of a private organization to deliver services to eligible groups of people; examples of such contracting would include transitional homes for runaway youth, affordable housing, food, clothing, summer camps, and childcare. The benefits of this kind of service provision are typically understood in terms of indirectness (lack of direct state involvement), automaticity (utilizing an existing administrative structure rather than creating a new one), noncoercivity (they are elective), and visibility (transparency in both the administrative and political senses) (DeHoog and Salamon 2002:322).

Legal Structure

The legal structure of the nonprofit sector in the United States, perhaps more than any other feature of the country's associational sector, demonstrates the powerful presence of institutional logics of professionalization and bureaucratization. The country's third sector has evolved over more than a century's worth of legislation, all aimed at institutionalizing nonprofit work and making it part of both the political and social services systems in the country. The first tax exemptions for social organizations are found as far back as the Tariff Act of 1894. The first tax on corporate income represented an attempt to define the subjects of tax exemptions, beginning a long tradition of designating certain activities as socially constructive and therefore deserving of favorable tax treatment. In addition to charitable, religious, and educational organizations and activities, the Act exempted certain fraternal beneficiary societies, some mutual savings banks, and some mutual insurance companies. The 1913 Statutory Law of Tax-Exempt Organizations, stating that "any corporation or association organized and operated exclusively for religious, charitable, scientific, or educational purposes, no part of the net income of which inures to the benefit of any private shareholder or individual" set them apart from profit-making companies and has been the basis for nearly every important tax act since (Hopkins 2011). From this history of legislation, aimed from the beginning at integrating voluntary organizations with the economic and political workings of the state, an ever-more complex and comprehensive body of nonprofit policy has evolved.

Not all "nonprofit" organizations in the United States are afforded tax exemption, and not all tax-exempt organizations have the typical characteristics of a "nonprofit" organization: the term "nonprofit" generally refers to an organization's form under state law, not its federal tax status. State law generally does not prohibit "nonprofits" from earning a profit, but rather prohibits the distribution of earnings by nonprofit corporations to their members (US Congress, Joint Committee 2005:27). The US Department of the Treasury is responsible for the administration of the tax policies, including those pertaining to tax-exempt organizations. From an economic perspective, the Joint Committee on Taxation and the Department of Treasury measure the economic value of various tax preferences (including tax deductions, credits, and exclusions).

Nonprofit status in the United States is intended to confer two great benefits: tax exemption (the ability to not pay taxes) and the ability to receive tax-deductible contributions from donors (in which the donors "write off" their contributions from their own tax bills). For some organizations, the latter is far more valuable than the former, as it provides considerable incentive for donors to give. Fundamentally, federal income tax charitable contribution deductions enable individuals and taxable corporations who itemize deductions to deduct an amount equivalent to the value of their contribution to a registered nonprofit organization (Hopkins 2011). A dollar contributed to a nonprofit is (often roughly) a dollar less in taxable income.

Nonprofit status is delineated by a 501(c) tax designation, which refers to one of twenty-eight types of nonprofit organizations, which are exempt from some federal income taxes (US IRS 2010). These 501(c) organizations are:

- 501(c)(3): Religious, educational, charitable, scientific, or literary organizations; testing for public safety organizations. Also, organizations preventing cruelty to children or animals, or fostering national or international amateur sports competition
- 501(c)(4): Civic leagues, social welfare organizations, and local associations of employees
- 501(c)(5): Labor, agriculture, and horticultural organizations
- 501(c)(6): Business leagues, chambers of commerce, and real estate boards
- 501(c)(7): Social and recreational clubs
- 501(c)(8): Fraternal beneficiary societies and associations
- 501(c)(9): Voluntary employee beneficiary associations

The most common charitable tax status is 501(c)(3), often known as "charitable organization." Nonprofits granted tax-exempt status under this designation are exempt from payment of federal corporate income taxes and may receive both public and private grants. Individual donors can claim a federal income tax deduction of up to 50 percent of income for donations made to 501(c)(3) groups. Nonprofit corporations also enjoy the same limited liability protection as for-profit corporations, so that officers and members are typically not personally liable for the debts and obligations of the nonprofit corporation.

Every exempt charitable organization in the United States is classified as either a public charity or a private foundation. Generally, public charities include churches, hospitals, qualified medical research organizations affiliated with hospitals, schools, colleges and universities; or organizations that "actively function in a supporting relationship to one or more existing public charities" (US IRS 2011). Most organizations commonly referred to as "NGOs" or "NPOs" fall into this category. Organizations classified as public foundations most often have one major source of funding (usually gifts from one family or corporation rather than funding from many sources), and most have as their primary activity the making of grants to other charitable organizations and to individuals, rather than the direct operation of charitable programs. These organizations are commonly referred to as simply "foundations."

US NGOs, with their roots in the Anglo-American legal political system, have as their influence several overlapping legal concepts that have deeply shaped their formation (such as common law, legal precedent, rule of law, etc.). These ideas are designed to empower the NGO leadership and make it responsible; the intent is to inspire honesty, transparency, and individual responsibility, rather than expecting that there will be reviews, inspections, or a specific check on the organization's activities and staff (as is more normal in many other countries, where mistrust is institutionalized in detailed regulations.) These ideals are incorporated in many national and state regulations in the United States that govern the creation, maintenance, reporting procedures, punishment norms, and the de-authorization of the NGO status temporarily or permanently. While there is, of course, variation in the types of nonprofit regulation among the United States, UK, and Anglo-Saxon countries like Canada and Australia, the general idea is that an NGO must write up bylaws (a sort of constitution) and a set of regulations that it will undertake to follow in its daily activities, and that this charter, followed in good faith, comprises the bulk of accountability procedures. This question of self-policing is a major difference between NGOs that have grown out of this Anglo-American tradition and those in other parts of the world that have been treated more as parts of government agencies and monitored in a more hierarchical, supervisory manner. However, NGOs have so expanded globally in recent decades that these traditional distinctions have become somewhat less sharp than they were in the past in places such as France.

In practice, this means that many of these legal documents are supervised or approved by professional accountants and lawyers, which introduces a major dynamic of professionalization into nonprofit organizations that sometimes stands in tension with other institutional logics (such as activism). Professional accountants and lawyers try to supervise and assist the individual NGOs in respecting the many laws and regulations that are too complex and difficult for NGO staff members to remember or understand. Often insurance is required for certain NGO activities, which protects the NGO and its board of directors against lawsuits. Small NGOs may not be able to obtain or afford to pay such insurance. Very small organizations (primarily community groups) sometimes do not become incorporated or seek 501(c)(3) status for this reason.

Though individual board members are normally not individually liable in a court of law (if they are acting in an unpaid capacity), the nonprofit itself remains liable for breaches of legality. In the United States, the courts have granted large amounts of money in many such claims, making it dangerous for corporations or NGOs to engage in actions that are potentially the subject of a lawsuit. Thus again, the threat of a possible lawsuit is a major source of institutional self-policing that does not involve any specific inspection or supervision by a governmental agency.

The smallest charitable organizations in the United States do not achieve this legal 501(c) status because it is expensive to hire lawyers and accountants and to pay insurance each year. In fact, some estimates suggest that 90 percent of voluntary organizations in the United States are not registered with the IRS, and approximately half of the volunteer efforts taking place in the country occur in these informal channels (Gronbjerg and Paarlberg 2002: 567)—this estimation includes things like book clubs, neighborhood cleanup organizations, and the like. In order to file for a nonprofit status, an organization's gross annual receipts must be over $5,000 (Adams, Cahoon, and Hodges 2005). A nonprofit must file annual information returns, as well as Business Income Tax returns if it earns more than $1,000 a year from trade business. A 501(c) 3 application costs $400 for organizations whose gross receipts are less than $10,000 annually and $850 for organizations whose receipts exceed $10,000 annually (US IRS 2013).

It is hard administrative work to respect each of the required legal procedures and to submit proper reports; indeed, studies have shown that some large organizations don't even know what their own legal status is (Gronbjerg, Liu, and Pollak 2009:987). Federally, nonprofits that expend more than $500,000 in a single year are required by law to conduct an audit. Twenty-six states require charitable nonprofits to submit audited financial statements (a review of every single document concerning expenditures and revenues over the past year, and signed by an outside accountant indicating that there were no regulations violated by the organization) in order to formally register the organization (National Council 2013), and forty out of fifty states require formal incorporation in order to legally fundraise in that state. An audit can cost between $10,000 and $20,000 for a small NGO. Such procedures can be prohibitively expensive.

Because of these strict regulations and high costs, small charitable organizations do not hold a 501(c)(3) status, so they cannot receive grants from foundations or government agencies, nearly all of which require that the NGO be certified. Consequently, many of the large grants go to the large and medium-sized NGOs, not simply because of personal or political connections (which may indeed operate). Rather, these simple regulations may make it illegal for many agencies to award funds to non-incorporated NGOs. If they do, they can be sued or fined if their grantees do not act properly. The other consequence of this, of course, is that grant funding can create a feedback loop—an organization must be of a certain size to obtain funding, and small organizations that lack funding may have difficulty reaching that size without financial support.

One mechanism that helps make this system more "friendly" is that there are many lawyers, accountants, and related professionals who volunteer or work at low or below market rates to assist small and emerging nonprofit organizations and activities. Often the smaller and poorer NGOs may pay one-third or less than the normal fees for completing the legal and accounting activities that are required. These professionals may work through separate associations or organizations specifically focused on nonprofits (which hold conferences, maintain websites, etc.) or may be part of a larger accounting or law firm. These organizations are often led by lawyers and accountants who may earn high fees in much of their work, but feel a charitable responsibility to assist the less fortunate smaller and more charitable NGOs in their creation and maintenance of activities so that they can continue their work successfully and maintain a nonprofit status legally.

The dry and seemingly endless legal specifications within US nonprofit tax law are often inconveniences for both the nonprofit practitioner and also, potentially, the reader. But the important thing to understand about nonprofit tax law is that it is aimed at institutionalizing—professionalizing—third sector activities within the context of the state and ensuring nonprofits' position within the federal bureaucracy. Third sector organizations in the United States are understood as a basic building block of the country's democratic participation.

Funding, Legitimacy, and Evaluation in the US Third Sector

> The nonprofit system has tamed a generation of activists. They've traded in grand visions of social change for salaries and stationery; given up recruiting people to the cause in favor of writing grant proposals and wooing foundations; and ceded control of their movements to business executives in boardrooms.
> —Adjoa Florência Jones de Almeida, "The Revolution Will Not Be Funded"

If the benefit of extensive tax law is deep integration with the US state and economy, perhaps the most fraught aspect of the nonprofit sector in the United States is the funding structure. The search for funding consumes vast amounts of nonprofit time and administrative attention among organizations large and small, and the increasing professionalization of the industry has spurred a dramatic growth in fundraising professionals and consultants whose sole occupation is to assist nonprofit leaders with developing their funding base.

In 2011, public charities in the United States reported over $1.59 trillion in total revenues. Of those revenues, 22 percent came from contributions, gifts, and government grants, 72 percent came from program service revenues (including government fees and contracts), and 6 percent came from other sources (including dues, rental income, special event income, and gains or losses from goods sold) (National Center 2011). The relative roles of these different funding streams have important implications for the structure and character of the third sector (Salamon and Anheier 1996). In all cases, seeking, securing, maintaining, and evaluating funding is a time-consuming and carefully choreographed process.

There are deep implications for equality, distribution, and access within the US funding cycle. For example, wealthier third sector organizations tend to conform to objectives of elite workers, rather than donors or other constituents, creating a conflict of goals within the organization (Barnett and Finnemore 1999; Cooley and Ron 2010). Differing priorities among organizational stakeholders can transform supposedly apolitical funding relationships into brutal power struggles, as we demonstrated in the introduction regarding processes of accountability and evaluation.

Similarly, there are questions of appropriateness at play; some people suggest that (in addition to the technical difficulties of awarding money and creating meaningful relationships among stakeholders), charity and philanthropic activities simply lack the political teeth to change the basic structures of inequality in the world. Peter Buffett, son of the famous philanthropist Warren Buffett, wrote in a widely circulated op-ed in 2013:

> Inside any important philanthropy meeting, you witness heads of state meeting with investment managers and corporate leaders. All are searching for answers with their right hand to problems that others in the room have created with their left. . . . Philanthropy has become the "it" vehicle to level the playing field and has generated a growing number of gatherings, workshops and affinity groups. As more lives and communities are destroyed by the system that creates vast amounts of wealth for the few, the more heroic it sounds to "give back." It's what I would call "conscience laundering"—feeling better about accumulating more than any one person could possibly need to live on by sprinkling a little around as an act of charity. But this just keeps the existing structure of inequality in place. The rich sleep better at night, while others get just enough to keep the pot from boiling over. Nearly every time someone feels better by doing good, on the other side of the world (or

street), someone else is further locked into a system that will not allow the true flourishing of his or her nature or the opportunity to live a joyful and fulfilled life. (Buffett 2013, n.p.)

The process of seeking funds can arguably have positive effects on both parties. Nonprofits can capitalize upon fundraising campaigns to create awareness, attention for their cause generally and to programs specifically. At their best, fundraising programs can inform donors about the program's functioning, its components, and the characteristics of the nonprofits and can permit organizations to scale up certain programs. Frumkin and Kim argue that fundraising represents an opportunity for third sector organizations to engage in what they term "strategic positioning," which is in essence determining in the process of communications what information reaches donors. This is an important step, as it enables donors to decide where to allocate their philanthropic dollars (Frumkin and Kim 2001:267). Thornton (2006:204) argues that this process of active fundraising on the part of organizations can in fact reduce the cost (for donors) of finding a charity whose work they wish to support.

Contrary to popular belief, the average amount of total nonprofit income originating with private donors (charitable giving) is rather small. Private giving in the United States accounts for 19 percent of nonprofit revenue; this relatively high rate (compared to other countries) may have something to do with relatively modest rates of US taxation compared to places like Western Europe (Salamon and Anheier 1996:68–69) and the relatively low rates of government involvement in this sector. For example, in France between 1991 and 1992, giving to nonreligious nonprofit organizations amounted to only .15 percent of personal income, whereas the comparable US figure was 1.9 percent (68–69).

Broadly speaking, nonprofit organizations doing social welfare and human service activities receive the most funding from the public sector, mostly in the form of government grants and contracts. Most of these public sector contracts are Medicare and Medicaid (publicly funded health insurance programs) reimbursements to nonprofit healthcare organizations. After those reimbursements, the primary source of public payments is grants (representing payments for services rendered to the government). Cultural and recreational organizations (which serve a broad cross-section of the population) receive much of their funding from private fees and charges, such as not-for-profit theater companies, museums, and parks. International relief agencies get approximately the same amount of support from private giving and government support (Salamon and Anheier 1996:74). Obtaining and maintaining government grants and contracts can pose major challenges for nonprofit organizations; those that successfully do so are apt to be older, more formalized, and working in institutionalized fields (Gronbjerg and Paarlberg 2002).

Public nonprofit organizations receive the bulk of their state and local government support either as grants (POS) or fee-for-service payments on behalf of individuals. A good deal of money passes through state-administered programs that are financed by the federal government such as food stamps (Bowman and Fremont-Smith 2006:191). Government financing of public services has expanded to include grants, contracts, tax credits, tax-exempt bonds, tax deductions, vouchers, and fees for service. This diversification masks the extent of public funding of nonprofits and the increased centralization of government funding at the federal level in main service areas (Smith 2006:220).

Beginning in the 1960s, as part of the War on Poverty and similar efforts by Presidents Kennedy and Johnson, government financing of nonprofits increased dramatically, spurred by extensive federal spending on social and health programs; government support prior to this point had been largely restricted to child welfare or high-profile institutions. This rate of funding again increased in the 1980s as the central government continued to outsource social programs to third sector organizations, such as low-income housing and immigrant assistance (Smith 2006:221). Beginning in the late 1960s and within little more than a decade, nonprofits became the principle vehicle for government-financed human services in the United States, and perhaps unsurprisingly, the government had also become the largest financer of human service nonprofit organizations (Frumkin 2005:71). For example, the number of nonprofit service providers in the United States more than doubled between 1977 and 1997, from 40,983 to 92,156.

As the table 4 demonstrates, the overall rise and diversification in government funding of the third sector spurred growth of nonprofit organizations during this time and since. Note that the table represents only public charities, not private foundations or other types of nonprofit organizations.

For conservative policymakers, this nonprofit growth was a positive phenomenon, because it brought services and decisions closer into the local communities that those organizations served (Frumkin 2005:71). Interestingly, this shift represents a dramatic diversion from, for example, the Japanese model, wherein nonprofits began as state partners and gradually diversified their interests.

The presence of these state-funded nonprofit agencies runs directly counter to one of the prevailing theories about the origins and rational for the non-

Table 4. Growth in registered public charities over time

Date Created	Number of Organizations
1969 or earlier	177,303
1970–1979	85,872
1980–1989	113,720
1990–1994	77,261
1995–1999	99,187
2000–2001	49,114
2002–2003	54,959
2004–2005	59,697
2006–2007	65,492
2008	29,454
2009	40,838
2010	43,136
2011	42,096
2012	35,807
Total	973,936

Source: National Center for Charitable Statistics 2011.

profit sector, held dear by academics and practitioners alike—a theory that emphasizes the third sector's role as independent of the state. We argue, based on the data above, that far from growing away from the state, the nonprofit sector appears to be facilitating the expansion of governance by assuming the task of delivering the services that government is called on to finance. It is thus making possible the expansion of government-financed services *without* a corresponding (visible) expansion of the scale of the state itself. This system of "third-party government," long present in the American and German contexts, seems to be expanding elsewhere as well (Salamon and Anheier 1996:76). There are, however, potential threats to the third sector as a result of this dramatic shift toward government funding of service activities, including a loss of autonomy vis-à-vis state imperatives, mission creep, and excessive bureaucratization.

In part as a way to retain their (both political and economic) independence from government contracts, American nonprofits have moved toward providing fee-for-service options. This shift generates income that is independent of (and in some ways, more reliable than) government contracts or public philanthropy, but also reflects increasing pressures to marketize and privatize, moving further away from Keynesian-esque welfare policies. Even with religious congregations included, nearly half of the growth in nonprofit revenue from 1977 to 1997 was composed of fees and charges. From 1977 to 1997, the percent increase of fees-for-service and charges was 145 percent in the US nonprofit sector. Though this number also reflects the inclusion of colleges and universities, the trend of charging for services grew rapidly throughout the sector. Adjusting for inflation, "fee income" for arts and culture organizations rose 272 percent during this time, fee income for civic organizations grew 220 percent, and fee income for social service organizations increased over 50 percent. During the same timespan, government support to the nonprofit sector also increased by 195 percent (Salamon 2003:52).

Individual charitable fundraising has also changed dramatically in the United States in the past thirty years. The "industry" of soliciting individual donations has undergone a tremendous professionalization, evidenced by the birth of organizations such as the National Society of Fund-Raising Executives (in 1960), now the Association of Fundraising Professionals (AFP), and the National Committee for Planned Giving, among others. Between 1979 and 1999, the AFP grew from 1,899 members to more than 20,000; interestingly, this dramatic expansion has been facilitated by mechanisms such as workplace solicitation, direct mail, telephones, e-donations, workplace matches, and other means (Salamon 2003:57).

Notably, for-profit financial service companies have been able to popularize some planned giving mechanisms, enabling people to earn tax-sheltered income on funds deposited into trusts whose beneficiaries are charitable organizations (Salamon 2003:57). Such examples can include everything from leaving real estate to charities in one's will (the organization receives the property, or cash after the property is sold, while the individual makes use of it during his or her lifetime), transfer of retirement funds to NPOs (that donation is tax-free), or charitable remainder trusts (the trust provides income to the donor during his or her lifetime and then pays the remaining balance to a third sector organization upon the donor's death). Though some of these measures are not unique to this era, they are increasingly available and constitute a more standard part of individual financial planning, reflecting an increasingly institutionalized and professionalized approach to charitable giving.

Despite its comparatively low percentage in total funding, individual giving has its place in the United States, and all signs indicate that the tradition is alive and healthy and is outstripping that of other countries in this book. Research from the Survey Research Center at the University of Michigan and the US Census Bureau notes that charitable giving increased from approximately $29 billion in 1975 to an estimated $295 billion in 2006 (reviewed in Hopkins 2011). That same year, giving by individuals totaled an estimated $222.89 billion; individual giving constituted an estimated 75.6 percent of all US charitable giving in 2006. Grant making by private foundations was an estimated $36.5 billion in 2006, accounting for an estimated 12.4 percent of total giving in that same year. Charitable bequests were estimated to total $22.91 billion, some 7.8 percent of the estimated contributions. Gifts from corporations, including corporate foundations, totaled $12.72 billion, 4.3 percent of the total giving that year (Hopkins 2011).

These percentages, however, vary greatly by field. For example, in 2006 giving to religious organizations amounted to $96.82 billion, about 32.8 percent of total national charitable giving that year. Education giving totaled $40.98 billion, an estimated 13.9 percent of total giving. Social services organizations received approximately $29.56 billion, 10 percent of the total for the year. Individual contributions to grant-making foundations were estimated to be $29.5 billion, again approximately 10 percent of total giving, while public-society benefit organizations received about $21.41 billion, or 7.3 percent. Following were healthcare organizations, with $20.22 billion, or 6.9 percent of all gifts, gifts to arts, culture, and humanitarian organizations, which was about $12.51 billion, or 4.2 percent of giving, and donations to international affairs organizations, which received $11.34 billion, or 3.8 percent of total gifts in 2006 (Hopkins 2011).

Despite the extensive legal structure, the heavily institutionalized giving apparatus, and the sector's long history, associations in the United States still periodically struggle with legitimacy, vis-à-vis private, for-profit organizations, and this struggle plays out both in searches for funding and in questions of evaluation. As a result of this, some scholars (such as Dichter 1999, 2003) have explored problematic mismatch of corporate values onto philanthropic organizations (see also Wirgau, Farley, and Jensen 2010). We assert that these pressures for legitimacy have been, in part, responsible for the rise of professionalization within the US third sector.

Verbruggen, Christiaens, and Milis use the organizational sociology notion of isomorphism (see also DiMaggio and Powell 1983) to describe the pressures on third sectors to demonstrate legitimacy. These pressures may manifest most obviously among other organizations on which their support depends—that is, pressures that are external to the organization itself. An example of "coercive isomorphism"—coercive pressures toward a new behavior—might be a pressure from the organization's board of directors or a state agency that demands changes in an organization's methods or strategies. "Mimetic isomorphism" is a kind of "best practices" approach, one of copying other organizations in a state of uncertainty (agencies mimic each other's techniques in pursuit of field-wide legitimacy around an unproven technique or technology). "Normative isomorphism" is, in essence, profes-

Table 5. Change in foundation gifts received, adjusted for inflation, 1978–2008

Year	Gifts Received (Current) Amount ($ in billions)	% Change	Index (1978=100)	Gifts Received (Constant) Amount ($ in billions)	% Change	Index (1978=100)
1978	1.61	—	100.0	1.61	—	100.0
1979	2.21	37.5	137.5	1.99	23.5	123.5
1980	1.98	(10.4)	123.3	1.57	(21.0)	97.5
1981	2.39	20.6	148.6	1.71	9.3	106.6
1982	4.00	67.4	248.6	2.70	57.6	168.0
1983	2.71	(32.4)	168.1	1.77	(34.5)	110.0
1984	3.36	24.1	208.6	2.11	19.0	130.9
1985	4.73	54.2	321.7	2.87	48.9	194.9
1986	—	—	—	—	—	—
1987	4.96	—	307.9	2.85	—	176.7
1988	5.16	4.1	320.4	2.85	(0.1)	176.6
1989	5.52	7.0	343.0	2.90	2.1	180.3
1990	4.97	(10.0)	308.8	2.48	(14.6)	154.1
1991	5.47	9.9	339.5	2.62	5.5	162.5
1992	6.18	13.0	383.8	2.87	9.7	178.4
1993	7.76	25.5	481.8	3.50	21.9	217.4
1994	8.08	4.2	502.0	3.56	1.6	220.9
1995	10.26	26.9	637.3	4.39	23.5	272.7
1996	16.02	56.1	995.0	6.66	51.6	413.5
1997	15.83	(1.2)	983.4	6.43	(3.4)	399.5
1998	22.57	42.6	1402.1	9.03	40.4	560.8
1999	32.08	42.1	1992.3	12.55	39.0	779.7
2000	27.61	(13.9)	1715.1	10.45	(16.7)	649.4
2001	28.71	4.0	1783.5	10.57	1.1	656.6
2002	22.16	(22.8)	1376.6	8.03	(24.0)	498.9
2003	24.86	12.2	1554.0	8.81	9.7	547.1
2004	23.99	(3.5)	1490.0	8.28	(6.0)	514.3
2005	31.46	31.2	1954.3	10.50	26.9	652.4
2006	36.60	16.2	2277.6	11.84	12.7	735.4
2007	46.84	28.0	2915.1	14.73	24.4	914.9
2008	39.55	8.1	2461.4	11.98	1.2	744.0

Source: Foundation Center 2010. Years are approximate; reporting years varied.

sionalization—a spread of pressures that are based on norms of education and professional networks, which subsequently create institutionalized models and rules. "In the case of nonprofit organizations, both loci of power (at least partially) coincide, as the government is the institution that sets the rules as well as controls important resource flows" (DiMaggio and Powell 1983; Verbruggen, Christiaens, and Milis 2010:4–5).

These legitimacy pressures play out in large part around questions of accountability and transparency in nonprofits as regards funding. As nonprofit sectors worldwide have expanded and begun to receive funding from governments, so too has come an increased demand for accountability and transparency procedures; financial reporting by nonprofit organizations is no longer the exception but the rule (Verbruggen, Christiaens, and Milis 2010:1). Formal entities (such as the state, Congress, or regulations) may demand transparency measures. Informal pressures, such as the demands and expectations of stakeholders, especially donors, may also demand transparency. It is not uncommon for both to demand them. A transparency procedure necessarily requires defining the organization's stakeholders (to whom organizations are accountable) as well as settling on the issues that these stakeholders have decided to measure (Gugerty, Sidel, and Bies 2010) (what constitutes "success" or "failure" of a project). To return to a quote from this book's introduction, a nonprofit leader articulates these challenges:

> [In the United States] they want to know: what is the objective [of a project], what are the results. The emphasis is much more on results that you can measure, and for that reason it is much more difficult to seek funding, for example, for peace. With an economic project you can say, "these chickens will lay twenty eggs a week", but the question of peace is a question of values, of change, of mentalities, of activities, and it's difficult to subject it to a measure. (Kallman 2013:57).

These questions of accountability have engendered the growth of whole industries devoted to monitoring, compliance, and program evaluation (Ebrahim 2003, 2005), which critics blame for taking up time and resources. While accountability is not inherently bad, it also signals a loss of political control within an organization; such a loss of control has consequences. Yet, as organizational forms and public values merge, the traditional boundaries of governance that have relied on legal and organizational measures of answerability are no longer adequate for measuring public accountability. With the growing involvement of third sector organizations in governance, accountability takes on new meanings and implies institutional transformations (Choudhury and Ahmed 2002).

Transparency can also be an essential element of legitimacy and trustworthiness in this growing sector, and some argue that the practice emerged precisely from this sort of concern. But the concern with transparency is itself powerful evidence of the growing influence of an institutional logic of professionalization that both engenders credibility and discourages other types of legal auditing:

> Professional staffs want to bring a new rigor to their work and develop standards to measure their performance, both as the basis for their own advance-

ment within the field and in an effort to build a growing body of expert knowledge. For these professionals, the techniques of reengineering processes, quality management systems, and benchmarking are appealing because they hold out the promise of supporting and justifying the move from volunteer labor to well-compensated professional staffs. With their desire to avoid the charges of amateurism that have plagued this sector in the past, the growing ranks of non-profit professionals have turned out to be the perfect audience for claims that cost effectiveness represents the new frontier of nonprofit management. (Frumkin and Kim 2001:268)

Specifically, self-regulation can be seen as a way both to strengthen organizational governance and to "signal quality and attract funding." Some organizations have also pursued a strategy of self-regulation in order to discourage potentially stricter government regulation, and also "as a means to lend legitimacy to nonprofits operating in contexts where government regulation and nonprofit infrastructure are weak" (Gugerty, Sidel, and Bies 2010).

Dependence on governmental resources and loans increases nonprofit compliance reporting, namely because of the audited financial statements necessary to receive that funding. In other words, if you get your money from the government, you must be prepared to send the government the documentation that it wants. Levels of reporting and transparency compliance increases among third sector organizations that are part of a larger group (e.g., Save the Children) (Verbruggen, Christiaens, and Milis 2010:18). Others suggest that in countries with younger third sectors, the primary concern of transparency mechanisms is to *preempt* more intrusive regulation from the state, while in those places with more established third sectors, its primary concern is to increase legitimacy. The multiple motivations of the third sector toward transparency can also include enhancing the collective reputation of the sector, avoiding further regulation, allying strategically with government, eliminating nonprofit competitors, taking advantage of entrepreneurial opportunities for self-regulation facilitators, and minimizing the impact of "low quality actors." This may be especially the case, they suggest, in China, where third sector organizations take the initiative to develop transparency mechanisms in a way to stave off stricter governmental regulation (Gugerty, Sidel, and Bies 2010:6).

The United States is perhaps the clearest example of both the benefits and perils of extensive professionalization among NPOs, as the country's associational sector encompasses a wide range of organizations. Professionalization in general implies more fundraising, undertaken to support industry infrastructure and the need for more paid staff. The benefits to such a system also include, as we have shown, transparency, credibility, the ability to attract resources, field-wide best practices and institutional durability, and the ability to scale up.

The problems with increased professionalization, however, are those to which Jones de Almeida alludes in the passage near the opening of this chapter: that fundraising and formal organizations in general may serve to de-radicalize activists across the political spectrum, binding them to institutionalized, professionalized mandates that remove them from their activism. This dynamic is meaningfully distinct from the clientelist approaches that we explore in other countries—which can also de-radicalize—and is particularly visible in the United States because of its enormous third sector and the sheer number of professional nonprofit organizations that comprise it. More generally, studying the professional structures of a contemporary third sector requires that we be conscious as to what the incentives, limitations, opportunities, and dynamics of any given organizational structure are.

Bowling for a Paycheck: Professionalization and Arts Organizations

Robert Putnam's famous account of the drop in US participation (Putnam 2000) has spurred a great deal of soul searching in the United States about why democratic activities have seemingly decreased in the past several decades. This is a complicated issue that we take up in cross-national comparisons in chapter 8. It has occurred, however, alongside a mushrooming of selected types of NGOs and new forms of citizen participation (including more paid work in third sector organizations). Together, this information suggests that the purported "drop" in participation is multifaceted and may in fact simply be a reshuffling of third sector allegiances: people may participate in fewer bowling leagues, but they support other kinds of NGOs in far greater numbers. They may also be finding their careers in such organizations.

Other dramatic examples of these changes are the rise of cell phone and Internet-based activities—blogs, social media, texting—that are intertwined with changes in all sorts of physical participation. Even if families go "out to dinner together," or people "attend a meeting," they also may simultaneously communicate with others via their smartphones or tablets, sharing and amplifying their experiences. They may Tweet about it when they get home. The relationships between the new electronic communications and more classic concepts and measures of "participation" are being acted out in dozens of new and creative ways that many are just beginning to describe. Similarly, there has been a recent and dramatic rise of arts and culture activities in the

United States, doubling in some twenty years in the World Values Survey for the country, even while membership has dropped in many classic types of civic organizations. These specifics vary in subtle ways that new work is identifying (T. Clark et al. 2014).

The major theme of the US nonprofit sector, particularly as it has expanded in recent decades, is the dramatic and increasing presence of the institutional logic of professionalization, at times in conflict with that of activism. The selection of brief case illustrations below are intended to provide examples of how some of these dynamics play out in practice.

Case Studies

The Women's Intercultural Center

The Women's Intercultural Center, based in New Mexico, was founded during the summer of 1991 by two Catholic Sisters of Mercy whose mandate was "a commitment to learning about multi-cultural realities and concern for women and children." The sisters had learned of the isolation that immigrant women were suffering in that region of the country; women who had migrated recently were hesitant to reach out to others and restricted by their inability to speak English. There was clearly a need for community building and social services in this small city, so, drawing on the skills of bilingual social workers, the sisters began a program on health and self-esteem for recent immigrants from Latin America. Activities grew and expanded organically, and the group began to receive funding from the New Mexico Department of Health. Noticing a (very relevant) general lack of understanding about the border and border issues, the Women's Intercultural Center began to organize "immersion" experiences for others who were interested in learning about immigration. By 1993, the group had found larger quarters, thanks to a sizable donation from an anonymous individual and assistance from the Sisters of Mercy of Omaha.

Local businesspeople joined the board of directors when the Women's Intercultural Center was legally incorporated as a 501(c)(3) nonprofit organization in the state of New Mexico. The center was now home to a number of different classes and programs: participants learned and taught sewing, carpentry, English, art, hair styling, Reiki, and other skills. There were programs to help women empower themselves; they learned to speak in front of others, to be on committees, to make decisions, and to give opinions about how the center should be run, and to interact with the immersion groups. Some of the women who were most involved in the center were eventually hired on as staff, a practice that continues. Other women, as they learned English and gained skills and confidence, moved on to higher education or employment. A testament to the underlying funding shortages, since its inception, the center has depended on volunteer teachers of English as a second language.

The center uses what it calls a "flat model of management," meaning that there are few levels between executives and employees. The structure is intended to empower "employees and participants by including them in a larger part of the decision-making process and help[ing] us maintain our integrity and values in all the decisions we make for the operations of the Center" (Women's Intercultural Center 2011). The model is also intended to minimize bureaucracy and promote empowerment and horizontal decision making; the center says that it expends only 15 percent of its annual budget on administration, which is relatively unusual for nonprofit organizations, pointing to relatively low levels of professionalization.

Uniquely, many of the staff at the Women's Intercultural Center were previously clients or were referred to the organization as volunteers through social service agencies, subsequently were offered positions, and stayed on. The organization is visibly proud of this diversity, and its website notes that, of their six employees, five are primary breadwinners of single-parent households; two are working on attaining higher education; and one is working on her GED (high school degree). Of the six full-time employees, five were participants in center programming before being hired (Carter 2011). The center's paid positions are those of executive director, director of programs, consciousness-raising coordinator, hospitality manager, buildings and grounds technician, and receptionist.

The center has four key programs. The Economic Self-Sufficiency program is designed to "foster the entrepreneurial spirit of women through the development of diverse and creative opportunities that promote an exchange of knowledge and skills that will enable women to produce and market quality goods and services." In order to do so, the program tries to tap the existing talents and marketable skills, working toward small business possibilities. The program currently provides training in catering and food sales (and hires from this group to assist with catering jobs when necessary), marketing and selling handcrafts and other products through galleries, fairs, and conferences in the Southwest, and the organization offers classes through the Small Business Development Academy. The academy teaches its students about strategic planning, law, accounting, marketing, and human and business resources in a twelve-week course. Another center program, called Consciousness-Raising for Change, helps women analyze social, environmental, immigration, and economic justice issues, in order to help them organize themselves and others. The program does outreach through workshops, forums, guest speakers, and cultural events, all designed to address issues that impact communities. The Alternative Education and Personal Development program provides nontraditional learning for women in safe settings and is designed to work with women who have had limited access to or bad experiences with formal education or traditional schooling. The program offers a comprehensive ESL program, as well as classes on such topics as computer skills, financial literacy, health and fitness, job readiness, cooking, parenting, public speaking, and arts. The Border Awareness Experience is an immersion program that takes place in the southwestern United States, along the Mexican border, and is designed to call attention to how so many issues (economics, human rights, ecology, law, labor, migration, and health) interact in this contested space. The participants have the opportunity to interact, visit, and attend workshops with local residents, professionals, and grassroots organizations that work in these issues, and they often stay overnight with local host families.

Three of the center's four programs (excluding the Border Awareness Experience program) are designed to support and complement each other. The main focus of those three programs is economic self-sufficiency and self-reliance; they are designed to empower women to improve their personal situations, as well as to improve their participation in economic and civic life. The logic behind such a design is independence: in order for a woman to overcome the traditional barriers facing her, she must be independent. She will be able to make decisions for herself, her body, her family, and so on, based on what she perceives is good for them, not because she is economically or otherwise reliant upon someone else (Carter 2011).

The center also cites a growing concern with civic engagement, as one avenue toward social justice organizing. As Mary Carter, executive director of the Women's Intercultural Center, put it, the center does not want to "create a generation of sheep that can be led, or taken to any rally whatsoever. We want people to be engaged, independent, critical, and to make appropriate decisions on anything that is impacting their community, state, or nation" (Carter 2011). The center is slowly building up this piece of its programming, emphasizing the process of becoming informed on all sides of an issue before taking action. Toward this end, the center is sending community leaders to capacity-building training run by the Industrial Areas Foundation, with the expectation that those leaders return home and teach grassroots organizing to their local (neighborhood and city-wide) communities.

The center works fairly closely with its board of directors—executive director Mary Carter notes that board members range in levels of commitment. The organization runs a training every year designed to teach current board members (and new board members) how to fundraise, which is one of the main responsibilities of such a position. Carter says that asking for money can be very difficult for people who are not used to it. The annual training is designed to refresh everyone's memory on the roles and responsibilities of board members and to test them on the organization's mission.

Current board members are expected to be on the lookout year-round for new potential board members; selection of candidates, interviews, and nominations for additions to the board take place before the annual meeting in January of each year. New board members then join the annual training session. The board selection process is designed to make sure that board members are aligned with the organization's mission and strategy, but further, to ensure that personalities will gel appropriately with one another and that the group can have a cooperative dynamic (Carter 2011).

The Women's Intercultural Center has a permanent endowment fund and accepts donations through planned giving, general unrestricted donations, or donations that are restricted programmatically. The organization also has an emergency food pantry and accepts donations of food, which it then distributes to families in need. The center also makes use of "in-kind" donations of services or products that can help lower administrative costs (such as printing, postage, supplies, volunteer time, accounting services, etc.). It receives 47 percent of its funding from grants and foundation support. Support comes from foundations such as the W.K. Kellogg Foundation, the New Mexico Community Foundation, the Albert Allen Foundation, and others. Carter mentions that the organization has a window of opportunity in this regard, as the center is not tapping the same wells of funding as other NGOs in the area. She does all of the grant solicitation herself. The remaining 53 percent of support comes from the Border Awareness Experience, in in-kind donations and support from individuals, and from the organization's services (such as catering and rental services) (Carter 2011).

The center's programming continues to grow. Since Carter's arrival in 2010, the center has grown from serving seven hundred people per year to over three thousand people per year. Additionally, the center has begun to integrate a male component, trying to create allies and advocates among men, and to help women share their newfound strength and independence with their partners and families. As Carter puts it, "the needs of the community change all the time, and the center has to be ready for the evolutionary process" (Carter 2011).

Prize4Life: Accelerating the Discovery
of Treatments and a Cure for ALS

Massachusetts-based Prize4Life administers public health and research programs, a combined approach that is not atypical of US nonprofit organizations. Prize4Life is a 501(c)(3) organization that is focused on seeking treatments and cures for Amyotrophic Lateral Sclerosis—ALS, or Lou Gehrig's Disease—a rare, fatal illness that has no treatment or cure. The organization was founded in 2006 by a group of Harvard Business School students when one of them, Avichai Kremer, was diagnosed with ALS at a young age. Frustrated by the lack of scientific progress toward a cure, twenty-nine-year-old Kremer and his classmates and colleagues decided to pilot a new way to accelerate ALS research. They formed Prize4Life, using their business school training to design a new way to induce participation: the prize model.

Prize4Life's founders were frustrated by the fact that few scientists or drug companies work on finding an ALS cure, because the anticipated profits are relatively low compared to other diseases, given the small number of people who suffer from it. The organization offered an incentive prize of $1 million, trying to convince drug companies, academic research teams, and other scientists to turn their attention to finding treatments and cures for ALS. Prize4Life, as an organization, has administered two prizes of $1 million each: a prize to find an ALS biomarker and a prize to find a treatment for the disease. In addition to the two prizes, the organization manages a range of other scientific-infrastructure programs, including a web-based forum on current ALS research for scientists. Prize4Life awarded its first $1 million incentive prize for the creation of an ALS biomarker in February 2011 to a neurologist from the Boston area (Venkataraman 2011).

The organization received a $1 million donation from an anonymous donor in 2006 to fund its first prize. Since then, funding and support has come from individual donations, corporations, fundraising events, and foundations. The organization has a Champions program—a volunteer program designed to help members of the public who have been affected by ALS raise funds for Prize4Life. Prize4Life Champions host parties, film screenings, and other fundraisers in their homes or offices and donate the money to the organization. Prize4Life also puts on a five-kilometer road race annually and has organized video screenings, galas, and auctions in order to raise money for its programs. Its fundraising apparatus is diversified and professionalized and makes use of a broad array of institutional revenue streams.

Prize4Life's governance structures are typical for a nonprofit of its kind, a 501(c)(3). It has a board of directors with fourteen members; the board includes a well-known auctioneer, professors at respected universities, consultants, bankers, and nonprofit professionals. Because the organization is scientific in focus and requires professional scientific guidance for its programs, it also has a scientific advisory board, which consists of a group of well-known scientists and researchers from the northeast United States who provide input on the organization's scientific programming and projects.

Prize4Life has eight paid staff members: a president, a chief scientist, a scientific program officer, a communications professional, two fundraisers, a financial officer, and an administrator. As with many other nonprofits, the finance and administrative positions comprise at least half of the staff, representing high degrees of professionalization of both the programmatic and administrative functions of the organization.

The scientific staff members are responsible for administration of the scientific programs—they liaise with competing scientific teams, administer infrastructural projects (such as a portal of current ALS news and information), and actively seek out new researchers to recruit for competition. A critical part of their jobs is to keep abreast of current ALS research, which they do by reading the latest scientific articles and attending conferences and trade shows. The fundraisers spend their days seeking support from grant makers and individuals alike—they may visit prominent community members to ask for gifts to the organization, meet with current funders, or write grant applications to foundations. Additionally, the fundraisers are responsible for the organization's transparency measures, including the compilation of Prize4Life's financial reports, activity reports, and annual reports. The communications manager is responsible for managing several newsletters and communicating the organization's progress to the general public, maintaining the website and other publicity materials, and attending conferences and events on behalf of the organization. The organization's president is primarily dedicated to fundraising as well, by seeking individual donors, overseeing events, and providing input on programmatic decisions and general operating procedures.

In order to keep its administrative costs down, Prize4Life uses donated office space, occupying a small corner of a pharmaceutical company building. The organization received a total of $107,722 in unrestricted grants and donations in 2009 and $686,900 in restricted funding (designated for specific prizes or programs). The organization also received in-kind contributions valued at $60,000 (including its office space). Prize4Life has funds set aside and designated for each of its prizes that have not yet been awarded, and it earned approximately $250,000 from those investments.

Prize4Life faces two main challenges: like most nonprofits, it has been plagued by underfunding. However, because its work is very scientific in focus, fundraising is particularly difficult. Because the organization does not do advocacy or patient-focused activities, communicating the need for increased scientific infrastructure to the general public and potential donors presents a unique challenge. On the other hand, because its ideas and approach are fresh and provocative, the organization has generated a herd of "copycats"— programs and organizations that have seen the promise of the prize model and have implemented something similar in their own issue areas.

Prize4Life has limited contact with any sort of governmental entity and functions largely autonomously. For more information on the organization, see www.prize4life.com.

Farm Fresh Rhode Island

Farm Fresh Rhode Island is based in Providence but is a Rhode Island–wide 501(c)(3) NGO that works to support a statewide local food system. Its organizing principles value the environment, health, and quality of life for Rhode Island farmers and eaters. Founded in 2004, the organization has blended professional resources—farmer's markets, infrastructure, and the like—with farm-related and food-related advocacy on a state level.

Rhode Island is the smallest state in the United States, with a total population of 1,052,567 in 2010; thus, its statewide local food movement is rather small and to a great extent mimics the dynamics of district-wide food initiatives elsewhere. However, for a small state, Rhode Island has a growing food movement and growing interest in local food production and farming. The latest numbers on farming (from a 2007 federal census) show that in 2007 Rhode Island had 1,219 farms, up 42 percent from 858 farms in 2002 (Lord 2010).

Reflective of this growing interest and commitment to local food, Farm Fresh Rhode Island's programs work to build Rhode Island's local food capacity in three areas: by focusing on food producers, markets, and food eaters. It counts among its objectives the preservation of Rhode Island farmland, culinary and agricultural traditions and knowledge, the creation of healthier communities, increased access to fresher food, the strengthening of community-based businesses, and the improvement of the impact of food production and distribution on the natural environment.

Farm Fresh Rhode Island is best known in the city of Providence for its seven summertime farmers markets in the city and its surrounding suburbs.

These markets take place at different locations on different days (they rotate through zones of the city in order to ensure accessibility to residents in different neighborhoods), and are designed to expand urban access to local fresh food and to connect urban consumers with rural producers while revitalizing public spaces. The Wintertime Farmers Market is a market that is designed to offer year-round fresh food to consumers and year-round income to producers by selling seasonal foods indoors on weekends during the cold season. All the farmers markets are home to other collaborative efforts, such as weekly collection of compostable materials. The week after Thanksgiving, the Winter Farmers Market's Green Team (another local nonprofit covering Rhode Island's environmental and social justice issues) staged a collection of turkey carcasses, which would be reused for animal feed. "Bring us your Turkey Carcass . . . we'll feed them to some pigs," said a sign taped to a barrel (Ziner 2010). These markets accept WIC (Women, Infants, and Children) and Seniors Coupons, federal subsidy programs for low-income families, and work in active collaboration with these government initiatives. This collaboration represents an important linkage with state social services.

Farm Fresh Rhode Island also administers a local food forum designed to increase direct farm-to-business sales (such as to restaurants and catering services). The organization liaises directly with independent schools in the area, as well as with chefs.

In addition to its summer and winter farmers markets in Providence and throughout the state, Farm Fresh Rhode Island has a number of programs aimed at cultivating what it calls "local eaters." The organization administers an online database with information about what food is in season and how and where to obtain it. The portal is intended to increase contact between farmers and buyers. Farm Fresh Rhode Island also has a Healthy Foods, Healthy Families project, working to share information about seasonal and local eating in schools and in low-income communities.

The Harvest Kitchen Project is a fifteen-week culinary and job-readiness training program for youth within the Division of Juvenile Corrections, to create preserved foods using ingredients sourced from local farmers at a certified kitchen.

Finally, the organization administers a number of programs to help support farmers and food producers. It advocates open space and smart growth policies for the state, coordinates beginning farmer apprenticeships, works with farmers to market their products through malls and trainings, and operates a shared food-processing site for farmers that provides affordable training and rentals.

For all these programs, Farm Fresh's budget is about $650,000 and is funded through grants and private donations. Contributions, gifts, and grants totaled $231,016 in 2009, and program service revenue was $148,760 (Farm Fresh 2011). Farm Fresh Rhode Island receives grants, donations, and in-kind support from a large number of corporate sponsors, in addition to individual donors. They count among their supporters a local bank, the local branch of a national insurance company, the Rhode Island Division of Agriculture, and a local charitable foundation with emphasis on funding Rhode Island community projects. The organization's 2009 year-end appeal sought donations to support the next phase of warehouse upgrades for the Wintertime Farmers Market. The organization sought to raise $20,000 to pay for this piece of infrastructure, which was intended to allow for expanded distribution in the area.

Staffing and infrastructure has proved a challenge for the organization; thus, Farm Fresh Rhode Island also makes use of the national Americorps VISTA program, a federal service program working to fight poverty that is administered by the national government. VISTA volunteers (government-recruited volunteers) do a year of service at nonprofits around the country (whose missions are matched with volunteers' interests and talents). Farm Fresh Rhode Island counts among its staff members three Americorps VISTA volunteers, an outreach coordinator, a culinary educator, a Wintertime Farmers Market manager, an executive director, a program director, and a managing director. These volunteers are subsidized by the federal government and through their volunteer years are trained in nonprofit administration. The organization has a board of eleven directors of diverse and relevant experience, including farmers, CEOs of small businesses, the director of business development of a medium-sized coffee company, a restaurateur, an attorney, and several marketing professionals. The distribution of the board expertise reflects Farm Fresh Rhode Island's triangulated emphasis on food production, food marketing, and food consumption.

Additionally, Farm Fresh Rhode Island is affiliated with several other organized groups, including a regional Farmers Union, the Northeast Sustainable Agriculture Working Group, and the Rhode Island Farm Bureau (Farm Fresh 2011).

Farm Fresh Rhode Island is but one piece of a small renaissance that has begun promoting farming and local food infrastructure in the smallest US state, as well as across the country. Rhode Island, a state of a little over a million people, produces less than 1 percent of the food it consumes and leads the nation in percentage of farmland lost to development in the last twenty years. However, a federal survey found three hundred new small farms in Rhode Island in the last several years, with agriculture one of the few growth industries during the recent (2008 onward) recession (Lord 2010). Community food and farming organizations have rapidly sprung up to support this wave of farming; a survey from the Rhode Island Agricultural Partnership found that Rhode Island farmers have much appreciated and continue to rely on the services of nonprofits such as Farm Fresh Rhode Island.

Other similar organizations include the Rhode Island Agricultural Partnership, a voluntary organization that administers a web portal to access information on Rhode Island agriculture, and a strategic plan composed by farmers for farmers. The strategic plan called for, among other things, better marketing and branding, so Rhode Island meats, vegetables, and fruits are more identifiable as produced in the state. Representatives of Farm Fresh Rhode Island serve on the Rhode Island Agricultural Partnership's Board of Directors, indicating a strong climate of cooperation and cross-germination among the two organizations (Lord 2010).

The Healthy Families/Thriving Communities Collaborative Council

Social services are by far the segment of the US third sector with the most financial support from national government. The Healthy Families/Thriving Communities (HFTC) Collaborative Council of Washington, DC, is one such example of "third party governance." It is a highly bureaucratized, professionalized social service delivery organization that fulfills federal mandates through a local NPO. This council of six community "collaboratives" brings together local community leaders to create and sustain a network that empowers families and communities with a mission to improve their quality of life across the District of Columbia.

The HFTC is a 501(c)(3) organization that provides leadership, advocacy, resource development, technical assistance, and training to its six Healthy Families/Thriving Communities Collaboratives. Each of the six collaboratives is an independent nonprofit organization working in communities that face intergenerational poverty, social challenges, and issues of safety and violence in different neighborhoods of Washington, DC. Each collaborative is also an independent 501(c)(3) led by its own community-based board of directors (Healthy Families 2011).

Each of the HFTC's six participating collaboratives has a number of different social service programs targeting the needs of the neighborhood, including general case management services, housing placement, job support, crisis intervention, and therapeutic counseling. The goal of these programs is to build strong families and communities in which people can safely and productively live and thrive. The collaboratives are staffed by professional social workers, but like the Women's Intercultural Center, they often draw into their staff people who have successfully participated in programs and are ready to seek permanent employment. Though the collaboratives have different strengths and are independent organizations, they share a set of core neighborhood-based prevention services and philosophies.

Collaborative workers (some licensed social workers, and some not) spend their days primarily in case management, that is, working one-on-one with individual clients confronting a range of problems. Workers may accompany clients to look at housing, assist them with applications for education or employment, connect them with other services (such as food stamp programs, clothing subsidies, or subsidized childcare), and advocate for them during the application process to such programs. Some collaborative workers accompany wards of the state (foster children) to their quarterly court reviews.

The collaborative movement was born in 1999, when Dr. Jerry Miller, the first court receiver of the state's Child and Family Services Agency, brought together government, community, and families to develop an intervention strategy to create safer and stronger communities. Miller's vision was designed to draw on the strengths of individuals and communities, to prevent child mistreatment and neglect, and to promote success. The collaboratives were born of this concept. While the city's child welfare system becomes involved with a family only when an allegation of abuse or neglect is made, the collaboratives are designed to build networks of support that are accessible to families *before* a crisis. In 1997, the individual collaboratives decided to form the Healthy Families/Thriving Communities Collaborative Council in order to address more abstract parts of their work (data collection and evaluation, documentation, training, quality assurance, etc.). The council also provides a unified body that can advocate for public policies and present a face to the general public.

The collaboratives and the collaborative council (jointly called the HFTC initiative) were established under the Federal Family Preservation and Family Support Act of 1993. The law was intended to reflect the belief of many child advocates that at-risk children and families need a continuum of social services that includes prevention, family preservation and reunification, out-of-home care, and adoption and post-adoption services. The law, then, encouraged individual states to create such continuums of family-focused services and required them to engage in comprehensive planning processes to develop more responsive family support and preservation strategies (US

Department 1993). The HFTC is supported financially by the DC Child and Family Services Agency (CFSA), the state agency for the oversight of children and families as part of the Partnership for Community-Based Services program. Because the HFTC receives government funding for its work, it also complies with outcome measures, transparency measures, and progress reports as specified within the grant contract, though the specifics of such information are confidential.

The HFTC Collaborative Council is involved in several programmatic initiatives, apart from coordination of its six member collaboratives. It advocates family and social policy at a DC-wide level; it runs a program that gives attention to the presence of a father figure in children's lives; and it administers the Fatherhood Education, Empowerment and Development program that is designed to help enhance fathering skills, improve co-parenting relationships, and reconnect fathers with children.

The HFTC and its council face many of the same challenges that social services in general face, including issues of safety for both clients and workers, client and participant attrition, and larger challenges that have to do with the socioeconomic position and intergenerational poverty among client communities. Because social work is an emotionally taxing position and the pay is low, turnover rates among social service professionals are very high. However, the HFTC also faces a broad challenge in balancing the demands of the federal bureaucracy with the community-based work that it does.

The HFTC Collaborative Council's work is carried-out by a diverse staff of ten, which includes child welfare professionals, program administrators, and researchers. Positions include that of executive director, deputy director, director of policy and planning, financial officers, data analyst, and several support staff. The council's board of ten directors, and five alternate directors, is composed of community stakeholders, as well as experts in the fields of child welfare and family advocacy. It also includes three members from each of the six collaboratives, four associate members from the Consortium for Child Welfare, the Center for the Study of Social Policy, DC Action for Children, and the DC Children's Trust Fund (Healthy Families 2011).

San Francisco Community Health Organizations

Nonprofit community-based health and advocacy organizations played a key role in the first response to the beginning of the US AIDS epidemic of the 1980s. These organizations showcase a fairly typical NPO trajectory within the United States—that of a small advocacy organization that grew, institutionalized, professionalized, and eventually contracted its services to the federal government. A 1984 survey of fifty-five US cities reported that 60 percent of local health departments had established relationships with community health organizations to provide a range of AIDS-related services (including education, counseling, housing, and social services) to community members. The city of San Francisco, like many other US cities, contracted AIDS-related services to community-based organizations during the mid-1980s. During this time, city funds constituted a substantial portion of the total revenues from these nonprofit community-based groups. Among those groups were the San Francisco AIDS Foundation (SFAF), the Shanti Project, and Hospice of San Francisco (Arno 1986:1325).

SFAF was founded in April of 1982 as a direct response to the AIDS epidemic. With its roots as an activist, all-volunteer, grassroots organization, composed of gay community leaders and physicians, it began as a storefront information referral hotline that soon became known as a source of accurate medical information on AIDS. In October of that same year, SFAF formally contracted with San Francisco's Department of Public Health, working to provide educational services, information, materials, and media presence that included accurate information on AIDS. The following year, SFAF established a social services department to assist AIDS patients with shelter, financial assistance, and medical attention. In addition to educational materials, the foundation established a privately funded food bank to assist those in financial need, providing eligible persons with a weekly bag of groceries. In the middle of the AIDS epidemic in 1986, approximately 150 people were using the service monthly (Arno 1986:1327).

Currently, the San Francisco AIDS Foundation provides a number of services and programs in support of its clients and participants. The organization has a team of financial benefits counselors who help HIV-positive individuals understand and navigate the complex private and government benefits systems, including the AIDS Drug Assistance Program, food stamps, Medi-Cal, Medicare, Social Security, and private disability plans. SFAF's Housing Subsidy Program assists with rent for more than 350 individuals—the organization notes that through the work of its client advocates and the clients themselves, more than 95 percent of these individuals remain stably housed. Additionally, Black Brothers Esteem is "a prevention and support program from San Francisco AIDS Foundation to empower men who predominantly live in the Tenderloin/Polk Gulch and Sixth Street Corridor neighborhoods of San Francisco. These men struggle not only with issues related to HIV, but also with racism, addiction, poverty, homophobia, violence and marginal housing. Facilitated by our expert staff, Black Brothers Esteem designs activities and events to provide a place for African American men to gather and to gain support from each other. The goal: provide education, skills and enhanced social connections to reduce sexual risk-taking" (San Francisco 2016).

SFAF's HIV Prevention Project operates a sterile syringe access program that targets the users of intravenous drugs. It distributes more than 2.3 million syringes per year, helping thousands of needle exchangers and their partners avoid HIV infection and hepatitis C. Program staff and volunteers, nurses, and drug treatment counselors offer free, anonymous exchange at ten locations throughout the city of San Francisco.

The Magnet program provides sexual health services, including HIV and STD testing and screening, and operates in the neighborhood with the greatest number of new HIV cases in the city. Magnet also hosts community events, art exhibits, and open mic nights.

"El Grupo" (Spanish for "The Group") is one of the longest-running bilingual support groups for Latinos living with HIV in the United States and is open to all HIV-positive Latinos/as and their families. The program exists to share information on living with HIV and to reduce the isolation and stigma that often accompany it. Finally, the Stonewall Project offers counseling and treatment programs for queer, gay, bisexual, transgender, questioning men who use crystal methamphetamine. Its website provides information about the use of meth to over two thousand visitors per day.

The San Francisco AIDS Foundation has a board of nine directors, including two physicians. Its CEO oversees all foundation programs, advocacy, research, finance, and operations (the current CEO was a past mayor of a large city in Arizona). The vice president of research and evaluation is responsible for managing the foundation's research endeavors and for evaluating its programs (the current holder of this position has a PhD in sociology). The vice president for development oversees all foundation philanthropic work and events. The vice president for marketing and communications is responsible for branding, communications, and online programming. The vice president for programs and policy is responsible for HIV prevention and care programs and for federal, state, and local policy initiatives. Finally, the chief financial officer oversees all accounting, budget, and information technology operations. Each vice president oversees a relevant and fully staffed department (San Francisco 2011).

Founded in 1974 as a community-based 501(c)(3) organization dealing with the problems of dying, the Shanti Project shifted its focus to AIDS care in 1981. In 1982 it began contracting with the San Francisco Department of Public Health to provide counseling services and housing assistance to people living with AIDS.

In response to the emotional toll taken by the disease, Shanti Project's trained professional and nonprofessional community volunteers offer free long-term counseling to people living with AIDS and their partners and families. During the AIDS epidemic of the 1980s, clients were matched to counselors within forty-eight hours of their initial request for assistance, and meetings could take place at their home, hospitals or outpatient clinics, or any other location. During the fiscal year of 1984–85, estimates put Shanti services at more than 56,000 hours of counseling to those living with or affected by AIDS in the San Francisco area. Shanti also worked at San Francisco General Hospital, the only hospital at the time providing acute care, and donated more than 6,000 hours of counseling in that context. Because of the debilitating nature of AIDS, patients can no longer care for themselves, and thus Shanti's support programs use volunteers to assist patients in day-to-day activities, such as cooking, cleaning, and shopping. During the fiscal year 1984–85, Shanti and Hospice provided 17,000 and 2,000 hours of this support, respectively. Further, since housing can become a severe problem for AIDS patients, the Shanti AIDS Residence Program was established to operate low-cost independent housing for area residents living with AIDS. The program owns housing units and rents each tenant a private bedroom, and tenants cooperatively run the residence. The residences also offer links to other health-care service providers. In 1986, Shanti administered eight such residences, which housed eighty-seven people in 1984–85 (Arno 1986:1327).

Shanti continues to offer what it terms a "continuum of services" for people living with HIV/AIDS. All the programs are designed to inform about HIV as a disease and its treatments and how to enhance health outcomes and quality of life. Shanti administers the Drop-in Service Center, a gathering space where clients can come for emotional or practical support from a peer advocate, a treatment advocate, or a volunteer and for access to resources regarding the disease, medication, current studies, medical and health care, housing, food, support groups, free showers, and information on other community services. The Drop-in Service Center also provides free local phone service. The Shanti Peer Support Volunteer Program trains volunteers and matches them with a single client. The volunteer provides weekly emotional or practical support, based on the individual client's needs. Practical support may include assisting with laundry, house cleaning, grocery shopping, medication pickup and delivery, and the completion of forms related to housing, disability, medical and mental health services, and so forth. Shanti also offers individual health counseling, the goal of which is to support clients in developing health-protective routines and addressing the psychological, social, and biological factors that can impact overall health and well-being.

Shanti peer advocates and treatment advocates have knowledge and experience with HIV disease and treatment and other HIV-related health issues; they help clients navigate through the systems of support administered both privately and publicly. This final program is similar to the one that the San Francisco AIDS Foundation administers. Finally, the Shanti Project offers a number of support groups, seminars, and workshops for individuals living with HIV (Shanti Project 2011).

Formed in 1978, Hospice of San Francisco was designed to provide physical, emotional, and spiritual support for terminally ill patients and their families in the San Francisco area. It followed a similar trajectory from community activism to bureaucratization to professionalization; in 1983, it contracted with the San Francisco Department of Public Health in order to expand its services to AIDS patients in the area, and by the following year it had a per-project contract to provide home health and hospice care (Arno 1986:1327).

During the AIDS epidemic in the 1980s, these projects relied heavily on volunteer labor in order to do their work. The SFAF used volunteers as "staff extenders": professional staff designed the foundation activities during the peak of the AIDS epidemic, while trained volunteers assisted them in carrying out those activities. At the Shanti Project, volunteers provided the vast majority of services, once they had been thoroughly trained (Arno 1986:1328).

Volunteers at all these projects underwent intensive training processes to ensure the quality of their services. Would-be volunteers for Shanti's Emotional Support Program passed a rigorous application process, including a series of interviews and forty-four hours of training, which included orientation on the medical and psychological elements of AIDS, substance abuse, grief counseling, and information on other AIDS organizations. Volunteers were expected to commit at least eight hours weekly for a period of six months, two hours of which were committed to a support group that provided guidance, feedback, and support in their work (Arno 1986:1328). Volunteers in other Shanti programs underwent twenty-two hours of training and were expected to make a similar time commitment. Training for community support workers included an AIDS medical overview and information on assisting physically compromised people, risks of substance abuse, referrals, and other relevant information.

Hospice volunteers underwent sixteen hours of training that oriented them to basic hospice care and AIDS. These volunteers attended weekly support groups, and professional staff supervised their home visits. Volunteer licensed massage therapists received special training toward techniques of massage therapy for AIDS patients. All volunteer staff committed to a minimum of ten hours a week for a period of one year.

At SFAF, 40 percent of volunteer time was spent at the telephone hotline, dispensing basic information on AIDS and providing referrals to other AIDS programs and physicians. Hotline volunteers attended a ten-hour training program on basic medical information and listening skills and received routine "refreshers" to keep their knowledge current. All volunteers committed to six to eight hours weekly for a minimum of six months (Arno 1986:1328).

The above examples show how community-based organizations can work very much in harmony with city administration in the provision of critical services to local residents during a period of crisis. In addition to greatly increasing the quality of life for AIDS patients, these community organizations were successful in reducing the overall rate of hospitalization in the San Francisco General Hospital, as patients were receiving necessary care in their homes and in clinics. Arno finds that in 1984, the average length of hospital stay for AIDS patients in San Francisco was 11.7 days (and compares it to 17 days in Los Angeles, 25 days in New York, and 52 days in Trenton, New Jersey) (Arno 1986:1329). This represents a considerable alleviation on strained hospital resources and demonstrates how the efficient use of third-sector resources can complement institutionalized service provision.

Schooner SoundWaters

SoundWaters is a 501(c)(3) nonprofit organization founded in 1989 with a mission to restore, protect, and preserve the Long Island Sound and its watershed through environmental education for children and adults. The Long Island Sound is an important geographical area on the outskirts of New York City, and its health has profound implications for the environmental health of the region. SoundWaters has a two-pronged programmatic approach to meeting its mission: it administers programs at the Coastal Education Center on land and aboard the Schooner *SoundWaters*, a three-masted schooner that travels through field sites throughout the local area.

The organization offers a wide array of educational opportunities for students from kindergarten through university, both on board the Schooner *SoundWaters* and at classrooms on land throughout the region. Coming aboard the boat allows students to observe the life of the Long Island Sound and learn about coastal ecology through four onboard educational programs. Generally speaking, students board the ship for a day. They help to set and strike sail, learning a bit about maritime history in the process, and then divide into groups to circulate through the on-board "learning stations" taught by the *SoundWaters* crew. The learning stations concentrate on ecological topics such as salt marshes, local bird life, and weather.

The SoundWaters Center, on land, hosts a variety of courses, seminars, and activities for organizations, schools, and corporations. School groups can visit the Learning Lab to take part in exciting hands-on programs, many of which can be adapted to support the classroom curriculum. Evening adult programs focus on wildlife, history, culture, conservation, music, and other topics. Similarly, outreach programs take place throughout the local watershed area. SoundWaters educators lead explorations into the forests, rivers, marshes, and beaches of the Long Island Sound. These programs can be customized for the level of students.

The organization charges for its educational services and provides some of its income through this fee-for-service operation, in combination with some grant and gift support. Further, the schooner *SoundWaters* and the Sound-Waters Coastal Center offer charters for corporate events as a mechanism for supporting the center. Corporate groups and parties can charter the sailboat for cruises along the Long Island Sound or rent the historic SoundWaters Coastal Center for a corporate reception or ceremony.

Its onshore staff of eleven includes an executive director, three educators, the captain of the schooner *SoundWaters*, the camp director, an office manager, the director of education, the director of annual appeals and special events (fundraising), and the finance director. Onshore staff is responsible for the maintenance of the organization, and the administrative positions mimic the trends found elsewhere. The onshore director of education is responsible for the development of the educational curricula for both the schooner and the onshore Coastal Center. The organization's board of directors includes twenty-four individuals, an array of community members and those with relevant scientific and educational expertise.

Additionally, in season, the schooner *SoundWaters* has an educator and deckhand crew that ranges between three and eight people, not including the captain, who live below decks aboard the boat and teach educational curriculum to students. The onboard crew is responsible for the maintenance of the ship in the off-hours and rotate responsibilities for cooking, cleaning, and painting and maintaining the vessel.

3. France

The French third sector emerged under unique circumstances. It was not created as an aggregate consequence of private groups attempting to solve social problems, as in the United States, nor as a system of third-party governance organizations, as in many places in Asia. Rather, the non-profit sector in France (typically termed the "social economy") formed as a consequence of an ideological struggle—between the Catholic Church and republicanism over the rights of the individual. Until 1901, individuals had few legal opportunities to even associate in groups; associations were only permitted under specific conditions set by the government.

In the nineteenth century, Napoleon rebuilt the state following rational, hierarchical ideals. He adopted a state-institutional arrangement similar to that of the military, and as part of this process he reorganized or eliminated all intermediary groups in order to "replace richness of individual with the precision of general law." The political label was "republicanism," stressing the anti-monarchical character of leadership after the 1789 Revolution, which required a strong state for implementation. This ideology opposed individual spontaneity and bolstered the idea of positivism—stressing reason and order. The political leaders of bourgeois citizens supported these views in the mid-nineteenth century as a reaction to monarchical traditionalism and its supposed irrationality, corruption, and disorder. In its stead, they favored uniform governmental institutions and scientific thought over individualistic or unpredictable action. But the nineteenth century was defined for many as battles between "the red and the black," the red republicans versus the black coats of priests and conservatives. Policies shifted continually with coups d'état, insurrections, and wars. When, in 1901, the social economy law was signed into being, observers saw it as the "final victory of the Republic over the Catholic Church in France" (Lindsay and Hems 2004:266).

Even so, the genesis of the French social economy has been marked by a strong statist presence in which the institutional logic of bureaucracy was most prominent. In the midst of the social tumult that rocked the 1960s in the West, the French nonprofit sector showed evidence of institutional logics of solidarity and activism. Contemporarily, and similar to the United States, we see the emergence of the institutional logic of professionalization.

Etatism (statism) is one of the most important features in French history, and the struggle of the French central bureaucracy against local power in any form has stamped the development of the third sector. This tension manifested in the state's struggle against the feudal order, in its struggle against urban citizens' organizations during the Middle Ages, in its struggle against regional governments and religious minorities during the Old Regime, against the Church and its nonprofit branches, and against guilds during the French Revolution. During the nineteenth century, the central state fought the labor movement and political clubs. The liberal laws of about 1900 marked a deep transformation in this regard, making the nonprofit sector legal for the first time in French history. Yet the centralized state continued to grow, even as new social and economic concerns became public concerns, and a strengthened welfare state emerged after World War II, as elsewhere in Europe (Archambault 2001:205).

Quite unlike the United States, Great Britain, or the Netherlands, the French social economy (which differs slightly from the US notion of the third sector) developed against the background of mistrust in any organization that would undermine formalized state authority. The social economy is largely a twentieth-century phenomenon, still contested and resented by parts of the legal system and many political leaders and intellectuals. Specialized groups representing religious minorities, women, gays, and, particularly after the late twentieth century, immigrants are fighting for legitimacy in France as they challenge the universal, egalitarian central state, the strongest of any state tradition in Europe. A classic example in the twenty-first century is that no religious symbols may be worn in schools, so Muslim girls are not permitted to cover their heads if they wish to enter a French public school. French administration sees this policy as a denial of the legitimacy of separatist organizations and culture in France; it would violate egalitarianism to permit any girl to cover her head. But elsewhere in the West, the same policy is seen as a violation of human rights, especially by the individualist groups in countries like the United States and the United Kingdom. France is thus a valuable analytic counter to the view that there is one "Western" tradition of civic involvement. Even if many French legal policies, described below, resemble those in other Western countries, they are implemented and interpreted very differently. As should be expected, those political differences play out in the French associational sector, as elsewhere in French political life. The institutional logic of activism during the development of nineteenth-century French associational life positioned itself against mainstream statism and bureaucracy, promoting concepts of self-determination and regional cooperation.

In the late 1960s, social upheaval shook France. Similarly to other parts of the West, these movements challenged the relationship between the state and the citizens. One revolutionary consequence was termed "decentralization," and while this same process happened globally, it was more a fundamental change in France, representing a move away from Parisian dominance. The central French state delegated massive amounts of social services to nonprofit organizations. In France, as in the United States and other advanced industrial countries, this period saw a shift from thinking about welfare services as public to at least thinking about them as more local, or even as private, adding a new emphasis on citizen participation in policymaking and implementation (T. Clark and Hoffmann-Martinot 1998), and, following the economic shocks of the 1970s oil crisis, a concern with reducing welfare state expenditures (Ullman 1998:10).

Similarly, the social transformations within French society in the last quarter of the twentieth century gave birth to new forms of social organization during that period. The 1960s saw the number of new associations multiply: for environmental defense and protection; for the concerns of feminism, notably the fight against restrictions on birth control and the prohibition of abortion; and for international development. After the previous years of affluence, by 1977, while public service types still dominated, there was an increasing number of sectoral interest associations that were by nature more self-interested and consequently more divergent to the Republican model of a "collective social integration of society though its organization and management by the state" (Worms 2002:14). This expansion continued through the 1980s, 1990s, and early years of the twenty-first century. In the early 1980s the first socialist government in decades, led by President Francois Mitterand, brought major policy shifts. Most local governments had socialist mayors from 1945 to the 1980s, who welcomed decentralization policies. Many local associations had been funded by and linked to local governments—sports, leisure, culture, and social service groups—termed *le socialisme municipal,* as part of their mission was to continue support for socialist mayors. Decentralization provided more transfers of funds from Paris for these and similar local programs, although it meant cutbacks at the national level.

The late twentieth century simultaneously witnessed the emergence of more citizen-driven, issue-specific movements, such as movements for the environment, human rights, and the like, similar to other movements taking place across Northern Europe. These were a change in France from classic historical patterns, especially by sectoral interest associations, and are indicative of the orientations of new social movements; this desire for "personal autonomy and chosen solidarities" (Worms 2002:19) stood in contrast to the traditional French culture and the statist tradition.

In the early years of the twenty-first century, the French social economy gradually moved toward private initiative; more attention was paid to the tradition of Anglo-Saxon countries, and thus an institutional logic of professionalization can be seen emerging alongside decentralization. The Decentralization Act (1982) was a step toward a more typically European political structure and generated a host of partnerships between nonprofit organizations and local authorities and businesses, expanding both the bureaucratic and the professional impulses that we observed in the US case. The association boom of the past forty years that has been seen all over the world is also visible in France, nurtured in part by support from French central and local governments. (From fewer than 15,000 in the 1960s, the number of new associations created each year reached 60,000 to 70,000 in the years after 1980 [Archambault 2001]).

A third trend in France and Europe is the rise of the European Union, which has reinforced national developments and brought more bureaucratic and professional styles of management from Northern and Southern Europe. EU grants, audits, and other programs have reinforced classic French elements of bureaucratic and professional administration.

This contemporary era of public-private partnerships or third-party governance in France is meaningfully distinct from the pre-welfare state era, when responsibility for the poor was seen as charity's mandate. The state formally delegates to and links more with nonprofit organizations, operating within an institutional logic of professionalization, moving away from charitable relief that was more broadly paternalistic and state administrative structures that were heavily bureaucratic. Whereas before, public officials supervised public bureaucracies, contracts and agreements now more often define programs. More traditional hierarchies of authority and oversight have to work with more professional, impersonal structures of contracts and reporting, which "involves a recasting of public authority and of relations between the state and society. It calls into question traditional definitions of the state, as the boundary markers . . . become blurred" (Ullman 1998:11). In that sense, France more resembles the United States than other European countries, which generally experienced growth in public-private partnerships and a rise in institutional logics of professionalization, bureaucracy, and activism that articulate within its third sectors. Still, the French historical background still plays a visible role, certainly in the political rhetoric about the state and skepticism toward markets and capitalism, which most French citizens also support.

Legal Structure and Background

France is a world leader in its development of strong state institutions, its use of art, culture, and cuisine to legitimate this authority, and its Napoleonic legacy. It consolidated the strong-state tradition that had originated in the Roman Empire; its central state served as a model that continues in many institutions worldwide. And this kind of statist tradition has a political effect on both the presence and the character of formal organizations. In a statist context, formal organizing in society is linked to, subordinate to, and defined in terms of state action and functions. But there is less formal organizing in such societies themselves than in other social systems, and fewer societal domains receive formal organizing (Jepperson and Meyer 1991:223). The use of the strong state to implement citizen egalitarianism (and the corresponding intolerance of intermediary organizations such as civic groups) makes France a classic Western counterexample to the Calvinist model of local, democratically based citizen involvement discussed in the introduction.

The French social economy comprises four basic organizational forms: cooperatives, mutual societies, associations, and foundations (Archambault 1997:4–5). The social economy is defined broadly as the set of private, formally organized enterprises with autonomy of decision and freedom of membership, created to meet their members' needs through the market by producing goods or providing services, insurance or finance, where decision making and any distribution of profits or surpluses among the members are not directly linked to the capital or fees contributed by each member, each of whom has one vote (CIRIEC 2006:36), different from other third sectors (notably the United States) in the explicit *absence* of political engagement. The word "economy" within the term "social economy" points to the needs for goods and services, rather than debate, dissent, or protest: "social innovation in the economy is mainly about the (re)introduction of social justice into production and allocation systems" (Moulaert and Ailenei 2005:2037). These social economy organizations are private (not controlled in whole or in part by the public sector); they are formally organized; they have autonomy of decision; they have freedom of membership; and they are created to meet their members' needs.

As in other countries, the French third sector gained its foothold in the areas within which government function was considered inadequate. Three long-term trends have strongly influenced the development of the French social economy: restrictions on nonprofit organizations imposed by a centralized and interventionist state prior to 1901, the early secularization of the sector in a predominantly Catholic country, and the strong legacy of the revolutionary egalitarianism of 1789, which continues in socialist ideology. Formal civic organizing in France was condemned during the French Revolution—the Décret d'Allarde of March 1791 and the Loi Le Chapelier of June 1791 together suppressed guilds, as they were said to interfere with free enterprise and fair competition. The Catholic Church's charitable arms were either closed or nationalized at that time; the French government subsequently undertook the responsibility to provide public primary education and to address extreme poverty. After the French Revolution the third sector secularized rapidly, moving from a primarily Catholic concern to an almost entirely statist one. According to the Rousseau-inspired notions of the time, the state had the monopoly of public interest concerns; nonprofit organizations were actually illegal in France until the 1901 law was passed permitting their formation.

Utopian socialist activists such as Saint-Simon and Proudhon influenced the formation of French cooperatives, mutual benefit societies, and other types of associations. This political philosophy stood in direct contrast to mainstream statism, promoting instead ideologies of self-determination and localism. Further, at the beginning of the twentieth century, during a period of unprecedented development of the social economy, the basis of the French Republican government was solidarity, which stressed income redistribution and mutual benefit societies. The 1810 French penal code stated that no association of over twenty persons could be created without government consent. This code lasted through the nineteenth century, until it was finally supplanted by the Act of 1901. However, despite the legal prohibition of associations, mutual societies (many of which were linked to an underground labor movement) survived in underground networks (Archambault 2001:208).

Despite the general legal climate of suppression, exceptions mounted during the nineteenth century. Thus between 1815 and 1848, the Church was permitted to restore its nonprofit charitable activities. Other associations operated by the middle class, including health centers and social service organizations, also took root. Apart from these organizations, the authorized nonprofit sector included middle-class social and recreational clubs called *cercles* and employers' philanthropy (Archambault 2001:208). In 1864, the designated crime of *coalition* (which included strike) was legally abolished, and something of an associative revival followed. In 1884, following a decade of deliberation in Parliament, labor unions were legalized. In 1898, the Charte de la Mutualité gave a legal status to mutual benefit societies. Finally, in 1901, a law called the Act of 1901 gave a legal status to the bulk of social economy organizations. This law provided the foundation upon which subsequent nonprofit law was built (Archambault 2001:209).

World War II again saw restrictions on freedom of association in France. As of 1939, foreigners' associations had to gain special authorization in order for members to congregate; this law was repealed only in 1981. Under the Vichy administration, any association could be dissolved by an administrative order, though clandestine networks of associations survived. After the war, the Act of 1901 was reenacted without restriction (Archambault 2001:212) and persisted until the 1960s and the social movements that emerged during that time.

In the 1960s and 1970s, following the patterns of the rest of the West, space opened up in the French consciousness for new social issues, such as environmental defense and women's rights (New Social Movements), and these concerns gave way to new organizations addressing the same. Still their activities and legitimacy were unlike other countries. As a climax of these social issues, the brief May 1968 general strike paralyzed the whole French economy for a month. In response, the French government got Parliament to pass an act in 1971 that reintroduced the nineteenth-century requirement that political associations secure authorization from the state. But the Conseil Constitutionel, the French Supreme Court, dismissed the 1971 act as an infringement upon the constitutional guarantee of freedom of association (Archambault 2001:212). Additionally, during this time period traditional nonprofits concerned with all kinds of issues expanded. Regardless, Moore notes that the events of 1968 to 1971 indicate a strong tendency for the French state to take action to reclaim power when threatened by independent groups (Moore 2001:711), indicating a persistent uneasiness in state–third sector relations.

Coinciding with its tenth anniversary, in June 1980 the National Liaison Committee for Mutual, Cooperative and Associative Activities (CNLAMCA) published the Charte de l'économie sociale (the Social Economy Charter), which formally defined the social economy (EESC 2005), thereby instilling it with a newer version of legitimacy. Two years later the 1982 Decentralization Act was another victory for the French social economy; the state's responsibilities were cut back and those of local communities increased, and this decentralization stimulated both privatization and the development of the nonprofit sector, similar to both NPC (New Political Culture) and neoliberal political dynamics occurring elsewhere. Interestingly, the United States was decentralizing during this time as well, but under a Reagan-esque political approach; in France, decentralization happened under Mitterand, a Socialist. These coincident decentralization impulses point to a strong New Political Culture dynamic of citizen participation.

The French social economy was reinforced as a solid source of jobs in the financial crisis of 2008 and onward (Clinton 2010). This also encouraged efforts to better capture the economic contributions of the social economy within France and the European Union.

As of 2014, financial accounting in Europe relied on aggregated economic information that made contributions of the social economy nearly imperceptible. National accounts systems, rooted in the mid-twentieth-century ideologies, were based on tools for collecting the major national economic aggregates in a mixed economy context with a strong private capitalist sector and a complementary—and frequently interventionist—public sector. Logically, in a national accounts system revolving around such a bipolar institutional situation, there is little room for a third pole that is neither public nor capitalist, while the capitalist pole can be identified with practically the whole private sector (CIRIEC 2006).

The French Social Economy

More than in other places, the French "social economy" (as opposed to the "nonprofit sector" generally defined) reflects the wide, real-life spectrum of initiatives and institutions that lie between unfettered market function and state administration in France. The social economy generates an unusually varied stream of market exchange, state initiatives and collaborations, and collective action (Moulaert and Ailenei 2005). Partly because of this, the varied institutional logics present in France are coexistent and stand less in tension with one another than in the United States, because the components of the social economy are so clearly delineated.

The US nonprofit sector and the French social economy do share important similarities. They share a requirement for a formal legal-institutional structure; they share an emphasis on the private nature of organizational governance; the nonprofit criterion of self-governance is close to the requirement for independent management in the social economy; finally, the legal statuses of both social economy and nonprofit sector organizations stipulate that membership is voluntary (Defourny 2001:10).

The 1980 French Social Economy Charter formally acknowledged the existence of this sector, notwithstanding the legal diversity of its elements, and yet attempted to specify the basic prerequisites of sector membership. It stressed organizations that embodied an ethos of personal and voluntary participation, solidarity among members (this solidarity implies interdependence, a sense of belonging, income redistribution), democratic management, independence from government, volunteer leadership (in the form of a board of directors), and a not-for-profit orientation (Salamon and Anheier 1997:120–21). This social economy includes undeclared associations, declared associations (which are subject to the 1901 Act), and public utility associations.

However, the European social economy and the US third sector also differ in important ways. First, the social economy has a deep commitment to democratic decision making, which represents a structural procedure to control the actual pursuit of the organization's goals (Defourny 2001:11). Within the third sector, however, such control comes from inside the organization through its governing bodies (such as its board of directors) but without any legal democratic requirement. Secondly, the nonprofit approach explicitly *disallows* profit distribution (like US nonprofits), thus excluding the component of the social economy known as cooperatives. Cooperatives typically redistribute a part of their surplus to their members. This prohibition also excludes some mutual societies for consideration under the rubric of "third sector," as some such societies return part of their surplus to members in the form of reductions or discounts. France retains a more anticapitalist view in its coops, similar to the United States in the 1930s and 1940s, but which changed during World War II (Cohen 2003).

The French state (including its local iterations such as public agencies and towns) created associations (which are governed by the 1901 Act) to manage social services; these associations grew more important after the Decentralization Act of 1982. In many ways, French associations resemble their counterparts in the United States and Japan, which were created for localized service provision. However, the French associations are technically dependent on public subsidies; they are not self-governing and therefore not part of the social economy, but rather third-party service providers that are more bureaucratized. Likewise, much public housing is excluded from consideration as part of the social economy because it is part of the welfare state and, consequently, is not self-governing. As another example, most universities are public, but business schools are private and managed by the chamber of commerce or trade association and therefore part of the social economy (Salamon and Anheier 1997:122).

The 1901 Act allowed for freedom of association, and the resulting creation, the *Association*, was then legally prohibited from earning profit. *Syndicats* (trade unions) have been legally recognized since 1884 and are structured in order to protect the rights of employees, though this category excludes profit sharing among membership (Archambault 1997:58). These syndicates are generally considered to be a category of association. French associations are allowed to generate profit, as long as it is not distributed among the members and is not the primary purpose of this association. Profit making (even in the form of fees-for-service), however, subjects the organization's profit-making activities to economic and business regulations, including on questions of insolvency, pricing, competition, and paracommercial practices (Archambault 1997:60–61), a further regulatory complication.

Associationalism rose in France, especially after the social transformations of the 1960s. Because associations are not required to declare dissolution, numbers are imperfect; however, Salamon and Anheier estimate that France had approximately seven hundred thousand associations as of 1990. Similar to the United States, the development of the French social economy was linked heavily to the emergence of charity, and that charitable emphasis persists in the large health and social services subsector that exists currently. Funded primarily by the French social security program (which covers 99 percent of the French population), these institutions are critical parts of the entire medical network in France. This subsector is an economic heavy hitter, representing 43 percent of the total resources and more than 55 percent of the employment in the French social economy (Archambault 1997:165).

French social economy law distinguishes between operating, advocacy, and sociability organizations (Salamon and Anheier 1997:114). Operating organizations generally provide services and receive most of their funding publicly through central or local governments or social security. Advocacy organizations encompass health, welfare, research, education, professional training, and recreation and are typically pressure groups working on issues such as feminism and minority rights that generally fall under the category of New Social Movements and operate under an institutional logic of activism.

Legislated by a 1955 code, mutual or cooperative societies have a different vision of profit sharing than their for-profit counterparts, despite the fact that they may in cases occupy the same territory. Mutual societies are essentially nonprofit organizations, descended from the friendly societies of the nineteenth and early twentieth centuries. Governed by the 1955 Mutual Societies Code, they are organizations that promote with their members' "subscriptions an activity of providence, solidarity and philanthropy to the benefit of families. This activity intends to prevent social risks, to encourage motherhood, to protect childhood and family, and to promote the moral development of their members" (Archambault 1993:10). Mutual society members and beneficiaries are one and the same (CIRIEC 2006:37)—they are self-interest groups—and demonstrate the persistently paternalistic, but also self-governing, deeply social, and autonomous impulses.

As the primary business group within the French social economy, cooperatives are legal entities whose principal objects are to satisfy their members' needs and advance their economic and social activities, with less of a moralistic bent. Cooperative activities are conducted for the mutual benefit of the members so that each member benefits from the activities of the cooperative in proportion to his or her participation; members are also customers, employees, or suppliers or are otherwise involved in the activities of the cooperative; control is vested equally in members, in accordance with the principle of "one person, one vote"; interest on loan and share capital is limited (though in some cases cooperatives may have among their members a certain proportion of investor members who do not use their services); voting rights of investor members, if allowed, are limited so that control remains vested in the user members; profits are distributed in proportion to the transactions with the cooperative or retained to meet the members' needs; there are no artificial restrictions on membership; there are specific rules on membership, resignation, and expulsion; in the event of dissolution, net assets and reserves are distributed to another cooperative pursuing similar aims or general interest purposes (CIRIEC 2006:40). Occasionally, "ancillary members" may contribute to the company without being users of the cooperative activity (such as capital investors or former user members who are no longer users for justified reasons such as retirement).

After the establishment of the public social security system in 1945, cooperative organizations shifted focus from meeting basic needs to essentially providing supplements to government health insurance policies alongside associations. As such, they provide health and welfare, insurance, medical clinics, hospitals, pharmacies, and the like. As of 1988, there were 1,070 such centers in operation. As managers of programs that belong to the national social security system, these institutions also provide compulsory social security for civil servants, students, teachers, professors, and so forth. Governed by a 1947 general Status of Cooperation Act, cooperatives include, among others, agriculture cooperatives and banks (Archambault 1993).

Foundations are legal entities that have been designated to nonprofit aims that benefit the public good. Until 1987 the country had no formal laws governing foundations (Archambault 1997:58). They play a far more limited role in France given its strong statist traditions. Numbers for 1990 put French foundations at 428 (Archambault 2000; unpaginated).

Funding

The distinctions between the French social economy and the US nonprofit sector somewhat befuddle comparative analysis, and the accounting system is full of exceptions. For example, the most important health and welfare associations are recorded in the government sector rather than the social economy, because public financing accounts for more than half of their resources. On the other hand, small associations hiring fewer than two people are included in the household sector for accounting purposes. Operating associations are treated as members of the business sector if their sales are more than 50 percent of total resources (Salamon and Anheier 1997:115). Generally speaking, however, French third sector organizations receive funding from three major streams—public, fee-for-service, and private donations. Government funding constitutes the largest component for most of the social economy activities on the list.

Declared associations are limited in capacity to engage in financial transactions in ways they are not elsewhere—for example, they may not own real estate or receive legacies, unlike in the United States. However, associations are exempted from gift and income taxes and profit taxes and are partially exempted from value-added taxes. Gifts are deductible to donors for up to 3 percent of taxable income (Salamon and Anheier 1997:13). French associations are expressly prohibited from owning property or exercising many rights; the stated purpose of this legal design was to stave off the risk of fostering secret or rebellious groups among associations (Archambault 1997). Additionally, expenses for voluntary activities that are part of recognized social activities receive favorable treatment; for example, trips with a person's own automobile can be listed for deductions in the tax declaration (Dehne et al. 2008:714).

Status Quo and Challenges

When the Mitterand government took power in 1981, the ground was laid for the nonprofit explosion that occurred in France as elsewhere, and in the decade that followed, the relationships between the French state and nonprofit social service providers changed dramatically. The new government offered these organizations unprecedented roles in administering the welfare state's reforms, and in the 1980s, the social economy "third party governance" agencies were heavily institutionalized; the institutional transformations from paternalism and bureaucracy toward professionalization became clear.

Further, these third sector organizations are becoming more visible vehicles of policy, at the same time integrating themselves more firmly within the government bureaucracy. The French population trusts local governments and third sector organizations to solve issues of public concern more than they trust political parties or labor unions (Archambault 1997:191). This is a telling detail, reinforcing the idea that these organizations can have dramatic impacts on issues of public trust and legitimacy. Indeed, the patterns of trust in different institutions in France vary dramatically from those in other countries: the French citizens have far more trust in the state, and much less

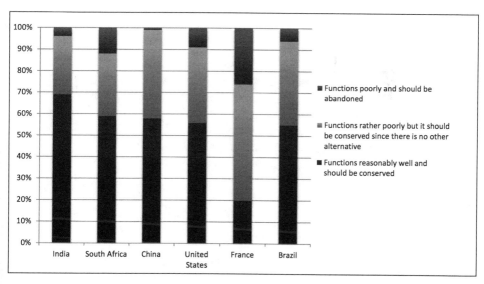

Figure 7. Comparison of attitudes toward capitalism and the market economy in six nations.

Source: Institut français d'opinion publique (French Public Opinion Institute) 2013.

in markets and capitalism than citizens in at least six other major countries surveyed. The French Public Opinion institute, for example, conducted a comparative international survey of a national sample of adults regarding their opinions on global capitalism. France, as shown in Figure 7, ranks far above other countries in its opinions that capitalism and the market economy function poorly and should be abandoned.

Interestingly in the context of these findings, the French social economy is much more "economic"—concerned with profit making—than is the US nonprofit sector. France is different from the United States in that its social economy is more economically and programmatically diverse, has more profit-making components, and retains a higher degree of bureaucracy than in the United States, in part because of its strong history of statism. As we demonstrate in subsequent chapters, the French experience of statism and decentralization parallels some Eastern examples, such as Japan. The tendency of the French nonprofit sector has been to move from a strong statist position, in which the institutional logic of bureaucracy was most prominent, to a solidaristic and activist approach, tempered both by dynamics of professionalization and the continued presence of bureaucracy.

Case Studies

Departmental Association for the Protection of Children and Adolescents (A.D.S.E.A.)

The Departmental Association for the Protection of Children and Adolescents, known as A.D.S.E.A., is a government-funded charitable organization that provides assistance to children, adolescents, and adults with special needs in the Seine et Marne (the seventy-seventh) department of France (see A.D.S.E.A. 77 2011). The organization was founded as part of a "humanist and personalistic philosophy" for children with disabilities who had been neglected or abandoned. A.D.S.E.A. has no religious affiliation, but is built upon the moralistic idea that each individual has fundamental rights that must be protected. Through advocacy, research, and education, A.D.S.E.A. works with children, their families, and the public to secure their safety and nurture their well-being. Each year, the organization assists about seven thousand people.

As a government-funded organization, tightly linked with the state and thus bureaucratic in nature, A.D.S.E.A. sustains a healthy and dynamic partnership with the General Council of Seine et Marne, Île de France, Education Nationale, and other key departments. A.D.S.E.A. was founded in 1944 with the mission to assist children and their families. In 2011 the organization was composed of seventeen different divisions and had more than eight hundred employees. While the association continues its original mission through individualized social work cases, it has expanded the scope of its attention to the national level. To facilitate effective operation on a large scale, each of the seventeen departments has a unique focus. The organization's research department is now a major center of scholarship and thought, producing publications and sponsoring national conferences that focus on best practices in emergency care, technological improvements in everyday care for those with disabilities, and developments in child psychiatry. With a legal department and strong governmental ties, A.D.S.E.A. is a formidable force in shaping public policies. Education outreach in local schools and community groups enables A.D.S.E.A. to affect public opinion about disabilities.

The General Council of Seine et Marne selects A.D.S.E.A.'s governing body. This council is composed of twenty-two to thirty members who serve six-year terms. These council members then self-elect a board, which consists of a chairman, one to three vice-presidents, a secretary, an assistant secretary, a treasurer, and an assistant treasurer. Additionally, two juvenile court judges and a representative from the General Council of Seine et Marne serve on the board. Local magistrates and professionals are often called to serve as advisers to this board. Membership on the board is purely voluntary, and there is no remuneration. The board meets twice a year.

The board's function is to oversee the activity of the professional staff of the organization, which is led by the director general, who reports directly to the board president. The director general's official function is to maintain unity and coherence of the collective work of the organization; that person is responsible for the implementation of the political and advocacy efforts, corporate communications, management of the internal staff projects, and all political and expenditure decisions. The director has support from a cadre of managers who are each responsible for developing projects within specific areas. Each manager commands a body of professional staff of social workers and academic researchers. A.D.S.E.A. places high value on its employees and encourages upward mobility among staff.

A.D.S.E.A. was legally recognized by the prefecture of Seine et Marne in 1944, and on November 29, 1971, the charity was designated as a Recognized Public Utility (under the category of "association"). The organization is formally authorized to provide care for individuals with disabilities, operate vocational training and rehabilitation centers, perform social work in an open environment, and supply resources for educational outreach. A committee of Seine et Marne municipal leaders, including the interior minister, the minister of justice, and the president of the General Council, has the right to visit A.D.S.E.A. and its affiliates.

The charity prioritizes accountability and rigorous management of spending because all operations are funded publicly through a government allowance. This dynamic—of government-funded social service—is one of the most common within the French social economy, and A.D.S.E.A.'s dynamics are illustrative of the kind of community-state collaboration that is so typical of service provision.

Committee for the Inter-movement of Evacuees (Cimade)

The Committee for the Inter-movement of Evacuees (Cimade) provides aid for immigrants and asylum seekers (La Cimade 2011). Cimade is governed by three key principles: "testify, inform, and mobilize." As Article 1 of its [translated] charter states, "Cimade intends to show solidarity with those who suffer, who are oppressed and exploited, to defend them, whatever their nationality, political, or religious position" by performing legal aid work for migrants, including managing individual case files, support in dealing with authorities, and drafting legal appeals. Cimade also provides housing, job training, and other resources for new immigrants, as well as advocating for migrant rights. The organization was established in 1939, in response to the rising numbers of evacuees during World War II as a result of the Nazi regime. During the war, Cimade partnered with the Red Cross, the Quakers, and other anti-Nazi organizations to help those targeted by the Nazis to hide, secure false papers, and flee the country.

Although it is difficult to measure the exact number of people assisted in Cimade's action, in 2009 alone, more than eighty-four thousand people benefited from education or advice provided by the organization. Cimade also operates two 200-person shelters: one in Massy for refugees and another in Beziers for asylum seekers. Cimade's other services include hosting national committee meetings to advocate for policy reform regarding the rights of foreigners. To this end, Cimade hosts two general meetings per year, in addition to the council board, which meets at least six times per year. The organization also publishes reports summarizing findings to the public and to policymakers. In 2009 the committees published two annual reports on reform of asylum procedures and visa policies and practices.

Cimade's Awareness Campaign was launched in late 2008 to denounce the current reform of refugee assistance and associated political and civic centers of refugee retention. The goal of the campaign was to inform the public of objective counts of deportations and to introduce citizens into the network of Cimade. The initiative involved an aggressive ad campaign in magazines and newspapers across France.

Cimade comprises a large network of members and volunteers across France, with sixty-nine local groups meeting in all twelve regions of France, two thousand volunteers, and over one hundred thousand people receiving legal advice, support, and housing. Permanent regional chapters in several major French cities provide centralized centers for development. These branches provide localized support for immigrants in the area, offering opportunities for migrants to engage in projects supported by Cimade. The organization is headquartered in Paris and led by Jerome Martinez, along with a six-member leadership bureau: secretary general, treasurer, vice chairman, secretary, and assistant secretary. General services, such as human resources and development operations, are also housed in the organization headquarters in Paris. A unique feature is that Cimade staff members live in the communities in which they provide assistance. The organization seeks to show solidarity with the refugees, migrants, and oppressed people by being "present" with them—focusing on enabling those affected by displacement rather than just delivering assistance to them.

As a nongovernmental advocacy organization, Cimade is somewhat unique in France in that it places a premium on securing funds from private donors rather than state or local governments, as this allows the organization to remain free from government pressure. Its model looks, in some ways, much more like organizations in the United States than those that are typical of France. Cimade is the lead agency recognized by French law working with undocumented immigrants; however, since the French Immigration and National Identity minister, Eric Besson, has authorized a number of other organizations to offer services to illegal immigrants, the organization's leadership has been challenged. This confrontation illustrates the persistent tension that exists between the French state and some of the advocacy organizations in operation or, more broadly, between institutional logics of bureaucracy and activism.

The Human Rights League (Ligue des Droits de l'Homme)

The Human Rights League (Ligue des droits de l'Homme, or LDH), is an international organization based in France. Specifically, LDH describes itself as a civic organization (rather than a humanitarian organization or charity) as it is involved in all matters relating to citizenship and the rights and freedoms of humans, collectively or individually. LDH also sees itself as a political association, committed to curbing dysfunction in the public sphere, yet it prefers to remain above the political system; LDH does not seek to become a political party and chooses not to involve itself in elections unless it considers its fundamental principles to be challenged. The organization does not describe itself as a union, because it views its mission as defending principles, rather than special interests. Further, LDH describes itself as a lay organization, which has no particular religious or philosophical agenda. Similarly to Cimade, and still somewhat uniquely for France, LDH reserves the right to criticize and publicize its opinion of the government, while acknowledging the government's responsibility to control the activity of state structures.

LDH was created in 1898 during the Dreyfus affair to defend against human rights violations, particularly those related to anti-Semitism. During World Wars I and II, the LDH worked with soldiers who had been wrongfully court-martialed, as well as fighting against the spread of fascism. In 1922, LDH helped to found the International Federation of Human Rights Leagues, of which it is still a member today. After 1958, under the new president, Daniel Mayer, the organization shifted its focus to civil liberties in general, although many of its initiatives focused on protecting the freedoms of those in the military.

LDH activists work with individual cases as well as broader advocacy efforts, meaning that the organization has a wide variety of programs and initiatives. For example, LDH provides legal services for individual and class action cases where human rights are concerned, although they have neither intention nor jurisdiction in private matters. In addition to legal services, LDH publishes position papers, press releases, brochures, and publications to disseminate the positions of the organization. LDH also collaborates with local authorities and other organizations, associations, and unions when necessary to achieve their goals, and organizes youth outreach, such as the Autumn School, which convenes in late November to discuss a key issue for the future of human rights. Recent sessions have focused on themes of "Culture and Citizenship," "Science and New Technologies," "Europe," "secularism," and "justice."

LDH presidents and officeholders are elected annually. The elected National Office includes a chairman, two presidents, five vice-presidents, a general secretary, two deputy secretary-generals, one national treasurer, and five general officers. This seventeen-member National Office is responsible for running the organization. In addition to the leadership team, the national headquarters employs fifteen employees to oversee administrative, financial, and legal matters. In addition to the centralized leadership team, each region elects a regional committee, led by a regional representative, to ensure communication between local headquarters and the Central Committee. The regional representative attends the Central Committee meetings, but neither the federation nor the regions supersede the sections. Working groups are open to all (members and nonmembers), and serve under the Central Committee. These working groups allow for specialized attention to local issues, which may then be brought to the attention of the national group. The overall budget, including the national treasury and its selections, is around €2 million. LDH is funded mainly by contributions from private donors, although it also receives public subsidies. Subgroups within the LDH are relatively autonomous, with each section managing its own budget and controlling an account at a bank chosen by LDH's delegation and national president.

LDH, like Cimade and unlike many other organizations within the French social economy, takes a highly activist—and not an explicitly economic—position toward its work. It thus represents a more activist approach than most French associations. As a member of the International Federation of Human Rights Leagues, LDH comes into more consistent contact with, and works collaboratively with, more foreign nonprofits than many other French social organizations, which may influence both its orientations and its tactics.

4. Japan

Japan shares with France a long cultural tradition that resisted organizations that were separate from the state. Unlike France, however, Japan never had a revolution with an egalitarian thrust. Rather, the Meiji "revolution" in the late nineteenth century was a powerful illustration of Japan's elites creating new institutions adaptable to the modern era. The emperor and the state have been the fount of traditional Japanese legitimacy, continued by sensitive administrators in the twenty-first century. This political history has marked the development of the Japanese third sector such that the prominent institutional logic visible is that of bureaucracy, as the state and nonprofits comanage service delivery through community organizations.

As in France, Japan's "strong state" undermined active involvement in formal civic or political associations. However, like some other Asian countries, Japan has long traditions of neighborhood and work-related associations. The difference from the West is that these associations were seen as more privately oriented and had less of a general policymaking emphasis. Indeed, until recently, activities typically provided by nonprofit organizations in many Western societies have generally been considered in Japan to be the task of government. However, with the gradual diversification of Japanese social values, a modest policy shift toward decentralized government, and an emphasis on efficient public administration, the range of nonprofit involvement in the fields of culture, education, welfare, and international activities expanded rapidly in the 1980s and 1990s (Atoda, Amenomori, and Ohta 1998:99).

The semantic debate about what exactly the third sector is or is not has been particularly pointed in Japan. According to scholars, the term "NPO" (nonprofit organization) came into use in Japan during the 1990s; prior to that, "NGO" (nongovernment organization) was the preferred term for civil society organizations. This evolution of terminology is revealing of the changing perception of the nonprofit within Japanese society:

> In Japan, NGOs could be defined as "nonprofit organizations providing a channel for civilians to participate in international volunteer efforts such as developmental aid, international relief, and environmental protection." This definition emerged from the fact that early civil organizations in Japan mostly concentrated on such public welfare domains as relief charity and developmental aid . . . the main attributes of these [early] organizations were "non-governmental" and "international." Such attributes fed the perception that these organizations were somehow antagonistic toward the governmental framework. They were emphasized as being Japan's "civil international organizations," which were sometimes referred to as international non-governmental organizations (INGOs). Looking at history, one could make the case that Japan's civil society grew out of the country's international welfare efforts. (Kaipin 2009:81)

Two different types of organizations characterize the third sector in Japan. Similar to organizations in the United States, the first type is heavily networked with the state and acts as mainstream social welfare service providers within an institutional logic of bureaucracy; as such, it is primarily government financed and dependent on the state for financial solvency. Those organizations that supplement the public sector are a distinctive characteristic of nonprofit activities, because neither the country's legal framework nor its greater social system encourage private or individual activities for public and charitable purposes (Atoda, Amenomori, and Ohta 1998:117). The second type of NPO, considered to be more "grassroots," is typically a product of local communities and generally independent of government (Osborne 2003:8), engaging in advocacy work rather than service provision.

Importantly, the highly social nature of Japanese political life is present, down to administrative decisions within the nonprofits themselves. In a comparative study, researchers found that Japanese nonprofit administrators based their organizational decisions on how such decisions would impact others (both within and outside the organization) in the context of personal responsibility to society and the maintenance of social order. In the UK, by contrast, nonprofit leaders are more likely to base their decisions on their own values and proclivities (Laratta 2011).

Background and Legal Structure

Charitable giving in Japan has been associated with different religious traditions as far back as the late nineteenth century (Young 2000:162). As Japan's economy expanded at the beginning of the twentieth century, wealthy families began to establish grant-making foundations to subsidize public service, which sometimes gave more support to social services than the government itself (Amenomori 1997:193; Young 2000:162–3). However, in the 1930s and 1940s, the Japanese military government subordinated all nonprofit organizations to the state, effectively rendering them extensions thereof. Traditional youth groups, rooted in individual communities, were merged into a single national organization. Further, every industrial sector was required to form a central coordinating body in Tokyo; religious organizations were consolidated or folded into common umbrella organizations. The *chōnaikai*, or community mutual organizations, came under government control (Amenomori 1997:192).

In the postwar period, despite the development of new social movements advocating human rights and peace, and increasing evidence of effective disaster response abilities, nonprofits continue to work largely in conjunction with the government. New foundations are widely seen as a mechanism to modernize Japan, and the administration has attempted to encourage charitable donations with tax incentives (Young 2000:163).

In 1989, the Japanese government officially launched a program of cooperation with NGOs in international development, intended to counter criticisms of being seen as a "faceless" and unaccountable state development agency. Government collaboration in this area was supposed to bolster NGOs' weak financial statuses, as well as give them access to some of the decision-making processes. This particular partnership was criticized by observers for being rather topical—the substantive decision-making process was still largely left to the state bureaucracy, and financial support was uneven and unpredictable (Nanami 2007). Critics have pointed to this pattern consistently in the relationship between Japanese NPOs and the Japanese government:

> Despite signs of a shift in government attitude in recent years . . . there remains an underlying assumption among government officials that nonprofit organizations are basically subsidiaries of government institutions, if not outright extension agencies for state policies. This is reflected in burdensome legal and extralegal requirements . . . intense bureaucratic involvement and oversight once established, and generally unfavorable tax treatment. . . . Frequently, obscure legal requirements for incorporation provide discretion-

ary power to government officials, and too little transparency characterizes government-nonprofit relations. (Yamamoto 1998:119)

Recent natural disasters and political events have increased public appreciation for both the presence and capacity of nonprofits in Japan. Following the 1995 Great Hanshin earthquake, for example, more than 1.3 million volunteers and thousands of civil organizations mobilized from all over the country to provide relief to the disaster zone. They far outstripped government response in both flexibility and efficiency, and the overall consequence was an increased respect and responsibility for the Japanese nonprofit sector: "Instead of stressing their 'nongovernmental nature,' Japan's international welfare activities now emphasized their 'nonprofit nature.' 'NPOs' replaced 'NGOs' as the term de rigueur to denote civil organizations" (Kaipin 2009:82–83). This new handle effectively encompasses the bureaucratic nature of these organizations, while also acknowledging their decentralized and nonmarket positions.

Japan has fairly extensive nonprofit law and structure, though its legal setup lacks a degree of consistency. Some writers claim that the legal treatment of Japanese NPOs is restrictive, reflective, in part, of the general character of Japan's civil law system. Article 33 of the Japanese Civil Code provides the legal base for private juridical persons. For an organization to be a legal person (for-profit or not), it must be recognized as a *koeki hojin* (public interest corporation) or a profit-making foundation under articles 34 and 35, respectively, or a legal person under a special law. Ultimately, many nonprofits become a legal person under these special laws because of the complicated requirements governing the approval of public interest corporation status (Yamamoto 1998:61).

Japanese tax law divides nonprofits into three categories of organization: those whose profit-making activities are completely tax-exempt (public legal persons), those who are granted specific forms of favorable treatment on their profitable activities (public interest corporations, who are taxed 27 percent instead of the 37.5 percent levied on profit-making corporations), and those who are taxed as profit-making legal persons (such as unincorporated associations)(Yamamoto 1998:62–63). Organizations that serve only one group of people (e.g., alumnae associations or organizations of like-minded persons) are generally not granted public interest corporation status, because they do not serve a wide and undefined group of people, (e.g., the public interest). The "competent authorities" within the government judge the degree to which organizations serve "the public interest" (Yamamoto 1998:64). In addition to public benefit corporations, associations or foundations (*shadan hojin* and *zaidan hojin*, respectively) also hold nonprofit status, as do social welfare corporations, private schools, and medical and religious corporations. Each type of corporation has field-specific laws that govern taxation, incorporation, and activities.

In 1998 Japan passed the NPO law, allowing for the creation of nonprofit organizations within specific regulatory guidelines. Most Japanese ministries (those of education, health, agriculture, etc.) have passed their own laws stipulating the kinds of nonprofit organizations they will authorize; therefore, although the country has a sizable nonprofit sector, it is divided into a good number of smaller, field-specific subsectors governed by a set of field-specific laws. The fields of education, research, and health dominate the nonprofit sector in Japan (accounting for two-thirds of nonprofit expenditures), and the corresponding nonprofit laws enable nonprofit organizations to perform a narrow set of functions within those fields (Salamon and Anheier 1996:92–94).

The NPO law includes numerous stipulations meant to govern the nature of the nonprofit sector. Some of its requirements specify that nonprofit legal entities are to not "engage in religious and political activities as their main purpose" (Article 2) and "to not recommend, support, or oppose any specific public official (including election candidates) or activities by any political party as their main purpose" (Article 2). These rules are intended to safeguard the role of the central state. Further, in addition to setting forth the legal parameters governing creation and taxation of nonprofits, the law defined terms such as "public welfare" and "nonprofit," thus creating a foundation on which other laws relating to civil organizations could be built (Kaipin 2009:87).

As in the United States, most Japanese universities and many elementary and secondary schools are legally incorporated nonprofits, as is much of the health sector (hospitals, clinics, and other facilities). Finally, there is modest representation of business and alumnae organizations in the nonprofit field. However, outside of those fields, nonprofit activity is relatively limited. Japan does not, for example, have extensive networks of cultural, recreational, or environmental nonprofits as some other countries do (Salamon and Anheier 1996:94).

Despite new legislation intended to streamline the registration process, the application requirements are so unwieldy that Japan has not seen the dramatic influx of incorporations that it (and international observers) perhaps originally expected. Thinking that the implementation of the NPO Law would prompt a large number of civil organizations to apply for legal status, the "Shinagawa City Hall set up seven windows specifically to accommodate the predicted influx of organizations. But until December 18, 1999, one year after the implementation of the NPO Law, the whole of Shinagawa Prefecture received only eight applications" (Kaipin 2009:91). The Quality-of-Life bureau found that between December 1, 1998 (when the NPO Law was implemented), to December 31, 2007, Japan received a total of only 35,065 applications. Of those, it approved 33,389 applications, rejected 443 applications, and processed 182 cases of disbandment. The bureaucratic demands placed on nonprofit organizations are one way in which the central state ensures conformity.

Funding

Some 60 percent of Japan's nonprofit revenue comes from private fees and charges (mostly tuition from private schools and universities). Outside the field of education, governmental support accounts for most of the support for health and social service organizations. Private giving is virtually nonexistent in the Japanese third sector, accounting for only 1 percent of total nonprofit income (Salamon and Anheier 1996:94). Japan's third sector, excluding religious organizations, had an operating expenditure of $214 billion in 1995, or 4.5 percent of the GDP. Apart from the fee-for-service income, it received 45.2 percent from the public sector. Support from individual and corporate philanthropy made up 2.6 percent (Imada 2003:189).

A large percentage of foundation grants made in Japan come from corporate foundations, unlike foundation grants in the United States or France. Over 40 percent of Japanese NPOs report receiving noncash support from business corporations (Bothwell 2003:127). In addition, most Japanese foundations are corporation-based and have no protected endowments belonging explicitly to them. The absence thereof renders the activities of these organizations somewhat more vulnerable to market fluctuations, but also to changes in perceived corporate self-interests (Estes 2000:16). This also limits the autonomy of professionally separate foundation officials who play such a visible role in US NGO activities.

Japan has recently experienced a growth of its foundations, though the overall number operating in the country still remains small. Most foundations were initially established in the 1960s and had as a focus research and technical grants. In the 1970s some expanded to include social welfare and international exchange, though most remained focused on natural science and technology research. An indication of this growing area of philanthropy within the third sector, the Japan Foundation Center (JFC), established in 1985, became a "source of up-to-date information on grant-making foundations and their grant programs and makes this information available to grant seekers, grant makers, and the public at large" (Japan Foundation Center 2012). It listed 849 organizations providing grant programs in Japan as of 2000; of these, 615 foundations expended 5 million yen or more per year in grant making (Imada 2003:192).

Individual giving to NPOs is almost insignificant in Japan and not incentivized by tax code. The first tax incentive given to nonprofit corporations in Japan was in the Corporation Tax Law of 1899, which stated that "income of corporations which are not aimed at the pursuit of profit" may be exempt from taxation. In 1950 the Corporate Tax Law was dramatically revised, and taxation from profit-making activities of nonprofits became institutionalized at a lower rate than for-profit corporations, as it remains. There is currently a deduction limit for those donations to nonprofit organizations from a corporate level. It was not until 1962 that tax deduction options for individuals were set up (Amemia 1998:81–82). Regardless, these incentives are small enough to be of only minimal effect.

Changes over Time in Japanese Civil Society

Some scholars argue that there has been a significant movement toward more social openness in Japan, largely due to the country's nonprofit organizations. In the Japanese context, the degree of institutionalization, professionalization, and the quality of state-NPO relationships (bureaucracy) are understood as providing foundations on which to build social mechanisms of political openness.

Hasegawa, Shinohara, and Broadbent (2007), for example, try to show that changing social expectations and newly internalized norms of openness have provided a central impulse for the passage of the NPO Law in Japan (179). Their work demonstrates that, throughout the late 1980s and early 1990s, Japan underwent a dramatic social, economic, and political transition, and a striking rise of third sector organizations was part of this transformation. These authors argue that initiatives spearheaded by association leaders, scholars, younger liberal politicians, and the media encouraged civil activism in Japan and did so by tracing the appearance of the words "nonprofit organization," "service labor," "volunteerism," and "nongovernmental organization" in newspaper articles, using their appearance as ways of tracking public acceptance of the third sector. There were two spikes in usage of the terms—the year of the Kobe earthquake and again in 1998, the year of the NPO Law passage.

> These simple newspaper article counts alone indicate at least growing interests in volunteerism and non-profit organizations, thus, citizens' increasing op-

portunities to encounter information for activism in Japan over time. By 2004, as much as 90% of 3902 randomly surveyed citizens ages 15 to 79 in Japan had heard of the foreign word, NPO, or its newly translated Japanese phrase, *minkan hieiri dantai*. . . . This also indicates growing "social expectation" among the public that could generate civic behavior. (Hasegawa, Shinohara, and Broadbent 2007:84)

Similarly, the number of independent volunteers rose from just over 100,000 in 1985 to nearly 400,000 in 2003, illustrating the rapid institutionalization of this kind of service. During the same period of time, the number of volunteer organizations went from under 50 to nearly 150 (Hasegawa, Shinohara, and Broadbent 2007:190). These numbers demonstrate the progressive development and "mainstreaming" of ideas of service and voluntarism, as measured by their presence in newspapers. These authors argue that social expectation moves through society in a collaborative process among certain Japanese social elites and opinion leaders, who have links with both the local and the global elite communities. The media reacted to those leaders, including philanthropists, intellectuals, and other social contributors; the subsequent coverage on association life represented a big step in diffusing this social expectation to the larger society (185–186).

Status Quo and Challenges

The nonprofit sector in Japan faces three unique opportunities and challenges. First is a growing social heterogeneity among citizens. That is, people feel that their needs are no longer reflected by the corporatist state approach and are turning to the third sector for assistance, representing a shift from a deeply statist bureaucracy to a more participatory (and pluralist) approach to social problem solving, and opening doors to the new institutional logics (both activism and professionalization). The Japanese state is also suffering, some suggest, from a crisis of legitimacy, and as shown below, third sector organizations can greatly help mitigate this through nimble liaising with community organizations. The national government's state of flux may open up new opportunities for the third sector in terms of funding opportunities. Thirdly, at the grassroots level in Japan, there has been growth of a desire for greater accountability of public services (Osborne, McLaughlin, and Miyamoto 2003:222). The combination of these elements creates a fertile field for cultivation of this third sector.

Like other places with a strong history of state involvement, however, lack of independence can be challenging to these organizations. A 1999–2000 study found, perhaps unsurprisingly, that nonprofits in Japan identified their relationship with the government as a primary challenge (Bothwell 2003). For example, in 2004, after fifteen years of official cooperation with NGOs in international development, the Japanese state abruptly cut off the partnership, supplanting the work of third sector organizations with that of the Japan Self-Defense Force. Although this particular partnership was criticized for being rather topical—the substantive decision-making process was often still largely left to the state bureaucracy, and financial support was unpredictable—observers attributed the breakup to state displeasure about how powerful the NPO sector had become in development during that time, in spite of the hurdles it faced. Japanese NGOs have become a powerful advocacy and political force, resulting in a tough series of negotiations with the central state about what, exactly, their role should be (Nanami 2007).

We can see in Japan a well-managed tension as the institutional logic of bureaucracy—product of a long history of highly centralized state administration—negotiates other emergent institutional logics, such as those of activism and professionalism. Though we say that Japan is bureaucratic (and it is, by Western standards), the degree and presence of nonprofit organizations in the country now is testament to its rapidly changing political culture. Several case studies illustrate these points further.

Case Studies

Neighborhood Associations (Chōnaikai)

Most cities in Japan have a system of neighborhood associations (called *chōnaikai* or *jichikai*). These chōnaikai are local neighborhood political and cultural organizations that range in size from ten to one thousand households, depending on the city and the character of the neighborhood. Chōnaikai are extremely common and continue to be the basic territorial and social institution of most Japanese cities; in theory they are voluntary, but social sanctions for lack of participation can be severe (Ansari and Nas 1983:96). Some such associations date back to feudal villages and the neighborhood units of feudal cities from before the Meiji Restoration of 1868. Others were spontaneously organized in the first wave of urbanization beginning in the 1920s (Suzuki 2007). Some scholars consider the chōnaikai premodern, because social sanctions are such that participation is more mandatory than voluntary and because they are generally headed by the conservative neighborhood elements; other writers suggest that the chōnaikai reflect their constituency and in fact have served as important organizing bases for the election of more radical leaders (Ansari and Nas 1983:105). A 2007 Cabinet Office poll reports that 93 percent of its Japanese respondents knew of a neighborhood association in their community; of those that did, 94 percent were members (Kamiya 2009).

During World War II, the Japanese government mandated the creation of associations in each community and designed them specifically as organs to assist the local government in the dissemination of policy. The Allied Occupation then issued a ban on chōnaikai in 1947. This ban expired in 1951, but neighborhood associations have not held legal status since then. Chōnaikai continue to be private organizations and thus not subject to either legal definitions or government control, though they continue to be points of engagement with local governance structures.

These chōnaikai generally do not overlap, as each is associated with a different zone or part of town. Households, rather than individuals, join, and though membership is not obligatory, consequences for failing to join can include damage to reputation. Each organization has its own set of rules, including expectations about dues (commonly a few hundred yen, which is the group's income) (Kamiya 2009). These rules and expectations are often similar across chōnaikai but, because the groups have no formal relation to each other, are not standardized.

The groups' activities also range widely. The *Japan Times* reports that many people associate certain functions with their neighborhood association rather than with their local government (such as disseminating information about community events and hosting festivals) (Kamiya 2009). Community cleaning and tidying events are also relatively common—for example, chōnaikai members are often responsible for enforcing recycling and garbage sorting in their residential areas. Some associations do neighborhood patrols and other forms of crime prevention, and still others organize outings and entertainment.

Most chōnaikai have clear rules of governance and formalized terms of leadership. Generally, they have an executive committee and a rotating chair who are elected to their posts. Both the chair and the executive committee often serve the same term (usually a year) and are responsible for organizing and running community events and for handling problems and complaints made by local stakeholders. When necessary, the executive committee is the body that negotiates with outside entities, such as the local government or third parties, and often carries information back from the local government to the neighborhood (Kamiya 2009). However, this organization can vary slightly: for example, a chōnaikai in the city of Ojima has a president, two vice presidents, two treasurers, and two supervisors. There are elected directors for each of the following issue areas: traffic, general affairs, women's issues, crime prevention, welfare, and youth welfare. The leading officials hold regular monthly meetings in someone's home to discuss activities. A general meeting of all chōnaikai members is held annually (Sargent and Wiltshire 1993:66). Some commentators suggest that young mothers are disproportionately active, which sometimes adds a distinct set of activities around women's issues as well as child care, especially in larger cities with highly educated women. Some scholars consider the chōnaikai bastions of political conservatism, as leadership has historically been assumed by older middle-class neighborhood residents whose social status is well established, and who retain traditional values (Ansari and Nas 1983:194). However, the *Japan Times* reports that these associations are having an increasingly difficult time filling their posts, as so many adults work full-time, and their free time is short; thus, the nature of leadership roles is changing somewhat (Kamiya 2009).

These associations are highly valued for their flexibility and responsiveness, especially in the case of natural disasters. For example, following the Great Hanshin earthquake in 1995, members of a neighborhood association lined up to extinguish small fires that broke out, and they were able to successfully contain a larger disaster. It is uncommon to see foreigners participating in chōnaikai, even though they are residents of a certain area, and efforts have recently been made to make the governance of such institutions more inclusive (Kamiya 2009).

Closely related to the chōnaikai are *shotenkai*, shop owners' associations. Like chōnaikai, shotenkai are community organizations of local business owners, including shop owners, restaurant owners, and retail business owners. While the nature of services is unimportant, the criterion of "local" is critical. The internal organization of shotenkai mimics that of chōnaikai in many ways; the main function of such organizations is to facilitate business through cooperative action, such as through coordinated special sales days, coordinated decoration for seasonal events, and so on (Sargent and Wiltshire 1993:67).

Though both chōnaikai and shotenkai are informal and technically voluntary, they are very common and constitute a backbone of political and economic organization in Japanese cities. They both remain independent and autonomous and are locally organized and administered. In some ways, chōnaikai especially can ease the administrative burden of local governments by disseminating information and organizing residents.

Elder Care: Volunteer Welfare Commissioners and Community Groups

Elder care, one of the most contentious and important elements of social welfare systems in any country, has found a unique resolution in Japan, and in many ways, Japan relies upon the third sector in order to effectively care for the country's aged. Several types of community groups are critical in providing elder care, activities, and lobbying on behalf of Japan's senior citizens. All but one of the examples below are neighborhood-based, and many are deeply embedded within the state governance structures.

Japan has a highly successful volunteer welfare commissioner system, one that has managed to adapt to changing social realities and remains an integral part of community life. Originally modeled after a similar program in Germany, the volunteer welfare commissioner system began after the 1918 Osaka rice riots drew attention to rising rates of poverty throughout Japan. The first welfare commissioners were social elites who somehow had contact with the poor (Haddad cites as examples police, teachers, and rice dealers), and who were responsible for determining eligibility and distributing public assistance to the needy (Haddad 2007a:70–71).

Following World War II, officials recognized that the welfare commissioner system had proved valuable and become a stabilizing influence in the social devastation that reigned in the war's aftermath. In 1948 the government passed the Volunteer Welfare Commissioner Law, which established national guidelines for the system to function; 1950 saw the amendment of the Daily Life Protection Law—cities then employed professional social workers to work within the system. Such a professionalization was intended to somewhat limit the role of the volunteer welfare commissioners (Haddad 2007a:70–71). In recent years, as Japan industrialized and as poverty rates declined, the organization's emphasis has moved from addressing questions of poverty to addressing eldercare.

As the system is currently structured, each city, town, or village appoints its own volunteer welfare commissioner to assist with social welfare issues in his or her jurisdiction. While original welfare commissioners were men, women now represent more than half, though the position continues to be linked to social status (Haddad 2007b:7).

In the case of volunteer welfare commissioners, their special notebook and stamp represent official symbols of office; however, the most critical source of status is successfully completing the long preparation process prior to obtaining an appointment. Potential commissioners must first be nominated by a special committee and meet with the approval of a number of selection committees before the volunteer post is confirmed. Such work requires a good degree of respect and influence, but also discretion; the public knows that nomination is selective, and welfare commissioners retain high social status even in contemporary society. National guidelines set the number of commissioners, who are appointed for three-year renewable terms. Many serve for decades. Commissioner duties range from certifying individuals as eligible for disability benefits to driving elderly to the hospital for check-ups or emergency care. In 2000, there were approximately 21,544 volunteer welfare commissioners in Japan, who dealt with a combined 13 million cases (Haddad 2007a:70–71).

While ideas of citizenship may be changing somewhat, people continue to believe that they need to participate in traditional organizations in order to be upstanding members of their communities. For older generations, peer pressure to participate was quite severe. One sixty-year-old retired volunteer firefighter reported that in his day a man who wasn't a member of the volunteer fire department wouldn't be able to find a woman to marry. Men who didn't participate were viewed as not fulfilling their responsibility to their communities, as being not quite real men (Haddad 2007a:47). While the social constraints are not nearly so strict these days, volunteers for traditional membership organizations still cite obligation to their communities as their primary reason for joining (Haddad 2007b:13).

Japan has other embedded community groups that work on behalf of their elderly, and they stand in distinct contrast to similar organizations elsewhere in the world. For example, the American Association for Retired Persons (AARP) represents 40 million retirees in the United States, has over 1,800 staff members, and is one of the most powerful lobbying forces in the country. It is primarily a political organization, and a very imposing one. The local branches of the AARP are nearly invisible. AARP members do not meet to converse, take outings, or organize community events, though the wide range of retiree services it offers to members (medical benefits, life event services, etc.) are highly popular and in great use across the country. The comparable organization in Japan, however, the Zenkoku Rojin Kurabu Rengokai (Japan Federation of Senior Citizens' Clubs, or JFSCC) has very few full-time staff members. Organized in 1962 and originally derived from neighborhood-based networks such as chōnaikai (Sodei 1993), the JFSCC has a budget of only $2 million (Haddad 2006). Whereas the AARP is primarily an advocacy organization, JFSCC was formed as the national representative of thousands of smaller seniors' clubs that met weekly or more often for outings, activities, and fellowship. They are primarily associational. When they do become involved in politics, they go directly to local bureaucrats. In contrast to AARP's 3,100 local chapters, JFSCC has 133,219 independent clubs with a membership of 8.7 million (Haddad 2007a:38). The Elderly Welfare Law, enacted in 1963, enabled the JFSCC to receive operating subsidies from the national and local government (Takao 2009:864).

JFSCC presidents are often former government welfare staff, and the organization works closely with the national government. However, its numbers have been slipping: in 2000 only about one-third of those aged sixty and over were participating, down from more than one-half in the 1980s. In 1997, participation was higher in rural prefectures than in urban ones, and Takao argues that this was because joining, as in the case of other Japanese civil society organizations, was prescribed by social norms rather than by pro-activity (Takao 2009:13).

Japan is also home to other voluntary associations focusing on ageing, such as the Koreika Shakai o Yokusuru Josei no Kai (Women's Association for Better Aging Society). Established in 1983, and numbering about 1,500 members, this organization has contributed to setting the agenda in public policy from the perspective of women. The Nihon Koreisha Seikatsu Kyodo Kumiai Rengokai (Japan Older Persons' Co-operative Union) was reorganized and repositioned in 2001. It developed twenty-three local unions across the country, and the national office launched a vigorous campaign targeting a membership of one million members in the years after 2008. The Union has developed as a service provider (modeling itself after the AARP). The Nihon Sekando Raifu Kyokai (Japan Association of Second-Life Service) was formed in 1992 for retired company workers and built itself on existing networks within corporate firms; it has a membership of more than half a million retired company workers in Tokyo, Osaka, and Nagoya. These members support each other in volunteer capacities, addressing issues such as recycling, pollution control, and social services (Takao 2009:14).

Changing Citizen Politics in Japan

In 1970, the owner of the Japanese Showa Denko petrochemical plant announced a plan to build the world's largest aluminum smelter in Saganoseki. Saganoseki is a small village in southern Japan in the prefecture of Oita, which was at that time governed by Japan's main party, the Liberal Democratic Party (LDP). This proposal set in motion a decade of political mobilization and conflict over the potential pollutants that such a plant would bring. Jeffrey Broadbent's book *Environmental Politics in Japan: Networks of Power and Protest* (1998) traces the development of this movement. He shows how, despite incentives from the company, nearby hamlets mobilized against the project's development.

The village of Kozaki, primarily women from the Kozaki Seinendan (a group of young people common to most small villages), led initial charges against the proposed smelter. These young women converted their association into a civic movement group and used it for new ends. The group formed a research team, traveled to investigate the company's aluminum smelters elsewhere, and gathered information about what their community would face if the plant relocated to their hometown. They then took it upon themselves to educate the other members of their community—in most cases their parents and grandparents—about the smelter. In his book, Broadbent argues that these young people, the first generation to grow up under democracy, passed on their new sense of rights to their elders throughout this process of political participation—for example, they were the first generation that could protest without worrying about beatings from the riot police. In February 1970, the Kozaki neighborhood heads signed a petition against the project and sent it to the governor, followed by a rally in Seki City two days later.

In response to the petition, the governor held an "explanation meeting" to discuss plans for the smelter. Broadbent sees this governor as a stronghold of the "political machine," which subsequently used tactics that combined financial motives, status considerations, and other incentives to stifle dissent about the relocation of the smelter. In keeping with entrenched systems of power, local bosses tailored their sanctions to the needs and weaknesses of each individual, using material bribery and patronage to mount a counter-argument against the civic protest groups.

In June of 1970, a second industrial proposal for the same landfill appeared; the Imperial Rayon Company and Showa Oil Company announced plans for the world's largest chemical fiber complex, which would include an oil refinery, a petrochemical cracking plant, and a synthetic fiber factory. The same youth group from Kozaki spearheaded the investigation for a second time. Again led by the young women, they mobilized more fiercely around the second proposal than they had around the first. "The dominant structure of gender roles in Japanese society defined women as outside the realm of politics and power. Ironically, this freed them from a degree of social control, giving them greater freedom to mobilize," Broadbent notes (1998:163), attempting to explain the extraordinary political appetite of these young women.

In 1971, the Saganoseki movement members made a trip to Tokyo to protest Landfill No. 8, meeting with both the Environmental Agency and companies interested in developing businesses in Landfill No. 8. That same year, prefectural officials began a campaign of "convincing" visits (so named because they were designed to convince people that No. 8 was a desirable thing) with opposition movement members in Kozaki, attempting to win them over to support the development of No. 8. In response, Kozaki movement members began to make linkages with other social movement organizations in the Oita prefecture.

In 1973, there were movement protests at the prefectural buildings for total cancellation of No. 8. The governor promised that Landfill No. 8 would not be built without citizen consensus, an end to factional fighting in the fishing union, and an environmental impact assessment, which together became known as the Three Conditions.

In 1975, the Oita prefectural government (OPG) and the Ministry of Economy, Trade and Industry changed tactics to back the movements for No 8. They employed citizens' movements to do so. That same year, a leader of the Kozaki movement was elected to the Sanganoseki Town Council. The mayor was able to push through a vote, reaching a form of "consensus" quite contrary to the traditional Japanese conception thereof. That consensus was not challenged.

In 1976, the Kozaki movement initiated a suit against the prefectural government. The OPG attempted to carry out an environmental impact assessment in Kozaki, but the citizens' movements prevented it with harassment tactics. Finally, in 1978, the OPG was able to finalize its environmental impact assessment, and the Three Conditions were fulfilled. However, the window of opportunity had passed; all interested companies had withdrawn their bids. The mobilization was able to delay the decision and therefore moved the proposed project past its window of opportunity.

A fascinating note on this movement is that it merged New Left politics with a vision of traditional village intimacy. The youth in these villages were the first generation raised and educated to believe in horizontal rather than vertical political relations, and this met with accusations of "individualism" and "Westernization" on the part of the entrenched political powers. "Accusation of irresponsible 'egotism' has long been a favorite tactic of the Japanese elite," Broadbent writes. To the new and the old, these "movements represented a challenge to the old ideology of vertical social order and the interest groups that benefitted from it" (Broadbent 1998:169–70). Such an illustration suggests that national, top-down imagery in some of these strong states is a normative assessment, one that can be broken by activists working from the bottom.

This case has become famous in Japan as an example of challenging traditional patterns. This brief case study shows that citizen associational involvement has, in some instances at least, changed Japan's politics in serious ways. It provides a very different suggestion for what is legitimate Japanese politics and who can be active. Associations and organizations (in this case informal associations) play an important role; these changing structures suggest that even more dramatic changes may be underway, although these issues remain sensitive and controversial as they challenge the classic Japanese gradualism.

The Japanese experience suggests a policy mechanism that could be used in other countries for handling social and political conflict: appoint a retired senior national civil servant to develop policies of compromise. For instance, many cities have two or three political parties elected locally, and no majority. They often invite a national civil servant to serve as mayor, who can help negotiate compromises in policies on a daily basis.

5. South Korea

In the past forty years, South Korea has undergone not only a massive democratic transformation but also an equally massive economic shift. Though once thought of as submissive, particularly under the military regime of the 1970s, Korean society is now characterized by active civic engagement and a proliferation of new types of community organizations and associations. As part of and as consequence of these rapid and far-reaching political changes, the nature and composition of the country's third sector has also been transformed. Activists and dissenters who participated in the transition to democracy now fill the ranks of the country's nonprofit sector, in which the institutional logic of activism remains highly visible. As the sector begins to make use of its comparatively new political freedoms, we see the emergence of other influences as well—particularly those of professionalization.

Korean history has been extremely politically volatile, marked by centuries of wars and foreign invasion, military dictatorship, and national government control of a wide range of policies. Some governmental innovations have been dramatic and highly successful, such as industrialization after 1945. But what is legitimate for government and politics is much less settled in Korea than it is in other places. Active citizen protest in Korea has also been visible to the international observer (exemplified in a long protest by thousands in Seoul in 2008 against importing American beef). But these demonstrations have often seemed spontaneous, not based on the work of organized groups. Indeed, the lack of integration of Koreans into organized groups may have *fueled* such demonstrations. Still, many groups of activists in Korea report less trust in government.

For a long time, Korean Confucianism contributed to weaken the "condition of necessity" for civil society by keeping political demand *inside* the familial sphere instead of in the public realm. Additionally, the contemporary Korean political context has, in many ways, prevented the emergence of collective identity outside of kinship groups (Bidet 2002:136; see also Weber 1968) because of the nation's religious background. This lack of collective identity, considered crucial in most organizing and social movement undertakings, in turn impeded the development of formal political or civic associations. There have been very few arguments made for a positive connection between Confucianism and civil society; when it occurs, scholars see the Confucian version of civil society mainly as being initiated by the literati or the elite—not by the lower classes.

Generally speaking, one of the main features of Korean NPOs (and the third sector generally across the world) is a relatively democratic ethos; by contrast, Confucianism stresses hierarchical principles. Further, Confucianism tends to promote homogeneity, uniformity, and orthodoxy, creating an environment that sits uneasily with those organizations that seek to challenge any component of the status quo. Because Confucianism stresses duty over rights, it helps create an environment that is not "conducive for a mediating level between the state and the individual, such as is typically provided by third sector organizations. . . . Confucianism promotes the development of family or family-like structures, whose functioning is closer to notions of obligation or duty, rather than volunteer action and rights" (Bidet 2002:136).

But these earlier accounts—the debate among South Korean social scientists during the 1990s and early years of the twenty-first century—dealt with how East Asian Confucianism dampened the region's civil society. Those debates, like Bidet's work cited above, treated Confucian values only as "a means by which to advance modern capitalism and by extension a market-oriented liberal civil society" (Sungmoon Kim 2007:5), rather than as a powerful force that could reshape the trajectory of civil society, rather than just impeding it. In other words, these accounts failed to imagine how civil society and Confucianism could emerge together.

As shown throughout this chapter, Confucianism does not necessarily stifle civil society; it simply reshapes it. Civil society in places like Korea can also look like an intermediary sphere between the private and the state, as autonomous from both. These new types of relationships enable community-based organizations, in non-Western contexts, to question, or challenge, both centralized state power and the assumptions that underlie neoliberal economic exchanges. Civil society, working within a context of social rights and self-help, but *within* the larger context of economic competition, emerges as a unique blend of Confucianism and Western civic traditions (Hahn and McCabe 2006:315–16). Indeed, civil society, along with other domestic factors, has been credited for Korea's democratic transitions; civic groups precipitated authoritarian breakdowns and have since deeply influenced the dynamics of posttransitional politics (Kim and Kim 2000).

Background and Legal Structure

The composition of Korea's civil society differs notably from that of Japan or the United States, for example, whose NGO distribution is heavily skewed toward social service and educational organizations. As in the United States and elsewhere, the Korean nonprofit sector is a sizable economic force, representing a $23 billion industry and a workforce of over 700,000 full-time equivalent (FTE) employees in 1997 (Park et al. 2004:201).

In Korea in 1999, however, of the 4,023 organizations, 25 percent were civil society groups, 19 percent were social service groups, and 7 percent were environmental organizations (Kang 2012). Of these organizations, religious groups play a strong role, employing over 20 percent of the paid nonprofit workforce and over 35 percent of the volunteer staff, and reflecting the degree to which religious, social, and economic life has been entwined in Korea (Park et al. 2004). Another strong feature of the Korean third sector is the credit-oriented cooperatives and nonbanking institutions. In contrast to the development of similar organizations in Europe, most Korean cooperative movements were not created by a bottom-up process at the initiative of farmers, consumers, or workers, but under a top-down process initiated by the Korean central government. Likewise, volunteer labor is relatively weak in Korea, with about 80,000 FTE employees (approximately 10 percent of salaried workers), whereas it is around 50 percent in Western Europe (Bidet 2002:135). In 1997 the economic contribution of Korean nonprofits accounted for less than 3 percent of the Korean GDP (US $12 billion), but for more than 5 percent of the total employment. Since the economic crisis of 1997, many third sector organizations in Korea have initiated social job-creation projects, which in turn have formed a key part of the Korean welfare-to-work system (Hahn and McCabe 2006:314).

The birth of more than half of Korean civil society organizations can be traced to the 1990s, soon after democratization, which suggests that political configuration had a powerful impact on rates of formal organization in that country. (There were 2,914 nonprofit organizations in 1996, increasing to 4,023 in 1999.) The first decade of the twenty-first century also saw the emergence of NGOs focusing on overseas aid and development work. The

Korea NGO Council for Overseas Cooperation (KCOC) had only 31 member organizations at its founding in 1999, a number that increased to 62 by 2007 and 66 by 2010 (Kang 2012:72).

The year 1989 was a formative one for the Korean nonprofit sector, in a newly democratic country, and cemented by formation of the ground-breaking Citizen's Coalition for Economic Justice (CCEJ) (P. Kim and Moon 2003:555). Unlike other organizations working against the military regime, the CCEJ claimed to be headed by ordinary people, pledged the use of non-violent and legal approaches to making demands, and undertook to propose alternative options (Kang 2012). This approach marked the first corner in a transition from active resistance to military oppression (more resembling an institutional logic of activism) to professional and bureaucratic projects that endeavored to create effective state-society relationships. That organization, along with the People's Solidarity for Participatory Democracy and the Korean Federation for Environmental Management, spurred a large growth in the number of nonprofit organizations in South Korea; the 1980s and 1990s were a formative time for the sector generally. Around the same time, activists mounted attempts to establish umbrella organizations to aggregate and coordinate actions. In 1994, thirty-eight citizens' movement groups created a coalition called the Korea Council of Citizens' Movements (KCCM), which was replaced in 2001 by the Civil Society Organizations Network (Kang 2012). These organizations in many ways echoed the emerging concerns of New Social Movements worldwide.

These new social organizations undertook several important initiatives to bring about political reforms, helping to visibly entrench the nonprofit sector's roles as political advocates as well as simply community assistance entities. For example, a group of organizations conducted a blacklisting and defeat campaign during the National Assembly election in 2000. Some 450 advocacy and community organizations came together, creating a group called Civil Action for 2000 General Election (known as CAGE). CAGE presented a blacklist of corrupt politicians, pressuring major political parties not to nominate those candidates. The result of this campaign were mixed (of the 113 blacklisted people, 11 did not seek nomination, 38 did not win nomination, and 40 were nominated). Following the nomination process, CAGE listed 86 candidates who were overtly targeted for defeat during that election (Kang 2012).

Dictatorship and military rule are widely marshaled to explain the stagnation of development of South Korea's third sector before the 1980s. Additionally, a main objective of the US military during its occupation of Korea (1945 to 1948) was to establish a strong anticommunist state and to maintain some of the traditional structures inherited from the Japanese colonization. The ideological divisions grew stronger after the Korean War divided the country into North and South Korea. The legacy in South Korea was a strong anticommunist and anti-leftist feeling, as well as a succession of dictatorial governments since the 1960s that contributed to a climate unfavorable to development of a third sector.

Most organizations that emerged in Korea after democratization did so without any real assistance from the US government or third sectors. The prevailing anti-Americanism present among many Korean activists during this time came from disaffection with US policy in South Korea (they did not try to prevent the military regime from taking power in the wake of the Kwangju incident of 1980). Those activists initiated and bolstered Korea's burgeoning civil society movement, some of them still harboring suspicions toward the United States. Conservative newspapers especially would often depict such organizations as radically leftist and pro–North Korean (Kang 2012:74–75).

The Korean third sector has been defined in several major terms, reflecting international debate about what the words mean and how civil society is constituted. Commonly used terms are "nonprofit organizations" (NPOs, or *beyoungri danche*), "nongovernmental organizations" (NGOs, *mingan danche*), "civil society organizations" (CSOs, *simin danche*), "civic movement organizations" (*simin woondong danche*), and "public interest corporations" (*gongick bubin*). Though each term evolved independently, there is a good deal of overlap, and the terms "NGO" and "CSO" are generally the most popular. The term "public interest corporation" is commonly used only in a legal context. The term "nonprofit organization" is more recently used in legal documents and academic circles (Asia Foundation 2001a:2). This confusion about terminology reflects the varied understandings of the third sector and its functions.

Korean foundations have typically been divided into three categories: (1) corporate- or company-sponsored foundations, (2) small- and medium-sized scholarship foundations, and (3) government-funded foundations established by special laws or decrees. Notably, since the economic crisis in late 1997, the formerly strong distinction between advocacy-oriented organizations and service-providing philanthropy has blurred, because many organizations have expanded their area of activities from a narrower advocacy role to a wider service-providing role (Asia Foundation 2001a:2).

Similar to Japan but unlike Western countries, there is no general law governing the creation of third sector organizations in Korea, and their establishment requires ministerial authorization, pointing to a persistent entanglement with state apparatus even in the creation of formal groups. There are several laws that could be applicable for an organization, depending on its occupation: the Medical Law governs nonprofit hospitals and medical organizations; the Social Welfare Activity Law oversees organizations involved in social services, including culture and arts; and the Private School Law is responsible for educational nonprofits, including most Korean universities (Bidet 2002:135).

As South Korean democracy developed, the relationship between government and civil society gradually became less contentious, reflecting a clear shift from an institutional logic of activism to the presence of both bureaucracy and professionalization. As a result of meetings between third sector representatives, government officials, and the National Assembly, two different political parties submitted separate bills to the National Assembly in 1994 seeking support for third sector activities. After several years of discussion, the South Korean National Assembly passed the Act of Assistance for Non-Profit Civil Organizations (AANPCO) on January 12, 2000 (Kim and Moon 2003:561–62). The bill not only was designed to politically foster the development of voluntary activities, but, importantly, it was understood in the classically Tocquevillian sense to help promote democratic principles and practices.

As a result of this bill, in 2001 the South Korean central government allocated 15 billion Won (US $11.5 million) to civil society activities. Of this, 7.5 billion Won (US$ 5.77 million) was designated for central projects, and the other 7.5 billion Won was for local projects. The central government selected 216 projects from some 400 applicants in order to allocate this money. These funded projects focused principally on participation, human rights, cultural events, the 2002 World Cup, voluntary service organizations, and environmental organizations. Of those projects, 74.5 percent received less than 50 million Won, 22.7 percent received between 50 million Won and 100 million Won, and 2.8 percent (6 programs) received 100 million Won or more (Kim and Moon 2003:562). The Ministry of Government Administration and Home Affairs (MOGAHA), the Prime Minister's Office, the Government Information Agency, and the Women's Commission are the best known supporters of the third sector (Asia Foundation 2001a:10).

January 2000 saw the passage of the Act for the Support of Private Nonprofit Organizations. Prior to the new law, the government did provide some fiscal support for some NPO and advocacy organizations, but the new law codifies this support for any private nonprofit organization that has been legally incorporated (Asia Foundation 2001a:9), bestowing upon them some institutional legitimacy that helps cement their place in democratic politics.

Importantly, two similar NPOs operating in the same field can be subject to different constraints according to the specific law under which they have been registered. Some analysis suggests that this lack of consistency can help explain why the third sector has not developed the collective consciousness found in some other countries (Bidet 2002:135).

Funding

Systematic information on fundraising practices for nonprofit organizations in Korea is rather scarce. However, donors to Korean foundations generally include companies, individuals, and the government (Asia Foundation 2001a:2). Under the current Income Tax Law, individual donors receive a tax deduction for contributions to nonprofit corporations. Individual donors may deduct up to 5 percent of their gross income as a special deduction to incentivize charitable giving (Bidet 2002:9).

In 1975, the Korean government launched a unique fundraising scheme designed to finance its own social services through NPOs. Through this program, funds donated independently (by individuals) were managed and allocated directly by the minister of health and welfare to various social service programs. Individual philanthropic contributions remained under control of the government. A scandal over governmental mismanagement of philanthropic funds was legally addressed in the mid-1990s with the passage of the Law on Social Fundraising. The law, intended to ensure philanthropic independence from government intervention, was passed on March 17, 1997 (Bidet 2002:5). Though a heated debate continues on whether receiving government money is acceptable for the healthy development of NGOs and civil society, the Act for the Support of Private Nonprofit Organizations marks a new era of government support in the third sector (Asia Foundation 2001a:9) and further entrenches the NPO as one option for government service delivery.

Korean foundations are a mix of corporate-run (80 percent) and government-run (20 percent) foundations. As in Japan, most Korean foundations are operated by corporations and have no protected endowments of their own, which makes them susceptible to changes in the market and to pressures for conformity, as well as to changes in corporate interests and self-interests. The annual budget of their sponsoring companies in large part determines the organization's activities and grant making for the year. As is the case in Japan, any substantial grant proceeding from a Korean corporate foundation is tightly entwined with perceived business interests (such as improving public image, opening markets, etc.). A good example is Hyundai Engineering and Construction's public pledge to "continue to strive towards

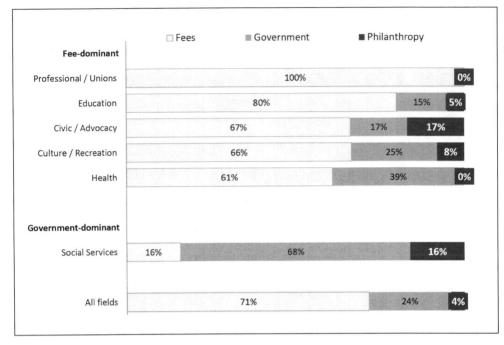

| | Fees | Government | Philanthropy |

Fee-dominant

Professional / Unions — 100% / 0%

Education — 80% / 15% / 5%

Civic / Advocacy — 67% / 17% / 17%

Culture / Recreation — 66% / 25% / 8%

Health — 61% / 39% / 0%

Government-dominant

Social Services — 16% / 68% / 16%

All fields — 71% / 24% / 4%

Figure 8. Source of civil society organization revenue in South Korea.

Source: Salamon and Sokolowski 2004:211.

productivity and quality improvements to better serve our global partners and the world community" (Newson and Deegan 2002). Similarly, the Samsung Foundation of Culture, created in 1965, works to preserve and promote the achievements of traditional Korean art, while simultaneously supporting emerging and established artists in all media. The foundation supports art exhibitions, performances, cinema, and literature, and its linkage to a well-performing company enables a broad scope of engagements and support (Samsung Foundation 2013).

Korean grant making is also often tied to government policies (Estes 2000:16), and this pattern has led some scholars to see Korean foundations as instruments of corporate and governmental policy and as reflecting the presence of an institutional logic of bureaucracy operating within the sector. Similar to the United States in the 1970s, the Korean third sector has recently seen a dramatic increase of partnerships between for-profit firms and nonprofit organizations, largely in the field of social services. Venture capital philanthropy, in contrast to traditional corporate or even government support, also emerged in Korea in late 1999 and early 2000, brought about by the surge of the stock market in early 2000 (Asia Foundation 2001a:6).

Private donations do not enjoy the flexibility or incentives in Korea that they do in some other countries, and as a result, levels of individual giving are quite low. Individual donors to Korean third sector organizations are permitted to deduct up to 5 percent of their gross income as a "special deduction," if they are earning wages, salaries, or foreign income. Unlike, for example, the United States, where even in-kind donations of used clothing can receive tax deductions, in Korea business, real estate, or timber income is not exempt, and thus the scope of eligibility for tax deductions is extremely limited (Asia Foundation 2001a:9).

Status Quo and Challenges

Formal civil society in Korea has grown dramatically since the 1980s and, in doing so, has expanded visibly from being largely activist to a sector that is institutionalized, professionalized, and bureaucratized in nature. However, Korean civil society still bears the stamp of earlier authoritarian regimes. Laws governing fundraising still serve to de-incentivize charitable giving; Korean NPOs are restricted in their abilities to seek funding—and thereby broaden their efforts. This dependence on the state impedes organizations' ability to be financially or otherwise independent from their state funders (Bidet 2002:138). The explosive growth of Korean NGOs in the past twenty years is both the result of the demise of authoritarian regimes and further stimulus to the transition solidifying democracy. The challenges for Korean NGOs will be to present themselves strategically to the state in the transitional period (H. Kim 2000), as credible bureaucratic and professional partners to state-led initiatives.

Korea does, however, currently face the same broad socioeconomic trends that led to the rise of a vibrant third sector in Europe. A continued emphasis on the nuclear (as opposed to extended) family, a shrinking of households, and decreasing fertility rates, coupled with an increase in the number of working women and double-income families, are likely to affect the traditional scheme of family organization and child care (Kang 2012), paving the way for new types of community interaction. The new earning patterns may give rise to new patterns of consumption like those that have been seen elsewhere (see, for example, T. Clark 2004). Additionally, the younger generation of Korean activists has proved exceptionally fluent in using online tools for coordination, organizing, and civic activism, as the 2008 beef protests (elaborated below) illustrate. These factors join together to create a fertile ground for the development of third sector organizations and associationalism generally.

Notably as well, Korea's academic institutions have taken an interest in NPOs and the third sector. There has been a dramatic increase in degree programs in NPO management at both graduate and undergraduate levels, as well as the development of academic associations' research institutes dedicated to the study of the third sector. For example, Sungkonghoe University has recently established the first graduate program on civil society, and Kyunghee University followed suit with the development of the Graduate School of NGO Studies (Asia Foundation 2001a:8).

Nonprofit organizations have as well emerged as arguably the most important shareholder advocates in Korea, Taiwan, and Japan. In Korea, the shareholders' rights committee of a large, diversified NPO known as People's Solidarity for Participatory Democracy (PSPD, founded in 1994) "has brought the only significant shareholder actions to date," winning two major court victories, including one against the chairman and managers of a leading *chaebol* (a type of business conglomerate). Likewise, in Taiwan, an NPO known as the Securities and Futures Institute (SFI), established with the support of the government and financial sector in 1984, has organized and filed class-action suits in securities and corporate fraud cases on the behalf of thousands of small investors. In Japan, with activist lawyers and academics, the Shareholder Ombudsman has litigated several of the most high-profile cases in Japan. This phenomenon of shareholder advocacy by NPO shareholder activists is not witnessed more extensively elsewhere (Millhaupt 2004:171–174).

Case Studies

2008 Beef Protests

In 2008, hundreds of thousands of South Koreans took to the streets to protest Lee Myung-bak's decision to import US beef under the Korea-US Free Trade Agreement. Following a documentary that cast doubt on the safety of this meat, Korean citizens began to fear mad cow disease. They debated on Internet forums, created online petitions, and held candlelight vigils; protests lasted from May 2 to August 15, nearly one hundred days. Social media platforms, including Internet and text messaging, played a large role in publicizing the protests. A teenage girl with a candle became the movement's symbol.

The protests initially swelled as the government stood by largely idle and as public discontent grew. Citizens complained that "the government was ignoring public outcry and waiting for the protests to die down" (Jack Kim 2008). Chung Hye-ran, a mother participating in a rally in the early stages of the protest, said she did not like being ignored: "I came out here as a mother and as a member of the public to protect the health of my child and that of the people of this country." In early June the police took action against protestors, blocking their progress through streets and plazas.

Critics described Lee's decision as a move to please Washington. "Not just the beef deal, but the Lee Myung-bak government's policies are anti-working people and are not right," said student Ju Ha-na (Jack Kim 2008). The protests were largely peaceful, considering both their size and their duration, though there were several occasions in which riot police clashed with protesters. On May 31 and June 1, police first used water cannons and fire extinguishers on protesters, and again later that month. The use of such tactics contributed to the mass resignation of all fourteen members of the Korean National Police Agency's human rights committee (Amnesty International 2008). Any serious attempt on Lee's part to change the conditions of the trade deal would have angered the United States (*Economist* 2008). The US government publicly rejected the idea that it had "bullied" South Korea into lifting a ban on its beef. From 2009 to 2010, the US Meat Export Federation undertook a lukewarm image campaign entitled "To Trust," aimed at restoring Korean trust in US beef.

This protest was important in several senses—it was the first substantive test of the rights to peaceful assembly that are enshrined in Korea's constitution, though such rights are complicated by a number of legal provisions requiring protesters to cease and disperse when ordered to do so by police. The trajectory of these protests (largely peaceful, well organized, and visible) was a powerful demonstration of the increasing strength, organization, and texture of Korean civil society. However, the residue of state animosity toward civil society in Korea remained visible throughout the months of protest, and the tensions between different leadership styles came sharply into relief. Lee's approval rating fell to below 20 percent during this time, and the administration sustained the resignation of all of the cabinet members.

The protests strained nascent and tense relationships between the state and civil society under President Lee's administration, which subsequently banned any financial support of organizations that took part in the protests. The administration cut off contact with civic groups that did not support his policies and did little in subsequent years to rectify the wounded feelings (Kang 2012).

Korean Federation for Environmental Movements (KFEM)

The Korean Federation for Environmental Movements (KFEM), founded in 1982, exemplifies the transition from bureaucracy to activism and professionalization in important ways (see Korean Federation 2011). Its founder, democratic activist Choi Yul, was imprisoned for activism against Korea's dictatorship during the late 1970s. He spent his six years in prison reading extensively about issues related to the environment, and after his release he founded South Korea's first environmental NGO. Originally called the Korean Research Institute for Environmental Problems, the group primarily addressed widespread pollution caused by South Korea's rapid industrialization.

The institute was successful in evacuating relatively large communities from areas contaminated by toxic waste in the coastal city of Onsan. Environmental movements came to the forefront of the democratic movement that took hold in South Korea, and in 1988, the institute merged with two other environmental groups and established the Korean Anti-Pollution Movement Association (KAPMA), and Choi Yul became the president of the new body. KAPMA was active in the fight against the government's attempts to construct nuclear waste storage sites, against dust contamination from coal briquette plants, and against the destruction of mountains to make golf courses and the reclamation of coastal tidal flats.

Reflecting a new emphasis on information, the organization also focused on providing information to the Korean public about the problems with nuclear power plants and nuclear waste disposal. Tens of thousands of people participated in rallies and signed petitions protesting the construction of new nuclear plants and nuclear waste storage sites in the late 1980s and early 1990s. In 1990, a demonstration of twenty thousand people was successful in halting a nuclear waste facility plan for Anmyon-do Island. In 1991, KAPMA organized massive campaigns to protest the toxic spill from an electronics company that contaminated the drinking water of two million people in Daegu City.

In 1993, KAPMA merged with seven other local environmental groups (the Pusan Citizens' Anti-Pollution Council, Taegu Anti-Pollution Movement Association, Kwangju Citizens' Association for Environmental Movement, Masan-Changwon Citizens' Anti-Pollution Council, Ulsan Anti-Pollution Movement Association, Jinju Citizens' Group for Nam River Protection, and Mokpo Green Research Center) to launch the Korean Federation for Environmental Movements (KFEM), Korea's largest environmental organization, and Choi became its secretary general. As an umbrella organization, KFEM has initiated a consumers' boycott of polluting industries, while continuing to oppose Korea's nuclear expansion policies. In 1994, KFEM was instrumental in the campaign to halt the construction of a nuclear waste storage facility on Gulup Island. KFEM was a participant in the UN Conference on Environment and Development in Rio de Janeiro in 1992, and as a consequence of that participation it became more involved in global environmental issues, such as depletion of the ozone layer, deforestation, biodiversity, and climate change.

South Korean NGOs are often oriented toward the capital city of Seoul, with branches that operate in provinces and in smaller cities, facilitating high degrees of coordination at national and regional levels. KFEM is currently the biggest and the most influential NGO in Korea, with its eighty-five thousand members and forty-seven local branches working on various types of environmental issues. Positioning itself as an "information clearinghouse" KFEM collects, studies, and disseminates information on global trends to Korean society and to NGOs throughout the region. KFEM has also organized international conferences and exchange programs with NGOs from other countries in Asia in hopes that such programming will foster more cooperative action among similar groups and stronger international bonds leading to more effective cooperative action on Asian and global environmental issues.

In addition, KFEM has been involved in many social issues, such as poverty, human rights, women's rights, and peace issues. KFEM raised these issues to Koreans intentionally, by participating in venues such as the NGO Forum on Women in Beijing in 1995, the World Summit for Social Development and the NGO Forum in Copenhagen in 1995, the UN Conference on Human Settlements in Istanbul in 1996, and the World Summit for Social Development in Geneva in 2000.

KFEM depends largely upon volunteers for its activities and, as an activist-oriented program, coordinates petitions and protests through its sub-organizations and at a regional level. Volunteers have formed a number of working groups and campaigns, including the Green Grass Reporters (elementary school students writing articles on environmentalism), the Green Voice (middle and high school students campaigning against fur coats), the Housewives' Environmental Watchdog Group (emphasizing activities that require the participation of homemakers, such as the reduction of the use of plastic bags and the campaign against genetically modified food), the Green Cyber Group (working on green software), the Eco-Related Engineers Group (those with environment-related licenses and in environmental industries), and Haho (a group working on wildlife protection and animal welfare).

KFEM as a national body has a board of advisers and a board of auditors, who work in conjunction with the General Assembly. In addition to these bodies, the organization has a co-president, a national committee, and a standing committee, which oversee the activities of the organization's local chapters. KFEM also has committees on personnel, policy, international issues, green politics, and wetlands, as well as departments that are dedicated to operations, planning, and campaigns. The Nature Conservation Department has subdepartments dedicated to wetlands, water/dams/rivers, wildlife, forests, pollution and research, peace, antinuclear action, and atmosphere and waste. The Policy Department has subdepartments dedicated to environmental policy, monitoring the Korean National Assembly and the national budget, international affairs, and green politics. The Planning Department has subdepartments related to planning, public relations, operations, local chapter coordination, fundraising, general affairs, and membership. The Seoul headquarters of KFEM has divisions dedicated to citizen participation, pollution and investigation, and organization.

KFEM counts among its supporting and partner organizations the Public Center for Environmental Law (PCEL), the Citizens' Institute for Environmental Studies (CIES), the Citizens' Information Center for Environment (CICE), the Environmental Education Center (EEC), and the Center for Energy Alternatives. KFEM is registered in Seoul, in accordance with Article 3 of the Law on Registration of Civic Organizations, and its Enforcement Ordinance.

6. Taiwan

Like Japan and China, Taiwan has also fallen victim to the scholarly claim that civil society is somehow incompatible with the nondemocratic features of Asia, including Confucianism; this chapter, along with the work of others (see Alagappa 2004) aims to demonstrate that civil society not only is present throughout Taiwan but also has experienced impressive growth in the last thirty years. Following global trends, Taiwan's civil society is professionalizing, although its relatively recent role in the transition to democracy is also empowering it to advocate on behalf of the underrepresented and underserved, pairing an institutional logic of activism with one of professionalization, much like in other Asian countries.

Taiwan's civil society is strongly related to its recent history; many of Taiwan's current CSOs were created during the struggle for democracy and against one-party rule during the era of martial law. In 1949, the Kuomintang (KMT—the Chinese Nationalist Party) lost a civil war in Mainland China and was exiled to Taiwan, where it established an authoritarian regime that relied heavily on clientelism as the critical mechanism for social control and for social mobilization (Gold 1991). Taiwan is unique among other industrialized countries in that the KMT controls (through public-owned, semi-public, and veteran-owned mechanisms) over 30 percent of productive enterprise, and this high degree of government control sets the stage for political and economic clientelism that leeches into civic life as well (F. Wang 1994:184). Clientelism is and has been so prevalent in Taiwanese civil society in part because most of the horizontal civic organizations are controlled (to greater or lesser extents) by the KMT itself.

During martial law (until 1963), as Hsiao explains, "Taiwanese civil society fell under the complete control of the Mainlander-dominated central state apparatus. Suppression and coercion were immediately applied to any autonomous demands from 'the society' that might threaten the legitimacy of the party-state" (1990:164). From the early 1960s to the late 1970s, economic promise gradually became visible, and the KMT state adopted economic growth as its primary aspiration in ruling Taiwan. As the economy developed, intellectuals especially engaged in "root seeking"—cultivating arts, culture, and civic practices that were distinctively Taiwanese—but civil society as such had not yet emerged in sufficient force to directly confront the power of the authoritarian government (164). Since the late 1970s, Taiwanese civil society has developed rapidly and has increasingly begun to make demands on the state, embodying an institutional logic of activism at the same time that, following the lead of other countries in this book, it inches toward professionalization.

But the social movement groups of the 1980s were instrumental in creating a political opportunity structure for democracy, which in turn has legitimized the third sector and helped it grow since then (Hsiao 2003:180). By the end of 1988, a total of seventeen broadly recognizable social movements had emerged to actively make claims on the state (166); these movements included consumer protest movements, environmental movements, women's movements, farmers' movements, and Aborigine human rights movements.

All of the movements were unique in recent Taiwanese history in that they demanded reforms of the KMT *state*, rather than other actors (such as corporations or groups of people). Additionally, class conflict was not a major source for mobilizing organized movements; rather, the movements targeted the state. At the same time, activists assumed a fairly depoliticized strategy by explicitly not aligning themselves with political opposition. In general, these movements jelled quickly and moved toward institutionalization and professionalization much more rapidly than movements elsewhere have done.

Similarly to China, a principal cultural factor influencing the development of CSOs in Taiwan was the *guanxi* ("culture of relationships"), which exists as well in China; a person's network of contacts, such as guilds, gangs, or clans, were the building blocks upon which organizations were built. "Given the traditional family-orientation of these organizations, people were unwilling to trust social organizations other than those made up of their own clan . . . in pre-communist China, folk organizations existed without a public character, thus preventing the development of community values and a public civil society" (T. Lin 2005:30–31).

Several factors (many of them evident in the New Political Culture worldwide), aside from formal democratic transition, have served to spur the growth of Taiwan's nonprofit sector. For one, higher levels of education brought an increased concern for political participation. "Overall economic affluence has allowed the general public release from worry about basic material needs and has freed them to pursue other goods, among them social and political reforms" (Hsiao 2003:183). This affluence, combined with political liberalization, has also enabled the intellectuals, or knowledge class, to develop cultural and civic activities autonomously from the state.

Globalization, and the accompanying spread of information, has also had an influence on Taiwan's third sector; this is evident both in the content and the structure of its developing civil society. During the 1990s, for example, and echoing the trend of New Social Movements elsewhere in the world, Taiwanese third sector organizations began to expand their focus from the traditional emphases on humanitarian assistance and took on issues such as women's rights and urban and rural culture.

Taiwan's liberalizing political culture is inextricably linked to the political culture in Mainland China, and thus, as changes in Chinese political culture occur, the reverberations are felt throughout Taiwan, especially as travel restrictions have been relaxed and movement between China and Taiwan becomes more common. Student movements in China have inspired similar movements in Taiwan. Following a series of outbursts on Mainland China, in 2013 Citizen 1985, a Taiwanese protest group in Taipei, organized a massive vigil to protest the death of the late army corporal Hung Chung-chiu, who was beaten to death while on duty, and to demand military reform. About 70 percent of those who attended were participating in a demonstration for the very first time. An editorial from the *Taipei Times* called the protesters

> sincere, irreproachable and passionate; . . . they truly want to create a new reality, a free future, in this tragic world; and . . . they are in this neither for fame nor gain. These people are the nation's future generation. If this movement continues in this way, it will not only show the world Taiwan's independent existence, it will also have an inestimable impact on the civil movement in China. (P. Lin 2013:n.p.)

Recognizing an opportunity for increased legitimacy, the Taiwanese government has increasingly sought help from third sector organizations to address salient social issues, such as disaster relief (Ku 1999), in much the same way Japan's and China's governments have. The Taiwanese third sector has been able to gain a considerable amount of legitimacy itself, through its increasing visibility and growth over the last thirty years, and new data show that a great number of Taiwanese citizens have some sort of engagement with nonprofit organizations. A 1999–2000 study commissioned by the Taiwanese government, entitled "Trends of Taiwan Social Development," surveyed 11,000 Taiwanese households to determine the extent of social participation and contributions to the third sector. The results showed that almost 11 million people (of a population of nearly 23 million), or 61.8 percent of the population, made charitable financial donations to a third sector organization during the time of the study (although this bump was partly due to the earthquake that spurred a raft of giving and charitable involvement).

The same study indicated that, by the end of 1999, Taiwan's membership associations had grown to 19,518, of which 21.5 percent were occupational or professional associations and 78.5 percent were classified as "social" associations. Within the second category, there were 4,740 social service and charitable associations, 2,111 literary and cultural associations, 1,943 international associations, 1,713 athletic associations, 1,574 economic affairs associations, and 529 religious organizations. Cultural and educational foundations were more than 70 percent of the total, with social welfare organizations following at approximately 16 percent. Other foundations dedicated to medicine, agriculture, transportation, economic development, and the like trailed at approximately 2 percent each (Asia Foundation 2001b).

Background and Legal Structure

As a semi-recognized state, the formal and legal development of Taiwan's third sector has been deeply linked with Chinese history and Chinese attitudes (legal and otherwise) toward nonstate organizations. The primary law governing third sector organizations in Taiwan is the Social Organizations Law of 1942, which established a corporatist registration system. This law allowed the formation of only one organization in each area of activity and administrative district, and the KMT was thus able to establish tightly controlled GONGOs (government-organized nongovernmental organizations) and to deny registration to independent NGOs (Heurlin 2009:234–35). In 1956, all social associations underwent a massive inspection, which required producing financial reports, activities, member lists, and personal histories of full-time members (Terao 2002:275). Organizations that refused inspection were banned, their assets confiscated, and in subsequent years organizations not under control of the state were largely repressed. Under authoritarianism clientelism ruled: only the wealthy, powerful, or well-established organizations were in a position to establish "charities" to assist the needy, and there were effectively no other autonomous organizations. International NPOs were the only "real" civil institutions that existed at the time, and were focused on social welfare, explicitly nonpolitical activities. Urban middle-class social clubs were also permitted to continue functioning (Hsiao 2003:181), as were clan societies, which were also subject to the registration rules; only one association per surname, for example, could be registered in each administrative area (Terao 2007:276).

From 1949 to 1987, the KMT enacted the Special Civil Society Organization Law, forbidding two organizations of the same nature from existing in same area, which limited the development of foundations—or, indeed, any type of ecology of organizations or organizational sector—in Taiwan. Consequently, the earliest *formal* NPOs in Taiwan (rather than loosely organized social movement and civic groups) came from abroad (organizations such as the Red Cross and the Christian Children's Fund). The appearance of these organizations paved the way for the development of other third sector organizations in the late 1990s (T.-C. Lin 2005:30–31).

In the late 1980s the KMT regime revised the laws governing third sector organizations and created a new set of rules under the Social Organization Law, which transformed what were previously considered protest groups into "regular" NPOs, in an effort to integrate them into a more complementary type of state-society relationship (T.-C. Lin 2005:31). Taiwan's political liberalization has been conducive to the mushrooming of its nonprofit sector, creating space for associational life to develop. Organizations that began informally have since become formalized, accounting for a percentage of this increase. The political opposition also reinforced the role of the NPO as a reformer (Hsiao 2003:182), underscoring its role as an activist agent of change.

Nonprofit organizations in Taiwan belong to one of five basic categories: business or professional associations, local community development organizations, social service organizations, "venture philanthropy" organizations, and social cooperatives. The boundaries between these categories are somewhat permeable (Kuan and Wang 2010:7). Functionally, however, the Taiwanese third sector can be divided into membership-centered civil organizations and endowment-centered foundations.

Most Taiwanese NPOs belong to the former category and are based on membership, meaning they derive political and social clout, and financial sustenance, from their members. Legally, associations must have at least fifty members to register (T.-C. Lin 2005:40–41). Formal civic organizations generally are clustered around the cities and span a range of issue areas: cultural and educational foundations are the most numerous, followed by social groups (including women's groups) and by charitable, medical and healthcare groups, agriculture, transportation, economic development, media, and environmental protection, among others. In 2000 there were nearly 3,000 foundations, 75 percent of which were new since the 1980s. Of these foundations, 70 percent are privately funded, about 25 percent are funded by corporations, and the remaining 5 percent are a mix and include governmental foundations (Hsiao 2003:183). As of 2001, the number of membership associations had increased to 15,000; this includes political organizations, showing more than a 50 percent increase over 1991. As of 2005, there was a total of 29,032 third sector organizations in Taiwan, of which 15.9 percent were located near Taipei and 10.4 percent near Kaohsiung (44–45). Taiwanese third sector organizations are required to register as a "legal person" with the relevant supervising government bodies; they are then reviewed and approved (Asia Foundation 2001b:5), and the 1927 Civic Code provided the legal basis for regulations governing Taiwanese NPOs. Foundations and associations are treated differently under this law: associations are regulated by the social welfare authorities of the central, provincial, and municipal governments, while professional, social, and political organizations are overseen by the Civil Organization Law (2001b:5).

Similarly to foundations in Japan, Taiwanese foundations may also have to apply for approval from different government agencies (depending on the organization's purposes), and these agencies in turn have different regulatory and administrative requirements—by way of example, each of twenty ministries and bureaus of Taiwan's Cabinet has issued its own "Regulations for the Establishment and Supervision of Foundations" (Asia Foundation 2001b:5). Establishing a Taiwanese foundation requires an endowment of between NT$500,000 and NT$30 million. The Taiwanese Tax Law grants special tax deductions for individual charitable donations, corporate charitable donations, and NPOs.

Funding

The Asia Pacific Philanthropy Consortium reports that no unified statistical data is available on revenues and expenditures for foundations in Taiwan because of their fragmented administration. Membership associations, however, totaled revenues of NT$43.3 billion in 1999—with a mean of NT $2.22 billion per association. Membership fees accounted for the largest source of income, followed by fundraising (NT$444,000) and fee-for-service income (NT$270,000) (Asia Foundation 2001b:1–2). Anecdotal evidence suggests that levels of corporate sponsorship for Taiwanese third sector organizations may be increasing as well.

For Taiwanese foundations, fixed interest from endowment and fixed assets are main sources of income, followed by donations and then fundraising programs (T.-C. Lin 2005:44–45). For associations, annual organizational goals are generally established based on the projected budget for the year, instead of vice versa (for example, the US model of creating a program and then fundraising in order to meet those programmatic goals). We find this difference noteworthy; on the one hand, it could circumvent the issue that many American third sector organizations face (professionalization of fundraising and cutting back programs at the last minute due to funding restraints), but it could indicate as well a lack of growth or innovation based on the constraints of projected budgets. Approximately a fourth of Taiwan's foundations are corporate, but unlike other parts of Asia, these foundations have access to both investment income and a share of corporate profits (Estes 2000:12).

Social organizations in Taiwan have been on the rise since the 1980s, but their activities peaked after the 921 (September 21) earthquake in 1999, because the government and donors shifted their distribution of resources and were focusing more on social organizations. A survey carried out in 1999 and 2000 by the Taiwanese Directorate General of Budget, Accounting, and Statistics on social development trends found that disaster relief efforts associated with the 921 earthquake created an 80 percent increase in donations from 1999 to 2000, suggesting that the crisis did a great deal to galvanize public commitment to nonprofit organizations. Among these new donors, 46.4 percent said that they would not have made any charitable contribution had it not been for the earthquake. The donation rate increased from 36.3 percent of the Taiwanese adult population in 1999 to 68.1 percent in 2000 (Asia Foundation 2001b). In 2003, 37.6 percent of Taiwanese had given to some type of charity, most of which was direct contributions (cash gifts, as opposed to in-kind donations) (T.-C. Lin 2005:40). NGOs in Taiwan faced the need to develop new channels to deal with such an influx of funding.

Taiwan's original donation policy, the Unified Donation Regulation, enacted in 1942 and revised in 1951, provided a vague guideline for social organizations to operate fundraising campaigns. Unrevised in six decades, the regulation was clearly outdated; the flood of donations after the 921 earthquake was an opportunity for the KMT to witness how disaster relief programs and social organizations could successfully mobilize resources. During this time, however, the public became concerned about how donation money would be used, and the government worried about how to monitor the money; social organizations needed to learn how to properly manage the money involved in rebuilding projects. A handful of nonprofit organizations thus collectively drafted a proposal for a new law to replace the outdated one. The new "Donation Law" would emphasize accountability and transparency. When running a fundraising campaign, the NPO would need to submit a clear plan to the government and have information available to the public about how the money is collected and allocated (Asia Foundation 2001b). NPOs would also publish the results of their work and financial reports. In May of 2006, the Ministry of Health and Welfare announced its regulations in "Charity Donations Destined for Social Welfare Funds Implementation Regulations" (Republic of China 2006).

As government-NPO efforts increase across Taiwan, so too does the importance of government funding of civil society organizations. In a study of nonprofit development, Twu (2001) found that since the mid-1990s, the Council for Cultural Affairs (a Taiwanese government agency) has proposed a series of community development programs that encourage local voluntary groups to understand the historical and cultural roots of their communities, organize arts or cultural activities, and share experiences in community building. Many of these development programs were financed by the central government but implemented by local voluntary groups (Twu 2001). City governments also frequently invite NGOs to joint meetings to facilitate dialogue between social organizations and the government, and local universities hold NGO personnel training workshops.

These types of government-civic partnerships, visible not only in Taiwan but also in third sectors across the world, have implications for the degree of professionalization within the Taiwanese third sector. More government and structured funding means more accountability measures—and more regulations. Civic organizations in Taiwan, in turning toward professionalization as a desirable end, have encountered many of the problems that newly professionalizing and young organizations face elsewhere, including resource scarcity, being shorthanded, workload and job overlap, financial instability, and modest wages with little room for increase. Similarly, NPO and NGO workers in Taiwan are not yet widely understood as professionals—a legitimacy challenge that third sector workers face around the world (Chang, Huang, and Kuo 2013).

Since the global economic recession beginning in 2008, however, public funds have diminished once more, and NPOs in Taiwan have had to turn to an income-generating business model of organization to sustain themselves (Pelchat 2004), echoing social enterprise tactics that we have seen elsewhere, particularly in the United States and Western Europe. Another (unique because of its prevalence) source of funding for Taiwanese NPOs is business corporations that are looking to be "model companies" that donate to charity. In general, in the past twenty years, Taiwanese nonprofits have attempted to adapt to both the changing needs of the population by dramatically diversifying the services offered and to the financial realities of a professional or semi-professional industry by diversifying funding and income sources. Finally, in this new climate of active nonprofits and scarce nonprofit resources, competition between and among nonprofits is becoming more apparent (Kuan and Wang 2010:8–9).

Status Quo and Challenges

Taiwan lacks some of the infrastructure for its rapidly professionalizing third sector that civil societies elsewhere possess. Whether or not such professional infrastructure is normatively desirable, its absence leaves Taiwanese NPOs in a liminal space between activism, clientelism, and professionalization, with weak infrastructure. Taiwanese NPO workers are few, and their ranks are shrinking; 70 percent of all professional Taiwanese nonprofit organizations have a staff of ten people or fewer (Chang, Huang, and Kuo 2013:6). As in most other countries, average salary is considerably lower than salaries in the business sector, leading to loss of professionally trained employees (T.-C. Lin 2005:51). There are very few overarching (umbrella) bodies or mechanisms of national coordination for third sector organizations (such as the American Council for Voluntary Action in the United States). The Taiwan Environmental Protection Union is composed of NPOs with similar aims, and such organizations generally operate similarly to professional associations, but in general the mechanisms for horizontal networking among civic groups are weak. This lack of coordination can lead to limited data and limited general understanding about the development of the sector.

One obstacle to this networking is the fact that Taiwanese organizations are generally protective of their limited resources (making collaborations difficult), and further, that there are dramatic regional differences between the north and the south of the country. However, recent developments in communication tools have had positive impacts. The Taiwan Philanthropy Information Center, launched and maintained by the Himalaya Foundation, works to develop mutual trust and sharing among Taiwan's CSOs and NPOS in the educational sector (T.-C. Lin 2005:37), a nascent attempt to build horizontal communication mechanisms.

Further, as in Japan, a fragmented legal framework makes oversight of Taiwanese third sector organizations difficult, and the process of registering per the relevant legal requirements can be frustrating. No single agency is responsible for collecting data from all third sector organizations (Asia

Foundation 2001b:9–10). In reaction to public complaints regarding this issue of transparency, some Taiwanese NPOs have worked together to draft an advocacy proposal for a new law to replace the Unified Donation Regulation to govern the ethical behaviors of third sector organizations receiving funds from the public (9–10).

Taiwan has undergone massive political and social change in the last fifty years, and its developing formal third sector exemplifies many dynamics of the process of change. Its activist roots institutionalized into a relatively professional sector comparatively quickly, following cues from third sectors throughout the world. This newly institutionalized sector has begun to liaise with the government. At the same time, political liberalization has enabled Taiwanese NPOs to advocate—at times contentiously—in new ways, making new and clear demands on the state, and meeting often with success.

Case Studies

The Children Are Us Foundation (CAREUS)

The Children Are Us Foundation (CAREUS) was founded in 1995 to provide support for people from ages sixteen to sixty-five with mental disabilities. The foundation promotes the potential talent of people suffering from Down syndrome, cerebral palsy, and other intellectual and physical disabilities by providing long-term care, education, and job training. It especially advocates the "self-support" of people with intelligence disability by providing adaptive technology and work opportunities so that they can lead normal lives (Hong 2004).

In 1997, Citibank donated US$100,000 to CAREUS after the Citi Foundation's CEO Paul Ostergard visited one of the bakeries that the organization had set up. Aside from Citibank's staff being able to fulfill requirements for its "3000 hour community service program," a continuing relationship with Citibank allowed CAREUS to set up more bakeries, restaurants, and bakery factories in Taipei, Hsinchu, and Kaohsiung. In 1998, Citibank also issued an "accepting mentally challenged children" credit card; with every purchase, 0.275 percent is donated to the organization. Today, the foundation has twenty-one bakeries and restaurants at which the mentally disabled work. Based on their individual status, students can then be referred to regular jobs in convenience stores, restaurants, cleaning companies, and so on. In addition, by creating a community group home, musical troupe, theater troupe, special scout troupe, and the Full Life Education Academy, the foundation addresses the holistic needs of people with intellectual disabilities in terms of daily life care, leisure, and education (Children Are Us 2011).

The foundation also has a community group home in Kaohsiung, housing six to eight children and two counselors who act as parents. Daily living training is available to help the children handle issues such as personal hygiene, social skills, daily routines, money, social integration, and so forth. Temporary and short-term daycare is also available for the mentally disabled who have family members that suddenly fall sick or have emergency situations.

CAREUS administers three workstations in Kaohsiung, Taipei, and Hsinchu, which are all headed by an independent director. For each workstation, there is a social welfare department that focuses on social work (special employee development, case management, temporary care service, and group home service), and a business department that oversees the operations of the bakeries and restaurants. The foundation is registered under the Ministry of Interior Affairs. The current estimated number of staff members is around two hundred.

CAREUS receives funding from a number of sources, as figure 10 shows. According to the organization, the government has provided up to US$1.6 million for the organization to carry out activities or projects. However, subsidies are only 12.9 percent of their total income. The organization also cooperates with corporations such as Citibank, Ritek Technology, Wang Steak Corporation, and Wanhai Lines. CAREUS is one of the social organizations that has adapted something of a social enterprise model, supplementing its grant support with income from various projects. Almost 60 percent of their income comes from the sales of the bakeries and restaurants they operate.

The Eden Social Welfare Foundation

Liu Hsia, a disabled writer suffering from rheumatoid arthritis, founded the Eden Social Welfare Foundation after she witnessed discrimination against people with disabilities. Liu donated her income from publications and initiated a group of Christians who shared her vision to bring people with disabilities out of their isolation. On December 1, 1982, the Eden Social Welfare Foundation was established to serve people with disabilities as well as other socially marginalized groups. The foundation provides "comprehensive human care" for people between birth and age sixty-five, including vocational training, employment service, rehabilitation, early intervention, long-term care service, new immigrant service, and community reconstruction for disaster victims (Eden 2011).

The foundation operates training and employment opportunities for disabled people such as sheltered workshops, a data key-in service, and a charity sales center. The foundation also focuses on developing alternative sources of income to donations in an attempt to maintain autonomy and stability.

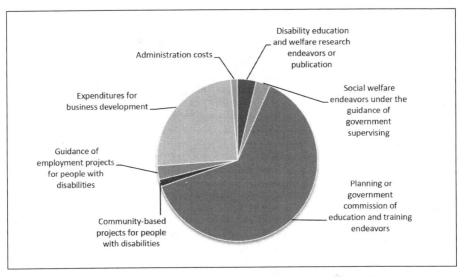

Items		%	Amount (NT$)
Social enterprises	Disability education and welfare research endeavors or publication	3.8%	13,550,823
	Social welfare endeavors under the guidance of government supervising	2.9%	10,249,011
	Planning or government commission of education and training endeavors	63.1%	226,445,732
	Community-based projects for people with disabilities	1.4%	5,011,979
	Guidance of employment projects for people with disabilities	2.8%	10,166,428
Expenditures for business development		24.7%	88,597,677
Administration costs		1.3%	4,697,677
Total		100.0%	358,719,327

Figure 9. Expenditures for Children Are Us Foundation, 2011.

Source: Children Are Us Foundation 2011.

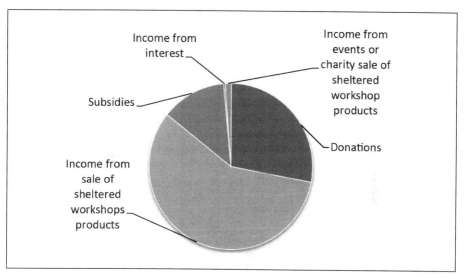

Items	%	Amount (NT$)
Donations	27.9%	100,011,506
Income from sale of sheltered workshops products	57.7%	206,886,529
Subsidies	12.9%	46,435,375
Income from interest	0.3%	1,112,552
Income from events or charity sale of sheltered workshop products	1.2%	4,205,345
Total	100.0%	358,651,307

Figure 10. Income for Children Are Us Foundation, 2011.

Source: Children Are Us Foundation 2011.

It has developed a "one-third strategy" in which it tries to balance government subsidies, donations, and earned income from social ventures. In 2004, the foundation set up a Charitable Enterprise Professional Team, a special group with its own structure of human resources and finances, to oversee the development and operations of the activities. The foundation does not receive regular government funding; at most around 2 percent of its budget comes from government-subsidized service projects. However, the KMT and Eden do collaborate in other ways (for example, Eden distributes wheelchair donations from the government to developing countries).

Since 1996, Eden has also been actively participating in international relief activities and promoting the welfare of people with disabilities around the world, in areas such as wheelchair donations, disaster response, food aid, and rehabilitation for war-injured people. It is one of the grassroots social organizations in Taiwan that has successfully expanded internationally. The foundation has also established overseas offices in Penang and Kuala Lumpur, Malaysia, as well as one service center in Vietnam.

The Eden foundation started out with only 2 part-time employees, but today it has expanded to a staff of over 1,200 people, nearly 40 percent of whom are people with disabilities.

7. China

China's long, strong statist tradition might initially suggest hostility to the third sector, especially a third sector of the Calvinist/decentralized variety as is dominant in North America. Still, our other chapters show that strong states (such as France, Japan, and Korea) can and do develop third sectors as vibrant as those elsewhere. They will look different, of course, from third sectors in the United States, with its long history of a weak central state and a strong associational sector. In China's case, some have argued that the development of the third sector is tightly linked to the operation of the market economy. Further, some of the dramatic changes of the New Political Culture that are occurring globally are also found in China. China's nonprofit sector had its roots in an institutional logic of bureaucracy (government-organized NGOs, or GONGOs, were long the most visible component), now opening up to professionalization and even activism in some places. This emphasis on cooperation with government is nicely captured in a comment that Fan Baojun, former vice minister of civil affairs, made in 1997, stating that the purpose of any social organization in China is twofold: first, to communicate the ideas of the people to the Party and government and, second, to engage in activities that serve the public (Hsia and White 2002:331).

Theorists working on civil society in China have historically treated it as part of a "revolutionary movement," a "counter-elite structure," or a reassertion of a culture that had spent decades suppressed (Chamberlain 1993:200). However, Clark and others have made a strong argument in favor of a New Political Culture in China, which sees associational life and civil society as less revolutionary per se and more related to ideas of participation, consumption, and service delivery that are unique to this political context. This New

Political Culture view does not see civil society as inherently being *counter* to the existing structures—or, to return to Young's (2000) typology, *adversarial*—but rather bases its analysis on patterns of values and consumption behavior that work differently within different national structures. Coupled with increasing bureaucratic collaboration between nonprofit and government structures, it seems that China may become an important example of how Eastern political structures may articulate with the kinds of civil society dynamics seen more commonly in the West.

There is a long history of what might be loosely termed "civic culture" in China. Early twentieth-century organizations of merchants, peasants, and intellectuals in some prosperous cities and in the upper areas of the Yangtze River developed features of Western-style civil society (Ma 2002b). Ma notes, however, that Chinese civil society has always lacked the Western civil society characteristic of opposition to state power (the proclivity for activism). Others argue that the purpose of early Chinese civil society was not to confront the government, but rather to harmonize the relations between it and society, providing autonomy with which to *assist* government. This point was mutually accepted both by the government and society. Scholars "in search" of Chinese civil society tend to focus on politically oriented organizations, such as workers', students', and women's organizations, groups of scholars, or illicit or underground organizations. The charitable and service-provision arm of Chinese civil society has, as elsewhere, received less attention despite its rapid growth (Ma 2002a:118).

Like the United States, China has strong informal organizational ties on which to build a third sector. Social networks have been critical components of the construction of every major social movement and every major civil society, from the United States civil rights movement, which mobilized through black churches, to Bolivia, where indigenous community networks brought the first indigenous president to power, to the development of the Taiwanese third sector. Yet how these networks specifically operate in China demands close analysis.

Guanxi (interpersonal, influential social networks) have historically functioned as a mechanism for coping with the absence of a formal system of third sector regulation and, in so doing, created the basis for sector organization and civil society itself. Like Japanese chōnaikai, guanxi fulfill functions that Western thinking would categorize as belonging both to the private and the associational sectors. Guanxi, like their counterparts in Catholic Europe and Latin America, fill an associational space in the absence of formal and institutionalized structures. While Western nonprofit organizations rely primarily on institutionalized and formalized procedures and structures to access information, policy processes, and the media, many Chinese NPOs rely more on their networks of relationships for access to information. Like Western civil society, guanxi also disseminate solidarity and mobilize members (Heurlin 2009:277).

China likewise has a considerable history of public philanthropy. Wang and Xu report that "quasi-foundations" can be found as far back as the Sui dynasty's public granaries and the Song dynasty's public farmsteads and lands (Ming and Yushan 2010:25). Under the *danwei* system that prevailed in China until the 1980s, state-owned enterprises provided for their workers' welfare needs; there was thus little incentive to allow for the development of NPOs working in those fields (Heurlin 2009:232). During the first three decades of Communist Party rule, people were deeply integrated into their work units, which provided most services—jobs as well as welfare. Following reforms, and the diminishing of those work units, community-based volunteer organizations began to move in to fill the void left by their units and to create community meaning (Ma 2002b:318).

Importantly, Chinese social organizations have had to adapt to three dramatic changes in the short period of time since 1949: the socialist reform period, 1950–66; the Cultural Revolution, 1966–76; and the post-Mao period from the late 1970s to the present (Ma 2002a:119). It would be reasonable to expect that these political changes have had an equally dramatic impact on organizational form.

In the 1950s and 1960s, only three types of Chinese civic organizations existed that were not explicitly run by the state. All three types of organizations were established originally by government and party departments and later labeled as "government-organized NGOs" (GONGOs) by some scholars. In fact, under an authoritarian regime with a planned economy before the reforms, social groups served more as links between the Chinese Communist Party and the people. One type was the private organization that had withstood the socialist reform period (here we refer to the program of economic reforms in the People's Republic of China, started in 1978 by reformists within the Communist Party of China), such as the Chinese Medical Association and the Chinese Red Cross; these adherents served the new state and were rewarded with compensation comparable to that of government officials. The second group was friendship, trade, or cultural exchange associations, most of which were initially established by the government during this time period to help facilitate relationships abroad. The third group of organizations, "mass organizations," were groups especially developed for workers and distinct populations therein. These organizations have consequently morphed into NPOs and CSOs (Ma 2002a:119–20). Like Japanese neighborhood and shopkeepers' associations (shokenai and chōnaikai), different types of private organizations that depended largely on geographic or family structure have been part of Chinese social fabric for a long time. Thus, as discussed at different points in this book, although the term "civic organization" seems like a Western concept, traditionally in China, civil society organizations have existed consistently in forms that variously emphasized both their private, public, professional, and market functions.

The development of civic organizations was hampered by the enormous chaos from the Cultural Revolution in the 1960s and 1970s. During this period, there were no new NGOs established distinct from new branches of the political movements. Most of the existing ones were also shut down or replaced by the Red Guards (*hong wei bin*) and the Rebellion Organizations (*zao fan zu zhi*).

Following Mao Zedong's death in 1976, Chinese society began to rethink its economic strategy, a process that culminated in a new package of reforms that shifted the focus from state planning to increasing reliance on the market. This move has implied the gradual liberalization of prices and "decollectivization" of agriculture. Such changes have clearly had implications for the character of Chinese social life. Social classes are forming and reforming, and the market reforms have developed new demographic categories like traders, entrepreneurs, and bourgeois (Howell and Pearce 2002:130).

As these market forces developed, other sources of power and influence emerged, and the social landscape of the country has differentiated. This differentiation, in turn, has created new sets of demands, needs, interests, and grievances, which have influenced the emergence of new types of social organizations. Whereas prior to 1978 the interaction of the state and society occurred mostly at the levels of state-owned enterprises (SOEs) and people's communes, at the beginning of the reform and opening period, the government realized that it would be unable to meet the vast array of citizen needs through a planned economy alone. It thus enlisted the assistance of NGO-like organizations (government-organized NGOs, or GONGOs, 官办组织) (Shieh and Knutson 2013). As in Japan, NPOs have stepped in or been contracted to provide much-needed services. The notion of "small government and big society" has become something of a slogan in the last twenty years, intended to reflect the generation of smaller, nonstate organizations to provide services (Ma 2002b:306). These organizations, first broadly established during the 1980s, began to appear in collaboration with multilateral agencies and INGOs, and with the Chinese government.

China's first formal foundation, the China Children and Teenagers' Fund, was founded shortly after the Reform and Opening (social and economic reforms beginning in 1978), and the subsequent Measures on Foundation Administration, passed in 1988, were meant to standardize the development and regulation of similar foundations (Ming and Yushan 2010:25). Following a period of restriction after the Tiananmen Square protests, the Regulations on Foundation Administration and the Accounting System for Civil Non-profit Organizations were passed in 2004 and 2005, respectively, both of which served to reinforce the legal foundation of third sector development (25). By the end of 2008, China had 1,597 NPOs registered at various levels of the Ministry of Civil Affairs, a growth of 19.2 percent in one year. Among these, 643 were private foundations, up from 253 in 2005 (32).

Furthermore, since the beginning of the Reform and Opening, mutual communication between China and the rest of the world has increased dramatically. During the beginning of this period, and consistent with its attitude for the past several decades, the Chinese government tolerated international NGOs and avoided setting up official policy that might serve to legitimize them. Though INGOs are able to provide valuable development assistance (ranging from capital to technology to expertise), the government is wary of such organizations as potential competitors for international funding and especially wary of the Westernized values that some of them represent, including values of democracy. "This suspicion of international NGOs became especially visible after the 'color revolutions' that took place in 2004 in some of the former Soviet republics such as the Ukraine and Georgia. Chinese leaders and their advisors saw NGOs . . . as playing a key role in bringing down authoritarian governments in these countries" (Shieh and Knutson 2013:12).

Similarly, more and more foreign NGOs have begun to launch their activities within Mainland China. Following the UN's World Conference on Women in China in 1995, international NGOs began to appear throughout China (moving out of their traditional spaces in Beijing), though actual numbers of INGOs in China are difficult to obtain due to the inconsistency of the legislation that governs them and the lack of publicly available data or directories. According to a recent report, the estimated number of American NGOs active in China is more than a thousand (Peng and Liu 2012). The conceptual framework of a "global civil society" has laid important groundwork for the expansion of NGOs in China. This influx of international interest and funding spurred the beginnings of official policy specifically on international NGOs. In December of 2009, the Yunnan provincial government issued a set of regulations aimed at foreign organizations. This type of regulation came about due to the rapid growth of small NGOs working on themes such as HIV/AIDS and receiving support from groups such as the Global Fund, UNAIDS, and the Gates Foundation (Shieh and Knutson 2013:37).

In today's China, although NGOs enjoy much more autonomy than they did, the government still worries about social "instability" and therefore imposes severe restrictions on many kinds of NGO activity. It bans the formation of any autonomous organization around politically sensitive issue areas (such as human rights, religion for the most part, and the free movement of labor). In fact, most of Chinese NPOs are only active in fields deemed less politically sensitive, such as economic development (this is big), environment protection, children and youth development, the disabled, and animal protection (Jie 2006).

Chinese Associational Life

Local climates for NGOs often vary drastically in China, a dynamic that creates NGO clustering in certain parts of the country. Such climates can include everything from the attitude of local authorities to the proximity of international funding sources to local interpretation of regulations to community needs and the general political climate of any given region. Historically, Beijing has experienced a heavy concentration of civil society organizations (by some estimates, nearly 30 percent of the country's NGOs are there), followed by Shanghai and Guangdong at 12 percent and 7 percent, respectively. All three regions are very urban, economically powerful, and leaders in NGO regulation. One study found that Shanghai was the most common location for GONGO and government funding, perhaps because it was one of the first cities to undertake large-scale government contracting during the reform period (Shieh and Brown-Inz 2013).

As a result of the changing political climate associated with Reform and Opening, associations of many kinds grew in the 1980s in China. In Shanghai, the total number of social organizations grew from 628 in 1981 to 2,627 in 1984, a dramatic leap in such a short timeframe. Likewise, student associations flourished. Associations of all types generally grew so rapidly that official policy lagged somewhat; there was neither a regulatory policy nor an official bureau for registering them (S. Wang and He 2004:501). In the next decade, private chambers of commerce and trade associations were approved for operation, at the same time that the government began to contract some of its own functions to associations, like many other countries (Ming and Yushan 2010:311).

Similarly, beginning around 1984 the Chinese government took steps to localize state management and to enlarge the autonomy of state-owned enterprises (SOEs); at that time, the nonstate-owned enterprises operated with minimal supervision. For example, in 1995, only 21.9 percent of the textile factories in Shanghai were under the supervision of the Shanghai Textile Bureau, and only 1 percent of plastics manufacturers were. "The state's withdrawal from the economy has created a huge vacuum of authority. China has no alternative intermediate mechanism, however, for the market economy to assume the government's role. . . . [It was] natural for the government to call for establishment of chambers of commerce and trade associations as intermediary managerial mechanisms for the industrial reforms" (Ming and Yushan 2010:312). From 1984 to 1988, more than one hundred associations appeared in the machine industry as the government started its experiment in this sort of decentralization:

> The development of industrial associations demonstrates a consistent and systematic multilevel effort by the government to originate cooperative mechanisms in the industrial reforms. By transforming the existing administrative bodies into trade associations that theoretically sit outside the state system, the Chinese government has quickly created a managerial intermediary designed to function in a market economy. This is the foremost reason behind the promotion of trade associations. (Ming and Yushan 2010:314)

The Ministry of Civil Affairs took over work of managing social organizations in 1989, and since then the number of social organizations has grown

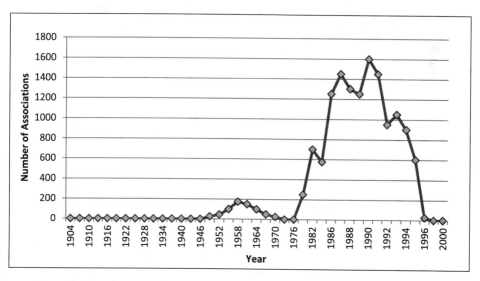

Figure 11. Founding year of associations in nine selected regions of China.
Source: S. Wang and He 2004.

even faster. From 1989 to 1990 the registered social organizations in nine selected regions (Jiangxi, Fujian, Gansu, Liaoning, Guangdong, Shanghai, Tianjin, Nanjing, Shaoxing) all surpassed the previous record (S. Wang and He 2004:501).

We can see, therefore, that the Chinese third sector appears to be following a trajectory similar to some of its Asian counterparts, and the founding of its nonprofit organizations (at least at the beginning) occurred in conjunction with government according to an institutional logic of bureaucracy.

Furthermore, in the last thirty years, Chinese neighborhood-based community voluntary organizations have been expanding rapidly. In some places up to 90 percent of the residential streets have established community service networks, and 80 percent have voluntary service organizations (Ma 2002b:318). Though community-based (highly geographically localized) associations do indeed exist in places like France and the United States, the degree to which the Chinese and other Asian third sectors emphasize this type of community group is unique, building on century-old traditions.

In China, as in Japan, young people and those with high formal education participate more in volunteer and public activities than others. This mobilization of young persons is distinct from many countries in the West, which are arguably dominated by older persons and established views (Steel 1996). According to the Central Committee of the Chinese Communist Youth League (CCYL), for example, there were about 29.5 million registered youth volunteers in China in 2008; a total of 380 million young people have spent nearly eight trillion hours of volunteer work during the last fifteen years (Hustinx, Handy, and Cnaan 2012:64). University students constitute the largest proportion of China's volunteers. For instance, college students represent only 1 percent of the youth population but form 53 percent of youth volunteers (Ma 2002b:321). During the Beijing Olympics in 2008, the number of applicants for volunteer work from Beijing alone was 256,000, of which 181,500 (71% percent) were students from universities and colleges (Hustinx, Handy, and Cnaan 2012:64). As Ma (2002b:321) puts it, "this finding reflects a tradition of Chinese intellectuals assuming social responsibilities. Whereas young and educated people have more career opportunities than ever before, the desire for personal fulfillment leads them to ask how much they can do for society and how much they should do."

Expressly philanthropic activity in China appears to be increasing as well. During the flood relief operation of 1998, private charities helped collect 6.6 billion RMB (about US$82.5 million) from individual donors. As an interesting comparison, in 1999, the government spent 1.08 billion RMB on disaster relief, and domestic and overseas private donations reached about 400 mil-

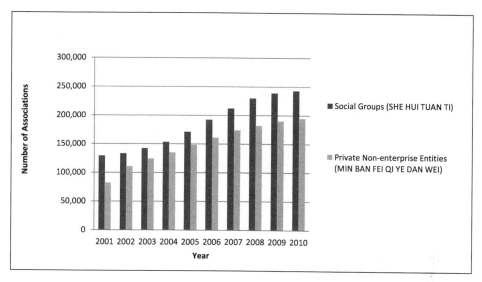

Figure 12. The development of associations in China, 2001–2010.

Source: Data reorganized from Ministry of Civil Affairs of the People's Republic of China 2010.

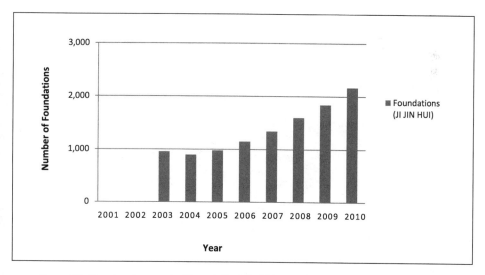

Figure 13. The development of foundations in China, 2001–2010.

Source: Data reorganized from Ministry of Civil Affairs of the People's Republic of China 2010.

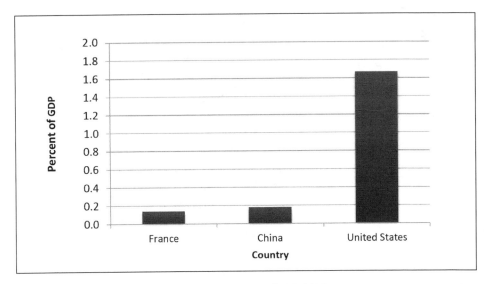

Figure 14. National giving levels as percentage of GDP, 2010.

Source: Tuan 2011.

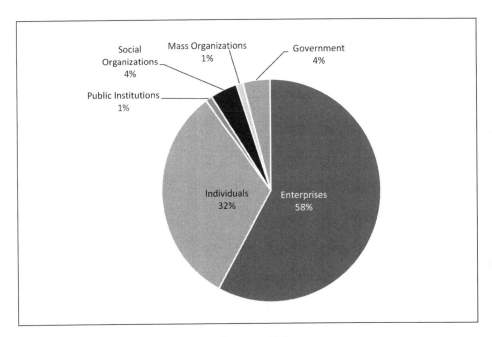

Figure 15. Chinese philanthropy development, 2011.

Source: Tuan 2011.

lion RMB (Ma 2002b:321). Led by Chinese celebrities, increasing numbers of public citizens have participated in philanthropy in recent years, especially after the 2008 earthquake. Some media even touted 2008 as the "Year of Civil Society" and expounded that "tribulations will revitalize a nation" (*Guo nan xing ban*), based on the widespread participation of volunteers and associations in earthquake relief.

The general philanthropic trend has been steadily increasing. According to the latest *Annual Report of China's Philanthropy Development* (Yang 2011), the total donations from various sources in 2011 reached 84.5 billion RMB and accounted for 0.18 percent of China's GDP, with an average per capita contribution of 62.7 Yuan. Business enterprises are still the leading contributors, while donations from individuals account for 31.62 percent of donations. Only a small part of philanthropic resources is from the combination of governments, public institutions, and other social organizations (Yang 2011).

Legal Structure and Funding

China's official classification divides all entities that are not managed by the state into two groups: community service organizations (CSOs) and non-governmental noncommercial enterprises (NGNCEs). CSOs include various associations, foundations, chambers of commerce, and federations. NGNCEs are income-making institutions that do not produce products but provide social or professional services (Ma 2002b:321). Functionally, however, four types of nonprofit organizations are represented in China: government-organized NGOs (GONGOs), grassroots CSOs, campus student groups, and INGOs.

CSOs in China are governed by formal mechanisms that serve to monitor their registration and activities. Following the Tiananmen Square protests in June 1989, the state created strict regulations on nonstate entities, requiring them to officially register with the Ministry of Civil Affairs to be viewed as legal. Those 1989 Stipulations on the Registration and Administration of Social Organizations represented the first legal attempt to recognize and regulate social organizations.

These stipulations require nonstate organizations to register under a dual management system; organizations are supervised by the relevant state unit as well as the Ministry of Civil Affairs. Because the state units can be unable or unwilling to undertake supervision of nonprofit activities, some organizations cannot register, which has the secondary effect of channeling nonprofit development into the areas in which the government ministries are most willing to supervise. Tellingly, organizational leaders refer to their supervisory units as "mothers-in-law"; these often-small CSOs register as for-profit businesses because they cannot find an organization to act as a "mother-in-law." During periodic mandatory re-registrations, many organizations are rejected and have their documentation revoked (for example, in 1991–1992, a total of 118,691 organizations applied for re-registration, but only 89,969 registrations were approved) (Ma 2002b:321). As in Japan, the dual registration process has taken its toll: numbers of CSOs fell from 184,821 in 1996 to 130,768 in 2000 (Heurlin 2009:233). New amendments to the 1989 stipulations further stressed that any unregistered social organization would be dissolved, and prohibited similar organizations co-established at the same administrative level. Organizations must register with the appropriate civil affairs department from the county-level upward—it is thus difficult for local groups from different areas to institutionalize. This has the net impact of creating centralized nonstate associations. It also points to a still-present institutional logic of bureaucracy that, despite the rapid recent expansion of the third sector, still defines the associational trajectories in important ways.

Further, this close linkage to the government powerfully shapes what the organizations are able to undertake. A 1997 survey of NGOs in Guangzhou showed that 50 percent of the boards of NGOs were composed entirely of government officials, 30 percent had at least some government officials, and 20 percent were staffed entirely by private citizens. According to the same survey, when asked about their most pressing need, nearly half of the third sector respondents indicated that they needed more government funds, and over 16 percent indicated they needed more government cooperation, while only 6.8 percent reported that they wished for more autonomy (Heurlin 2009), pointing to the presence of very different subtypes of organizations. In 1996, a high-level official estimated that fewer than 50 percent of CSOs were self-organized, self-supported, and self-governed; similarly, a study of that same era suggested that the majority of CSOs were semigovernmental (Ma 2002b:306).

Despite how closely linked they are to the central government, most Chinese CSOs do not attain the level of professionalization they might like, and they suffer from a deficiency in organizational development, program implementation, legislation frameworks, social support, cultural background, and funding. According to a report from Tsinghua NGO Research Center, 50 percent of CSOs in China still receive the majority of their funding from governments. This trend persists, despite the fact that Chinese government has begun to encourage organizations to seek independence. The Chinese government no longer provides funds to new NGOs and has not increased support to existing GONGOs. The trend is clear that China's NGOs are becoming increasingly independent, as Chinese economic reforms have deepened (Liu 2002).

Table 6. Financing resources of NGOs in Mainland China, 1998

Financing resources	Percentage	Rank
Membership fees	21.18	2
Operating revenue	6.00	3
Government interest	49.97	1
Governmental project fees	3.58	6
Grants (from international-NGO and foreign governments and organizations)	1.64	10
Grants from enterprises	5.63	4
Grants from other social organizations	0.50	12
Donations	2.18	7
Capital operating revenue	1.21	11
Individual fees (other than membership fees)	1.98	8
Loans	0.28	13
Capital surplus (preceding year)	1.83	9
Others	4.14	5

Source: Translated from Deng 2001.

There are distinct patterns, however, in these funding structures. For example, although China's NGOs receive a vast majority of funding from foreign governments and organizations each year (see line 3 in table 6), the bias toward government-controlled, Beijing-based grantees is overwhelming. According to a recent publication from Spires, between 2002 and 2009, eighty-six US foundations made 2,583 grants to 658 distinct grantees, for a total value of $442,925,349. However, of this amount, academic, government, and GONGO grantees accounted for 86.01 percent of total grant monies. By contrast, grassroots NGOs received only 5.61 percent of total grant monies. The top ten recipients were, again, dominated by government-controlled institutions based in Beijing, accounting for 37 percent of total monies received. In fact, almost 70 percent of the total grants, or $309 million, went to organizations in Beijing, a city with less than 1.5 percent of China's 1.34 billion overall population (Spires 2011:317). The lack of general financial support from the Chinese public has been one of the biggest obstacles to the growth of independent NPOs.

One might expect that due to the difficult registration process within the Ministry of Civil Affairs (MCA), the number of registered social organizations would be and remain low. However, a huge number of nonregistered NGOs are also emerging. These informal organizations are also referred to as "grassroots groups" or "bottom-up organizations." Moreover, tens of thousands of groups operating within government agencies, institutions, enterprises, schools, urban neighborhoods, and rural communities are considered "internal" organizations and not required to register with MCA (S. Wang and He 2004:490). In fact, only a small number of NGOs have been registered as legal social organizations. The total number of nonregistered NGOs in China has been estimated at 1.6 million by NGO Research Center at Tsinghua University and at 2 million by China Non-Profit Organizations Network (Edele 2005:15). Powerful consequence: the numbers of informal organizations are about ten times greater than the number of those that are formally registered.

Generally speaking, small grassroots groups organize more activities that target the general public, but membership and funding still present challenges. Though individuals and businesses fund organizations to assist with disaster relief, a sustained culture of philanthropic involvement does not exist in China as it does in the United States. Furthermore, whereas in the United States and much of Europe many NPOs have fundraising departments or staff, Chinese organizations often have less experience and capacity in this regard; further, there is minimal public trust concerning such activities.

For example, a 2011 scandal involved twenty-year-old Guo Meimei, affiliated with the Red Cross Society of China. That spring, blog posts went viral about Guo's extravagant, jet-setting lifestyle (complete with a Lamborghini and a Maserati); the blogs fueled existing suspicions of corruption in Chinese charities. Though the Red Cross of China denied ties to Guo, some speculate that she got her title of "commercial general manager" for being the mistress of a relative of a high-ranking Red Cross official. Guo was not the only complication that the Chinese Red Cross faced that year; in April of 2011, a photograph circulating on the Internet showed a $1,500 restaurant bill for a meal for a small group of Chinese Red Cross employees.

Then in June (in the midst of the Guo Meimei scandal), the Chinese National Audit Office reported that the Chinese Red Cross had financial problems, including an instance in which the organization, which had an approved budget in 2010 of almost $45 million, had overpaid an equipment procurement contract by $650,000 (Wong 2011). In December 2012, a widely popularized scandal "again attracted national attention—cash in donation boxes in Chengdu for disaster relief were left uncollected for four years, causing the money inside the boxes to grow mold" (R. Wang 2013).

In response to these ongoing problems, the One Foundation, which was previously founded as a branch of the Chinese Red Cross by movie star Jet Li—and whose donations were deposited directly into an account held by the Red Cross—sought more independence. Li moved One Foundation to Shenzhen, separating from Red Cross and becoming an independent NGO in a bid to increase its public legitimacy.

Such scandals understandably decrease trust in specific GONGOs like the Chinese Red Cross. However, the public fear of nonprofits in general is similarly rooted in the government's insistence on controlling much of the charity work in China generally through its own large organizations, while limiting the permissible involvement of private organizations. Further, "Many Chinese do not trust the Red Cross because of its special legal status—it is one of 25 large organizations that register with an office that answers to both the Communist Party and the State Council, China's cabinet. Virtually all other nonprofit groups in the country are supposed to register with the Ministry of Civil Affairs, which counts 420,000 such entities on its rolls" (Wong 2011, n.p.).

Furthermore, a new and controversial proposal for an appropriation, tentatively called the Charity Law, which first emerged in an interview with Zhou Sen, the honorary vice president of the China Charity Federation, sparked a new sense of public outrage. Sen described the proposal in an interview: "What is the concept [behind] the Charity Law? A certain amount from everyone's paycheck will have to be donated, just like a tax . . . and one single Charity Law can solve all problems facing charity in China" (Chuqing 2013). In response, historian Lei Yi remarked scathingly, "Is this [enforced donation] called charity? Government-backed organizations lack transparency, [so] donors are fewer and fewer, [so] you compel them? . . . [T]he right path is gaining public trust" (R. Wang 2013). In response to the public backlash (largely via online mechanisms such as Weibo and Twitter), the Ministry of Civil Affairs publicly distanced itself from Sen, saying his title was just "honorary" and that it did not reflect the opinions of the China Charity Federation.

The challenges of integrating a strong state with a robust civil society are important, as we have illustrated above. But we must also recognize that strong and robust civic associations can go together with a powerful and flexible state (Saich 2000:124–141; Shue 1994:66), as demonstrated in the example of France. New forms of civic activities, mobilization, and participation are on the rise in China as the country explores, through legislation and experimentation, how to better link popular engagement with state policies.

The NPC in China and Contemporary Trends

The data above suggest that, through this associational revolution, Chinese concepts of citizenship and public involvement may be changing. State legitimacy, social values, and types of civic engagement are all shifting as the economic and social reality of China shifts.

With the rise of social organizations documented in table 6 (beginning around 1980), civic activities and participation have dramatically altered the political culture of China. The rise of civil society in China has been extremely important politically. A "political culture" approach to studying China predicts neither that China will remain forever unchanged nor that China is headed down the road of convergence with the West or even former Communist societies of Eastern Europe, but instead, this change in political culture will inevitably "draw heavily on established cultural repertoires" (Perry 1994). This kind of analysis, emphasizing the political culture rather than the legal structure of Chinese associational life, suggests that the symbolism of social movements and protests must be taken into careful account, placed and analyzed within an existing domestic historical context as well as external international influences that have also shaped the society.

The percentage of actual formal membership in social organizations is low in China, leading many to believe that civic participation and engagement are also low. But this is in part because many Chinese associations are informal. Still, there has been a rise in participation in civic activities and in the level of public engagement in the decades spanning the last years of the twentieth and the early years of the twenty-first centuries. This can be seen from the China General Social Survey (CGSS) of 2003, a national survey of citizens, in which a question on willingness to join environmental groups was asked, and more than 70 percent of respondents either indicated that they would be willing to join or had already joined. In 2005, the CGSS shows that participation in charitable activities is higher than other social activities. However, in 2006, a question regarding formal membership indicated that membership levels were low (China General Social Survey 2006).

New forms of mobilization are emerging in China. The dynamics between the public, local, and central government have become differentiated from the past, due to the rising role of the media, the Internet, and cell phone technology in the context of the changing political culture in the country. Mobilization methods have altered; new channels opened up a new voice for citizen participation. For instance, on the first day of June in 2007, an estimated fifteen to twenty thousand residents in Xiamen city were mobilized by new media to protest against a chemical industrial project, prompting officials to locate the paraxylene (PX) factory elsewhere. Participators marched on the street around the city hall of Xiamen, including little children waving banners that read "oppose PX, protect Xiamen." Other big red banners read "no poison gas, no pollution of our river"; "protect our posterity, and defend our home." The protest went on for another day, demanding the project be discarded. Most of these protestors were organized informally by text messages, email, and online bulletin board systems.

As readers might recall, South Korea has had similar experiences with new media and organizing: the Xiamen PX movement is just one of many

Table 7. Response to the question: Would you join an
environmental social organization?

	Frequency	Percentage
No answer	11	0.22%
Yes, already joined	86	1.70%
Yes, hope to join	3,667	72.28%
No	439	8.65%
Don't know	870	17.15%
Total	5,073	100%

Source: Data from the China General Social Survey 2003.

Table 8. Response to the question: Are you currently a
member of a social group, club, or other organization?

	Frequency	Percentage
Yes	141	1.39%
No	10,010	98.61%
Total	10,151	100%

Source: Data from the China General Social Survey 2006.

cases in which social media created a platform for the expression of public opinion, opening new pathways for political participation. As of the end of December 2011, the number of Chinese Internet users was more than five hundred million (CINIC 2012). With the growing of the number of Internet users, scholars expect that these "new" media will become much more powerful in motivating large groups of volunteers to take action in different areas of concern.

The relationship between Chinese citizens and their government is also transformed by the Weibo, a Chinese social media platform roughly analogous to Twitter, which has already created a vigorous virtual public square since it was launched in 2009. The number of registered users has surpassed 350 million. Any ordinary registered user now can launch a public debate or try to elicit shame from government and corporate officials by posting photos, videos, comments, and messages in an instant (Magistad 2012). Interestingly, governments and NGOs in China have also begun to adopt Weibo as a mechanism of communication, using it to release information, to report on the status of ongoing projects, and to generate suggestions from the public. NGOs also use Weibo to advertise and collect donations. For example, the user "Weichengdu," registered in October 2010, reported 4,337,057 fans by September of 2012. Its 9,423 posts have been cited and commented on more

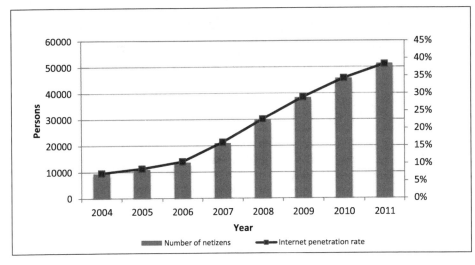

Figure 16. Number of Chinese Internet users and
Internet penetration rate, 2004–2011.

Source: CINIC 2012.

than two million times. In a high-profile example, Yao Ming, the international basketball star and founder of the Yao Ming Foundation, also uses Weibo to promote his foundation's work.

Globalization can have strong impacts, and China has been an interesting case study in that respect for some time. The involvement of new international actors (such as international nongovernmental organizations and other international web-based groups) has further contributed to changes in state-society relations. These organizations and groups offer new resources and opportunities for not only domestic NPOs but also for the state in areas of limited capacity. Though the government remains cautiously wary of these organizations, government agencies increasingly work on joint projects with NPOs in China. While the dynamics of the rise of civil society and social movements in China are still being analyzed, many elements of New Political Culture have emerged domestically and deserve further examination (see T. Clark and Lipset 2001). One element of the New Political Culture is the public emphasis on social problems that has gradually risen in salience (compared to financial and economic issues). The growth of people's wealth allows the dedication of more attention to lifestyle and consumption, not only to economic problems. Also, New Political Culture views are more pervasive among the younger, more educated, and more affluent individuals in the society. The above phenomena can be noted especially in some of the

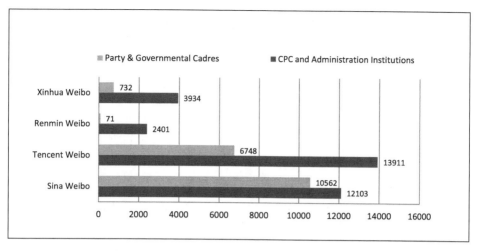

Figure 17. Registered governmental Weibos, 2012.

Source: Data translated from CNSA 2012.

economically developed coastal cities of China where student activism and other lifestyle-related movements have emerged, but such phenomena are not apparent in rural areas.

Another aspect of the New Political Culture is the rise of issue politics and broader citizen participation. As discussed, this new sort of citizen engagement has encouraged the government to respond more directly to its constituency. According to social capital theories like Tocqueville's and Putnam's, civic groups contribute to the generation of interpersonal trust. With the steady development of civic organizations in China, studies have also shown a relatively high level of interpersonal or "inner-circle" trust in society. However, membership in formal civic organizations does not seem to predict trust in China, but the lead international citizen surveys, such as the World Values Survey, lack information on citizens' informal participation outside of official organizational membership. In addition, there are different types of trust in China. Traditional trust, for instance, comes from family ties; trust that stems from the socialist system includes corporate trust, which is salient in many places in Asia; interpersonal trust has come about with market reforms in a country with new, higher levels of civic participation (Tang 2009). Different types of trust can simultaneously exist and can change from various different combinations of variables with civic development.

Many NGO "federations" have emerged, designed to permit horizontal interactions among organizations, especially in the field of environmental protection. Many of these federations are of government-organized NGOs

(GONGOs) and promote horizontal networking among organizations mostly in the form of conferences. This is a fairly new phenomenon and "cooperation" remains primarily in the form of attending joint conferences, rather than assuming projects or undertakings in a collaborative manner.

Status Quo and Challenges

With the rise of New Political Culture, Chinese citizens are, on one hand, becoming more willing to participate in different kinds of voluntary activities and join in NGOs. This is consistent with other findings suggesting that political transformations are acting on individuals' civic participation.

On the other hand, Chinese citizens are demanding transparency and accountability of their organizations, and public accounting of the money that such organizations spend as contracted agents of donors. Cases such as that of Guo Meimei, cited above, and other scandals have contributed to declining levels of public trust in NGOs and GONGOs especially.

In brief, the challenges of the budding nonprofit sector in China include (1) lack of social resources, such as funding and human resources limitations, (2) legislation limitations, (3) lack of professional capacity, (4) the lack of social monitoring mechanisms, and (5) lack of interaction among organizations within the sector. Still, despite these challenges, the development of China's social organizations has already become one of leading forces of China's coming social reform.

Case Studies

Anti-PX Protests

The Anti-PX movement in Xiamen in June 2007 was one of the most influential environmental movements in China in recent years (here we draw heavily on Zhang 2010). The case was so dramatic that it became widely discussed across China. It illuminates several general points of this chapter. PX, or paraxylene, a petrochemical used in polyester and fabrics, is understood to cause problems with the central nervous system. The 2007 movement saw ten to twenty thousand citizens marching along main streets and demonstrating in the city square on June 1 and 2 in Xiamen, a big industrial city in Fujian Province, southeast China, famous for its coastal resort.

In July 2006, the Xiamen government and the XL Corporation signed an agreement on the PX Plant, and construction began in August. However, as early as May 2005, some residents in the Haicang District had begun to meet to discuss the potential environmental consequences of the plant.

The citizens' groups appealed to groups from the bottom up, unsuccessfully. They first lodged a complaint to the Environmental Protection Bureau (EPB) of the Haicang District and the district government but received no reply. They then wrote a letter to the mayor of Xiamen. However, the mayor's office transferred the letter to the EPB of Xiamen and then to the EPB of Haicang District, and the letter was sucked into bureaucratic oblivion. Finally the citizens sent a petition with two thousand signatures to the SEPA and the State Development and Reform Commission (SDRC), the most powerful economic department in China and the strongest supporter of the PX project within the central government. The State News Agency refused to provide coverage of the citizens' objections, and the Green Cross (the best-known environmental group in Xiamen) refused to participate beyond providing basic information about PX. The Green Cross feared for its fate, as only NGOs that have a state department supervising them are considered legal, and the group was thus unwilling to engage in contention.

Thanks to the organizing efforts of Yufen Zhao, a Taiwanese-born professor of chemistry and member of the Chinese Academy of Sciences, the issue became one of salience, and national newspapers were able to report on it legally. The reports became issues of immediate concern to the public.

Mobilization around the PX plant took place primarily online because it was perceived to be safer than attracting the wrath of the Propaganda Department; in this case, the Internet served to amplify and disseminate public sentiment and provided a platform for organizing. Personal blogs, instant message programs, and text messages were understood to be more secure mechanisms of communications.

On May 20, an anonymous message began to spread throughout mobile users. It read: "The XL Corporation has begun to work on PX Plant, which would be like a nuclear bomb. Then our Xiamen citizens would live in a city with abundant diseases, and take a risk of total environmental pollution if a terrible accident happens to the PX Plant. We need life! We require health! International organizations have made a standard that this kind of project should be no less than 100 kilometers distant from the downtown, while PX leaves our city only 16 kilometers! For the good of our children, fight! Please join the march with another 10,000 citizens, beginning in the square of the City Hall from eight o'clock on June 1, 2008! Wear a Yellow Ribbon! Send this message to all your friends!" Activist Xiaolei Bao remembered, "we prepared for administrative lawsuit, but we knew that we would fail in the end. So the last solution was vote by foot: we move out [of] Haicang District and even Xiamen city."

Despite the anonymous mechanisms of social media and online communications, the state and the Propaganda Department did their best to crack down on the mobilization. The EPB printed hundreds of thousands of pamphlets and issued them widely. On May 26, messages sent through the Internet and mobile phones were checked. On May 28, the Xiaoyu online community—the platform on which a great deal of organizing occurred—was closed down; on May 30, an external *News Weekly* that had reported on the PX issue was prohibited from being sold in Xiamen, and all information about PX on websites around the city was deleted. Public school students were issued a notice that they were prohibited from participating in the mobilization. Also on May 30, the first deputy mayor of Xiamen announced that the PX plant construction would be postponed and that the city government would reevaluate the overall environmental impact using an independent organization. It was too late, however, for pacification—and the march occurred.

On June 1 and 2, tens of thousands of citizens assembled and marched; strikingly, the state did not repress the protest, and the march remained peaceful. Rank-and-file police officers, who were compelled by the same environmental concerns as ordinary citizens and did not have high positions to protect within the Communist Party, were able to protect rather than to police the protestors. They did so by permitting the protest to move throughout the city instead of corralling it, and by trying to minimize violence so that there would be no need for government repression. A participant remembered, "the policemen told us that we could do anything but [be violent]." Some police officers even wore the yellow Anti-PX armband that the other demonstrators sported. Further, and importantly, because of the unorganized and leaderless nature of the protest, the state had no way to negotiate with figureheads.

Because the Green Cross was hamstrung by its supervisory organization and other institutional mechanisms failed to produce the desired results, the Anti-PX movements emerged without organizational auspices; the mobilization occurred within the particular set of constraints in Chinese society. Social media and telephones played an important role, facilitating anonymous mobilization within a nondemocratic state, and helped participants evade regulators. The leaderless nature of the movement prevented negotiations, and the tacit support of low-level government officials (police officers) made the march both visible and nonviolent. This case study illustrates the particular set of tensions that civil society faces in China—high levels of government supervision even of purportedly independent agencies, the amplifying power of contemporary communications technology, and the value of quiet institutional support.

8. Looking Forward

*Understanding Associations
and Trust Patterns*

As we have shown throughout this book, associational life is common to human societies around the globe. Places like the teahouses of China, the Coliseum in Italy, and the Agora in Greece are surviving illustrations of how people throughout history have gathered, talking, sharing, and working out their differences, together.

Until Alexis de Tocqueville visited the United States, the political implications of associational life had not been considered in depth. When the young French aristocrat traveled America in the 1830s, he was impressed by the numerous civic groups formed wherein ordinary Americans voluntarily came together. Group theory emerged as a major perspective in the twentieth century, especially in US studies of government with Arthur Bentley, David Truman, Robert Dahl, and others. The focus shifted to how groups engage citizens after the late 1960s. Gabriel Almond, Sydney Verba, and Robert Putnam then stressed citizen participation and how it shifted political culture (e.g., Almond and Verba 1989). The core Tocquevillian theme has been a strong and consistent normative and positive argument for associational life—that it foments democratic participation and builds democratic values. Participation has classically been understood as voting and group activism, but in more recent years, scholars have added more focus on how participation can take multiple forms—demonstrations, advocacy, and even consumption patterns.

During recent decades, however, survey data have often shown that participating in elections has decreased. Those who do not participate in elections have also expressed less trust toward the principal institutions of democratic government, such as their representatives. This shift has occurred not just in the United States but in many democratic societies, creating what some have termed a "crisis of democracy" (Crozier, Huntington, and Watanuki 1975).

Various explanations have been proposed for this malaise, including a post-materialist value transformation (Inglehart, 1990), the rise of New Political Culture (T. Clark and Hoffmann-Martinot 1998) and critical citizen theory (Norris 1999). Putnam (2000) links the decline of democratic participation to a decline of civic engagement and erosion of social capital, arguing that in the last three or four decades common civic organizations, such as religious groups, parent-teacher associations, sports clubs, labor unions, and professional societies have also witnessed a substantial drop in membership. Putnam, in line with Tocqueville and with Almond and Verba, holds that many social benefits come from associational life: whether democracy works well largely depends on active civic engagement.

Among these social benefits, *trust* is particularly controversial. Trust is politically important because it acts as a social lubricant, decreasing transaction costs and enabling both social and market functions to transpire more smoothly. We here define trust broadly to include both trust in political institutions (what we term "political trust") and trust in other people (what we term "social trust"). Political trust is part of political capital and a cornerstone of political survival and development. Its absence may call the legitimacy of any regime into question (Easton 1975); when we do not trust political institutions, we have no incentive to uphold any specific set of social or political rules. Social trust is the core component of social capital (Putnam 1995), which is important for social integration, economic efficiency, and a healthily functioning government (Fukuyama 1996, 2001; Newton 2001; Putnam 1995; Uslaner 2002).

However, along with democratic participation, both political and social trust has been significantly decreasing in most democratic societies in recent decades. In this chapter, we ask whether this decrease in trust is specifically due to the decline in voluntary associations, as Putnam claims. Here, we probe some of the same data others have used, but we look more carefully at cross-national patterns. In contrast to Putnam, we find little evidence of a specific decline in associational life across fifteen countries, including the United States (Baer, Curtis, and Grabb 2001).

Specifically, we add more nuance to the claim that trust has "declined." For one, association and trust patterns vary dramatically by country. For example, Americans go to church and join associations; Chinese join few associations but trust their government and fellow citizens much more, confounding Putnam's theoretical claim. The puzzle makes the relationship between membership in voluntary organizations and trust one of the most important and widely discussed topics in the contemporary debate about democracy. If trust is declining but voluntary associations are not, then what generates this political trust, the glue that keeps democratic societies together?

In this chapter, we identify three patterns between associations and trust that emerge in different regions of the world. In some places and under some conditions, associations promote trust; in other places and under other conditions, associations increase *dis*trust. And in still other regions and under other conditions, associations have nothing to do with trust. We examine each pattern in turn below, arguing further that only with specific analyses of *types* of associations, firmly embedded in their specific contexts, can we capture coherent patterns linking associations and trust.

Pattern One: Associations Foster Trust

The first pattern is the claim that associations foster trust through their structure and the types of interaction that they produce. The relevance of associational membership for social trust was discussed long before the concept of "social capital" as such was introduced to political science. For example, Feld argued that voluntary associations fostered trust among citizens by enabling individuals to interact with others from different social realms (Feld 1981). Putnam, Fukuyama, and other followers of social capital theory have done work to support this idea.

Social capital refers to the components of social organization (including its networks, norms, and trust) that can facilitate coordination and cooperation for mutual benefit (Putnam 1993). Through face-to-face interactions, people learn to trust each other (Putnam 1995; Stolle 1998), and associations create networks that allow social trust to spread throughout society (Levi 1998; Putnam 1995, 2000). Different types of social connections, including informal social ties and nonpolitical groups (such as choral societies and bowling leagues, for example) can all benefit from citizens' trust (Putnam 1993, 2000). Fukuyama goes so far as to argue that sociability has the capacity to form *new bonds* of trust; for him, voluntary associations, together with the state and kinship ties, should be considered the three paths to sociability (Fukuyama 1996).

Voluntary organizations, the argument goes, provide a structure of norms, networks, and social sanctions that foster individuals' generalized trust. At the beginning, members of an association learn to trust each other by working together for common purposes in groups—by cooperating. They then develop social networks among themselves, which enhance and broaden their trust; finally, members spread their trust to a socially diverse group of others by the expanded voluntary association activities (Park and Subramanian 2012). The strong connection between associational life and trust has been frequently emphasized by systematic empirical investigations using survey data at different levels of analysis. For instance, using individual-level evidence, Brehm and Rahn demonstrated that people who participate extensively in their communities are more likely to have highly positive beliefs about the helpfulness, trustworthiness, and fairness of others (Brehm and Rahn 1997). This pattern holds internationally; having more connected voluntary associations increases trust across countries (e.g., Park and Subramanian 2012; Paxton 2002, 2007; Putnam 1995, 2000).

Similarly, people who are members of voluntary associations tend to be more politically active and show more trust toward democratic norms (Almond and Verba 1963; Hanks and Eckland 1978; Verba and Nie 1972). According to Almond, voluntary social interaction builds feelings of confidence and safety in the social environment, and the increasing of general social trust can be translated into politically relevant trust (Almond and Verba 1963). In fact, citizens' trust in other people and democratic institutions go together (Inglehart 1990). In other words, those who have a high level of trust in people are less likely to be cynical about politics and politicians (Rosenberg 1956).

Together, this work suggests that, at least in some cases, associational membership should foster social and political trust.

Pattern Two: Associations Do *Not* Foster Trust

Despite many empirical findings that suggest that associations and trust go hand-in-hand, there have been both theoretical and empirical arguments challenging this claim. Theoretically, Newton (1997) argues that relative to the family, workplace, school, and neighborhood, volunteering is a relatively unimportant source of trust. This is not only because people spend comparatively small amounts of time in voluntary associations, but also because those involvements involve lower levels of emotional commitment than, for example, families do. Paraphrasing Levi, Newton stresses that experiences and institutions, rather than membership specifically, are more likely to lead to the emergence of trust (see Newton 1997, 2001).

Others argue that by the time people join voluntary organizations (typically as teenagers or adults), their trust patterns are already formed; to attribute them to organizations is too little, too late (Brown and Uslaner, 2002). In other words, trust is a moral value and people learn it early in life from parents and other role models; it is thus more closely related to individual features of personality and subjective feelings picked up from early socialization. Social trust, for this intellectual camp, rests on feelings of optimism and agency at the individual level, and on economic equality at the aggregate level (Brown and Uslaner 2002; Uslaner 2000, 2002, 2007, 2008; Uslaner and Brown 2005).

Furthermore, participation in voluntary associations is just that—voluntary. Therefore, some scholars also argue that people who choose to join in associations *are those who trust others more than their non-association-joining counterparts in the first place*. Putnam himself argues that people who have faith in their fellow citizens are more likely to join civic organizations than those who don't (Putnam 1995), and thus the relationship between trust and associationalism may simply be a product of self-selection. Newton suggests that "social winners" are more trusting in general, and that those who join in voluntary organizations are often social winners with comparatively high levels of socioeconomic status. Instead of arguing that voluntary association experiences *build* trust, these scholars claim that the social backgrounds of being a social winner encourage both participation and trust (Newton 2001). Stolle finds that trusters are far more likely than distrusters to become members of associations (Stolle 1998). Even after joining, people with high levels of trust are more likely to engage in voluntary action, while those with low levels of trust may find problems in heterogeneous organizations and be more likely to leave them, or to not join in the first place (Bekkers 2012).

Empirically, the linkage between membership in voluntary organizations and trust has been questioned in much modern survey research. Stolle finds that, in Sweden, voluntary associations do not socialize their members into trusting other citizens, and the number of associations with which people are involved has no effect on levels of trust (Stolle 1998). Examining the origins of social trust in seven societies, Delhey and Newton conclude that there is only a weak link between voluntary membership and trust in some countries; in most countries in their study, in fact, voluntary organizations have no correlation at all with levels of generalized trust (Delhey and Newton 2003). In a sample of twenty-nine market economies from the World Values Survey, Knack and Keefer's study fails to find an association between memberships in formal groups and trust (Knack and Keefer 1997). More recently, a longitudinal study of time-intensive volunteering and social trust suggests that subjects' trust is relatively stable over time, and therefore associational life neither engenders that trust nor meaningfully alters it (Bekkers 2012). Glanville, by contrast, demonstrates that involvement in organizations has but a limited influence on trust, but that having a diversity of people in organizations does foster it (Glanville 2001).

In addition to the claim that voluntary associations don't foment political trust, other scholars argue that generalized social trust is not automatically transformed into political trust (J.-Y. Kim 2005). According to Newton, social trust and political trust do not have their origins in the same set of social conditions; they are different phenomena with different causes. Instead of voluntary associations, trust in political institutions is more likely to be determined by political factors (Newton 2001; Newton and Norris 1999). In a national study in Norway, for instance, researchers found no differences between passive and active organizational membership in creating social trust; they also found that there seems to be no real need for face-to-face interaction between members of associations for generalized trust and political trust to thrive (Rothstein and Stolle 2001). Similar results have also been found in Finland; passive members of associations are not categorically more distrusting than others (Kankainen 2009). This body of work argues as a whole that although associations are playing many crucial roles in society, we must not overestimate their importance in creating or enhancing trust.

In sum, in spite of a long and distinguished intellectual lineage suggesting that participation increases trust, this camp argues that the relationship between membership in voluntary organizations and trust remain empirically weak and somewhat patchy (Newton 2001).

Pattern Three: Associations Create Distrust

Finally, some studies have revealed an explicitly *negative* relationship between membership in voluntary associations and trust in both political institutions and in people. According to Tocqueville, the power of association is an assemblage of individual power primarily in combating the centralized power of government. From this perspective, it would be more reasonable to conclude that memberships in associations that stand in opposition to the government would only lead to *distrust* in political institutions (also see Brehm and Rahn 1997). We now examine scholarship on the third possibility—if and how associations might in fact cause *dis*trust.

Much political activity thrives on mistrust in political authority (Warren 1996). Thus, it would be odd enough to assume that joining in social protest groups or associations that stand in opposition to or are critical of the government would lead to *more* trust in government. Empirically, Kim suggests "bowling together" isn't a cure-all; in his study, when demographic factors were taken into account, associational involvement turned out to negatively impact political trust (J.-Y. Kim 2005).

The logic holds in some cases for social trust. In this vein, Rothstein and Stolle argue that instead of building trust, many associations destroy members' trust. The extreme examples are the parochial communities (Brinkley

1996) and the voluntary associations in Weimar Germany (Berman 1997), cases in which tight-knit associations foster fear of outsiders and exclusionary tendencies. Far from these extreme examples, many other voluntary associations (for example, some ethnic, religious, economic, and political organizations), have always been known to act in a way that distance themselves from the rest of the social world, therefore increasing members' distrust of each other (Rothstein and Stolle 2007). This empirical evidence suggests that some types of association are negatively related to trust (Glanville 2001; Kankainen 2009; Paxton 2002, 2007).

Do Types Matter?

As we have seen, studies exploring the relationship between associations and trust have emerged with mixed empirical results. What is clear is that voluntary associations are of crucial importance for people to gain social experience. For us, the real question here is not *whether* membership in associations influences trust, but *why* the effects of voluntary associations on trust are mixed. In other words, what is responsible for these differences?

Social capital theorists attribute the decline of trust to the erosion of civic associations, but the obvious rebuttal is that worldwide, the number and types of civic organizations are still increasing rapidly. To address the contradiction, Putnam distinguishes classic "secondary associations" from "tertiary associations," "nonprofit organizations" and "support groups," arguing that these vibrant new organizations don't typically play the same role as traditional civic associations (Putnam 1995), but rather they represent a different type of social involvement. Thus, *different types* of voluntary associations may have very different implications for trust. This suggests that paying more attention to types of association may help us understand variations in trust patterns.

Voluntary associations can be categorized in different ways. For example, there are "bonding organizations" that bring together similar people, and "bridging organizations" that connect dissimilar people (Putnam 2001). Members in bridging organizations are more likely to trust others, while those in bonding organizations do not trust others as much (Hooghe 2003; Stolle 1998; Stolle and Rochon 1998; Wollebaek and Selle 2002). There are "connected associations" that are linked to other voluntary associations through the multiple memberships of their participants, and "isolated associations" that operate independently of other organizations, and whose members hold multiple memberships. Studies have found that membership in connected associations creates more trust than membership in isolated associations (Paxton 2007).

Specifically, groups are organized around different themes: personal interest organizations, community organizations, economic groups, and political associations; and trust varies among them. Members in cultural, personal interest, and community organizations, according to Stolle and Rochon, have especially high levels of trust toward others and toward political institutions. Political associations, however, are less likely to be positively associated with both social trust and political trust (Stolle and Rochon 1998). Hence, at the individual level, members in bridging organizations, connected associations, and cultural, personal interest, and community organizations should be more trusting than those in bonding organizations, isolated associations, and political groups.

Moreover, the composition of associations also varies across countries and time periods. These differences may partially explain why scholars find that voluntary associations have mixed effects on trust at the national level (in other words, the *types* of organization in Sweden in 1949 may be different enough from the types of organizations in the United States in 2001 to produce different outcomes, even if membership rates are relatively stable). Based on the variations of voluntary associations and their different influence on trust, we might expect that countries (or settings) with *high numbers of bridging organizations, connected associations, cultural organizations, personal interest organizations, and community organizations would show more trust, while countries or settings with more bonding organizations, isolated associations, and political groups would demonstrate less trust.* Moreover, we must be sensitive to the ways in which types of organizations change over time. In Finland, for example, the flow of active association members has moved away from political and ideological associations and towards sports, cultural, and leisure associations. This may help explain the changing patterns of Finnish citizens' trust in recent decades (Kankainen 2009).

Keeping in mind that different types of associations are not equally beneficial in building trust, we aim in this chapter to bring *types* of association into the analysis, attempting to identify clearer patterns in a rather messy empirical debate. At the national level, we first explore the raw numbers. In other words, what are the most numerous types of associations in different national contexts?

Analysts using the World Values Survey have been exploring social and political change since 1981. The survey itself, widely held up as the gold standard of global research exploring individuals' values and beliefs internationally, consists of multiple waves of surveys with data from some one hundred countries. We use the fifth wave of the WVS, conducted from 2005 to 2008—the survey that specifically solicits information about membership in associations.*

In this wave of survey data, voluntary associations are categorized into eight groups: church/religious organizations; sports/recreation; art, music or educational organizations; labor unions; political parties; environmental organizations; professional organizations; and charitable/humanitarian organizations. More than eighty thousand individuals are interviewed across fifty-three countries. In this chapter, we combine "active members" and "inactive members" in voluntary associations. Our results show a huge difference in the types of voluntary associations people join across countries.

Religious organizations are among the most popular associations across the sampled societies. Roughly 40 percent of the total respondents indicated that they are affiliated with one or more religious organizations. However, the differences between countries are huge. In some places, such as Ghana, South Africa, and Zambia, most citizens (more than 80 percent) hold membership in religious organizations; while very few (less than 3 percent) in countries like Turkey and Egypt belong to any kind of religious organization. Dutch, English, Australian, Italian, and Norwegian citizens participate more in sports or recreation organizations than in any other kind. More than 30 percent of the populations of New Zealand, Britain, and Switzerland are active in charitable or humanitarian organizations, compared to less than 3 percent of Romanian, Turkish, and Egyptian citizens. Nearly 80 percent of Finns are members of religious associations, but they join few environmental organizations (9 percent); Sweden has the highest percentage of labor union membership in the world, while Ghana enjoys the highest level of membership in political parties.

The different configurations of associations are also striking among the six countries we have discussed in this book. Americans are generally quite religious (more than half say they go to church regularly). However, religion is no longer popular in France, despite its overwhelmingly Catholic history: only about 10 percent of French respondents say they hold membership in any religious organizations. French people are more active in recreation, charitable, and environmental associations. Even neighboring Asian countries show very different patterns. Religious people account for 10 percent or so of associational membership in China and Japan, but much more in

*The text of the question reads: "Now I am going to read out a list of voluntary organizations; for each one, could you tell me whether you are a member, an active member, an inactive member or not a member of that type of organization?"

Table 9. National differences in association membership, 2005–2008, as a percentage of total population

Country	Religious organization	Sports or recreation organization	Art, music, or educational organization	Labor unions	Political party	Environmental organization	Professional organization	Charitable or humanitarian
France	10.0	30.5	18.4	11.2	5.9	14.7	10.3	20.6
Great Britain	36.3	41.1	30.2	19.0	11.1	15.8	23.2	30.4
Italy	22.1	28.5	16.6	14.1	10.3	7.7	16.5	20.9
Netherlands	29.3	43.1	5.8	20.9	7.6	15.3	12.1	20.1
Spain	21.2	14.4	9.3	7.5	4.7	4.7	6.6	9.4
United States	65.9	27.9	26.6	16.8	47.7	15.8	24.1	28.5
Canada	50.4	43.1	35.7	26.0	17.4	16.5	28.6	24.7
Japan	11.7	26.2	15.1	9.5	6.4	4.5	13.1	4.5
Mexico	67.9	31.8	23.9	14.6	19.0	12.9	16.6	23.1
South Africa	82.3	35.5	27.1	19.7	35.2	19.8	17.7	19.1
Australia	42.7	26.7	26.7	18.3	9.6	13.5	25.3	27.9
Norway	37.9	42.1	20.3	49.2	17.1	7.3	25.2	31.6
Sweden	53.6	43.9	25.0	58.3	10.5	10.7	20.4	33.3
Finland	78.8	35.6	18.6	51.8	13.9	9.3	12.9	20.8
South Korea	43.4	34.6	22.6	9.8	7.4	7.5	8.6	9.1
Switzerland	53.9	49.9	20.8	14.2	15.5	23.8	29.7	33.6
Brazil	75.6	19.3	14.1	18.9	10.2	7.1	14.0	19.5
Slovenia	28.7	29.9	16.6	20.0	6.9	6.8	12.5	17.3
Bulgaria	4.3	2.9	2.7	7.0	5.2	1.4	2.8	2.0
Romania	9.7	2.0	1.8	6.6	3.8	0.7	1.7	1.2
China	9.6	16.6	14.0	12.7	12.7	10.1	6.8	7.8
Taiwan	19.2	19.0	10.1	9.0	5.9	5.4	14.6	16.2
Turkey	2.4	3.3	2.9	2.8	5.3	1.2	2.8	2.2
Russia	11.1	12.7	9.9	16.8	5.3	4.6	7.2	5.7
Ghana	92.1	39.8	39.1	21.8	50.9	26.1	19.0	20.8
Thailand	36.2	25.9	23.1	18.2	16.7	19.8	23.0	18.8
Vietnam	11.7	14.3	9.3	11.5	16.0	10.7	15.6	15.4
New Zealand	39.7	50.9	34.6	16.6	14.7	17.9	29.3	33.6
Egypt	1.6	5.3	1.5	1.3	4.4	1.2	10.9	2.5
Morocco	4.6	12.4	7.2	7.8	2.7	1.9	6.1	4.9
Andorra	35.2	47.7	40.0	10.3	9.5	14.3	16.8	22.4
Ethiopia	79.0	50.5	43.8	22.4	24.6	27.8	21.2	28.2
Zambia	94.5	47.3	40.1	22.0	39.4	20.8	28.4	25.1
Germany	36.0	35.4	13.7	11.9	5.0	5.0	8.8	10.2
Average	38.2	29.1	19.6	17.6	14.1	11.3	15.7	18.0

Source: Data from the World Value Survey 2008.

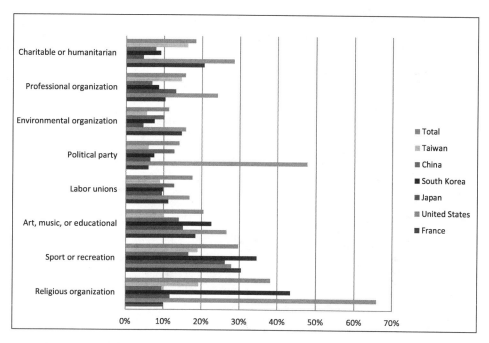

Figure 18. Membership in associations in the six profiled countries, as a percentage of total population.

Source: World Values Survey 2008.

South Korea and Taiwan. As shown in figure 18, other types of organizations also vary dramatically across these countries.

Our analysis also showed that *types* of voluntary associations in which citizens participate did indeed change across time periods. Membership in church-related groups, labor unions, and humanitarian organizations (such as the Red Cross) has been declining since the 1960s in America and elsewhere. However, some other types of associations have been growing during the same time period. For example, the United States, West Germany, and the Netherlands exhibit significant increases in working memberships (Baer, Curtis, and Grabb 2001). Similarly, Clark et al. find that some organizations may be dropping (bowling and Kiwanis clubs, for example), while arts and expressive organizations particularly are mushrooming (including cultural organizations, musical groups, dance companies, and sports facilities). Moreover, these developments are uneven: for instance, the strongest growth in cultural organizations is found in the Netherlands, Scandinavia, the United States, and Canada (T. Clark et al. 2014). Indeed, as shown in figure 19, there is overall growth in cultural organization membership from

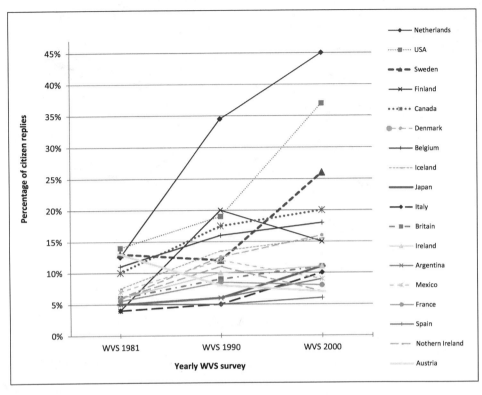

Figure 19. Variations in cultural activities, 1981–2000.

Source: Data are from World Values Surveys of national samples of citizens in each selected country. The Y-coordinate indicates the percent of citizens who replied that they participated in cultural or related activities across three study years.

1981 to 2000. At the same time, we find declines in some countries, such as Austria and Finland.

Other sources of data consistently support this observation: people in different countries join very different types of organizations (and it would follow, logically, that these different organizations produce different outcomes in terms of trust). For example, we downloaded information from the electronic Yellow Pages (often published as "telephone books") on thousands of organizations and associations and their street addresses for all of the United States and France, in order to look for the leading types of associations in each country. We found dramatic differences between the two countries. In France, we found many human rights and related social service organizations.

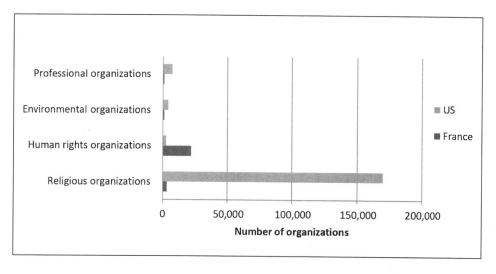

Figure 20. Total organizations by type in France and the United States.
Source: Data from the World Values Survey 2008.

By contrast, churches were a very small proportion of all organizations. In the United States, the opposite pattern emerges: churches are by far the most numerous type of organizations (some 70 percent of all US organizations are churches and church-related associations).

That voluntary association membership varies dramatically among nations has long been documented. Various studies show that national differences in economic development, religious composition, state structure, political institutions, culture, and so on channel the growth of very different types of organizations across societies and time (Curtis, Baer, and Grabb 2001; Duncan 2006; Schofer and Fourcade-Gourinchas 2001). At the individual level, although globalization makes people more alike, individuals from rich/poor, Western/Eastern, and even warm/cold countries still have different tastes toward different types of voluntary organizations. Therefore, specifically taking types of organization into account can offer new insights into associations between voluntary organizations and trust.

A Preliminary Examination

In this final section, we use data from the fifth wave of the World Values Survey conducted across more than fifty countries between 2005 and 2008 for a preliminary examination of how membership of different types of organizations may impact citizens' trust in both people and political institutions. Because of our large sample, we were able to delete all missing data of each in-use variable and still retain an N of 51,338 for analysis.

The study variable is trust, which we divide into "social trust" and "political trust." We use the question "Can most people be trusted?" in the WVS to measure social trust. Social trust then is coded as "0" for the response "we must be very careful in dealing with people" and "1" for "most people can be trusted." We use "trust in government" as the simple measurement of another dependent variable, political trust. For the purpose of comparison, we code political trust variable as "0" for response categories none at all (1) and not very much (2); we code as "1" response categories quite a lot (3) and a great deal (4). Therefore both social trust and political trust become binary variables.

For independent variables we drew on a list of questions in the WVS specifically asking about different types of organizations in which respondents may hold membership (either as active or inactive members). The list included groups such as religious organizations, environmental organizations, political parties, labor unions, and art, music, or educational organizations. We coded all of these independent variables by responder self-identification: "0" means "not a member," "1" is an "inactive member," and "2" is an "active member." Unfortunately, we could not find a way to categorize these organizations through either Putnam's "bonding organizations" and "bridging organizations" or Paxton's "connected associations" and "isolated associations"—a future research agenda would empirically test these. Instead, we test how each specific type of organization affects people's trust both in other people and in the government. Besides the types of associational membership, we included major demographics as our control variables, such as gender, age, education, and income plus several variables empirically identified as key predictors for social and political trust, such as satisfaction with life (Uslaner 2008), political interest (Putnam 2000) and postmaterialist values (Delhey and Newton 2003).

Table 10 shows the descriptive statistics for all variables analyzed. Most people (74 percent) in the world do not report trusting in others. Trust in government is much higher; about 46 percent of people trust their governments, worldwide. The mean score of "life satisfaction" is 6.85, which means that people in the most countries are moderately satisfied with their lives. The political interest score is also above the midpoint, suggesting that people are generally moderately politically interested as well. However, in these descriptive statistics, most people in the world are more materialist than postmaterialist.

Table 10. Descriptive statistics for key variables used in analysis, 2005–2008

Variable	Description	Percent	Mean	SD	Min	Max
Dependent Variable						
Social trust	1 = trust; 0 = distrust	26%	—	—	0	1
Political trust	1 = trust; 0 = distrust	46%	—	—	0	1
Control Variable						
Female	1 = female; 0 = male	51%	—	—	0	1
Age	Respondent's age	—	41.71	16.43	15	98
Education	1 = inadequately elementary to 8 = university with degree	—	4.54	2.0	1	8
Income	1 = lower step to 10 = tenth step	—	4.83	2.28	1	10
Life satisfaction	1 = dissatisfied to 10 = satisfied	—	6.85	2.19	1	10
Political interest	1 = not interested to 4 = very interested	—	2.41	0.95	1	4
Postmaterialist	1 = materialist to 5 = postmaterialist	—	2.03	1.20	1	5
Organization Membership						
Church/religious		—	0.62	0.81	0	2
Sports/recreation		—	0.44	0.75	0	2
Art, music, or educational		—	0.32	0.66	0	2
Labor unions	0 = not a member	—	0.24	0.55	0	2
Political party	1 = inactive member	—	0.22	0.53	0	2
Environmental	2 = active member	—	0.18	0.49	0	2
Professional		—	0.23	0.56	0	2
Charitable/humanitarian		—	0.27	0.60	0	2
Consumer		—	0.13	0.41	0	2

Source: Data from the World Values Survey 2008.

Religious organizations are one of the most popular organizations in the world, followed by sports/recreation organizations and art, music, or educational organizations. Environmental and consumer organizations are among the least popular organizations in general.

However, specifics vary across countries. Table 11 details the descriptive statistics for the six countries on which we mainly focus in this book. People from these six countries join very different types of organizations; trust also varies a great deal. Chinese respondents report the highest levels of both social trust and political trust, consistent with other surveys. Unlike in China, however, people in three other Asian societies (Japan, Taiwan, and South Korea) report lower levels of trust: 25 to 43 percent of people in these countries express trust in people and in government. France is a low-trust society, where social trust is only 19 percent and political trust is 29 percent. Americans have similar levels of trust as people in Korea, Japan, and Tai-

Table 11. Descriptive statistics for six countries (mean), 2005–2008

Variable	China	Taiwan	Japan	Korea	US	France
Dependent variable (%)						
Social trust	55%	25%	39%	30%	40%	19%
Political trust	93%	34%	30%	46%	39%	29%
Control variable						
Female (%)	49%	49%	53%	50%	49%	52%
Age	43.28	43.69	47.50	41.32	47.73	46.36
Education	4.08	5.34	6.06	6.37	4.80	4.01
Income	4.14	4.47	4.86	4.89	5.05	3.61
Life satisfaction	7.09	6.68	6.99	6.42	7.32	6.87
Political interest	2.92	1.97	2.78	2.28	2.67	2.14
Postmaterialist	1.32	1.22	2.12	1.88	2.01	2.62
Organization membership						
Church/religious	0.12	0.27	0.14	0.64	1.03	0.14
Sports/recreation	0.30	0.29	0.45	0.51	0.46	0.53
Art, music, or educational	0.26	0.14	0.26	0.36	0.42	0.30
Labor unions	0.23	0.14	0.14	0.10	0.23	0.16
Political party	0.24	0.09	0.08	0.09	0.70	0.07
Environmental	0.19	0.07	0.05	0.10	0.22	0.20
Professional	0.14	0.24	0.06	0.12	0.45	0.29
Charitable/humanitarian	0.14	0.24	0.06	0.12	0.45	0.29
Consumer	0.15	0.03	0.04	0.08	0.14	0.09
Total (N)	1046	1204	692	1154	1043	828

Source: Data from the World Values Survey 2008.

wan (about 40 percent). Compared to other countries, Chinese citizens also have the highest level of interest in politics. Citizens in China and Taiwan are more materialistic, while Japanese, French, and US citizens report more postmaterialist values.

Because we coded both social trust and political trust as binary variables, we applied logistic regression analysis to understand how these organization memberships affect trust. Three sets of logistic regressions were estimated. For the first (table 12), we included all surveyed countries and compared how the memberships of different types of organization impact social trust and political trust. For the second set of models (table 13), we detailed the six countries in this book and estimated impacts of different types of organizations on social trust for each country. Similarly, we estimated a third set of models on political trust for each country (table 14). In both the second and third set of models we also included all surveyed countries for comparison.

Table 12 (on p. 208) shows our first logistic regression results. Model 1 is the effect of the "membership of organization on social trust" multivariate regression. Model 2 is the effect of the "membership of organization on political trust" regression. These results confirm past findings that participation in voluntary associations *does* have impacts on both social and political trust.

However, we also find that the relationships vary for different types of organizations and for political and social trust. After controlling for major demographic factors, for life satisfaction, and for postmaterialist values, membership in religious, political, and consumer organizations has a negative influence on social trust. On the other hand, participating in churches and political parties has a positive influence on people's trust in their government. Memberships in labor unions and in sports, educational, professional, and charitable associations significantly increases people's trust in other people, but there are no noteworthy relationships between these organizations and people's trust in government. Environmental organizations have no significant impact on social trust but positively impact political trust. Members of consumer organizations have lower trust in other people, but their trust in government is not affected by their participation.

We should also note that, as in prior research, our study found that life satisfaction increases trust in both people and government. Interest in politics—a control variable for us—has a positive impact on political trust. Having postmaterialist values means being critical of common social practices, and critical citizens tend to have less trust in government (Norris 1999). We find, however, that people with postmaterialist values tend to have *more* trust in people. For now, we can conclude that joining different types of associations has very different implications for trust. Some types of associational life, as we have shown here, breed trust, while others will decrease trust.

Moreover, social trust is also very different from political trust. In fact, we find that organization memberships that increase social trust tend to have negative impact on political trust, while those memberships positively related to political trust are negative with trust in general. On close examination, we see that the organizations that increase people's trust in government tend to have close relationships with political institutions, such as political parties and religious churches, while organizations that build people's trust in others are more local and work more closely with grassroots groups, such as sports groups or art, music, and educational organizations. On the one hand, the rise of local social organizations is at least partly related to the failures of government, or social and market failures. Nongovernmental organizations often play a negotiating role with government, perhaps fomenting distrust of political institutions among people holding memberships in these types of organizations. On the other hand, more hierarchical organizations have a tradition of collaboration with the government, and joining in these types of

Table 12. Logit models predicting the effect of organization membership on trust

Variable	Model 1 (Social Trust)	Model 2 (Political Trust)
Organization membership		
Church/religious	−0.095***	0.095***
	(0.014)	(0.012)
Sports/recreation	0.117***	−0.002
	(0.015)	(0.014)
Art, music, or educational	0.035*	−0.025
	(0.018)	(0.016)
Labor unions	0.091***	−0.015
	(0.020)	(0.018)
Political party	−0.049*	0.237***
	(0.022)	(0.020)
Environmental	0.021	0.097***
	(0.025)	(0.023)
Professional	0.101***	−0.039*
	(0.021)	(0.019)
Charitable/humanitarian	0.095***	0.018
	(0.020)	(0.018)
Consumer	−0.61*	0.010
	(0.029)	(0.027)
Controls		
Female	−0.003	0.042*
	(0.021)	(0.018)
Age	0.015***	−0.003***
	(0.001)	(0.001)
Education	0.095***	−0.068***
	(0.005)	(0.004)
Income	0.041***	0.024***
	(0.005)	(0.004)
Life satisfaction	0.114***	0.092***
	(0.005)	(0.004)
Postmaterialist	0.157***	−0.116***
	(0.009)	(0.008)
Political interest		0.237***
		(0.010)
Constant	−3.519***	−0.939***
	(0.059)	(0.051)
Total (N)	51338	51338

Standard errors in parenthesis
*p < 0.05, ** p < 0.001, ***p < 0.001
Source: Authors' calculations using data from the World Values Survey 2008.

Table 13. Logit models predicting the effect of organization membership on social trust

Variable	Model 1 Total	Model 2 China	Model 3 Taiwan	Model 4 Japan	Model 5 South Korea	Model 6 US	Model 7 France
Organization Membership							
Church/religious	−0.095***	−0.178	0.172	−0.067	0.145	0.054	0.374*
	(0.014)	(0.174)	(0.124)	(0.190)	(0.091)	(0.084)	(0.182)
Sports/recreation	0.117***	0.080	0.112	0.069	0.018	0.108	0.125
	(0.015)	(0.138)	(0.115)	(0.106)	(0.097)	(0.091)	(0.118)
Art, music, or	0.035*	0.037	−0.106	0.172	0.037	−0.044	−0.091
educational	(0.018)	(0.142)	(0.159)	(0.136)	(0.118)	(0.102)	(0.149)
Labor unions	0.091***	−0.202	−0.040	0.286	0.359	−0.197	0.135
	(0.020)	(0.136)	(0.179)	(0.199)	(0.233)	(0.125)	(0.181)
Political party	−0.049*	0.292*	−0.510	0.457	−0.680*	0.133	0.104
	(0.022)	(0.135)	(0.261)	(0.268)	(0.323)	(0.094)	(0.283)
Environmental	0.021	−0.168	−0.061	0.242	0.557*	0.276	−0.101
	(0.025)	(0.201)	(0.238)	(0.315)	(0.246)	(0.142)	(0.202)
Professional	0.101***	−0.042	−0.214	0.059	−0.062	0.024	−0.011
	(0.021)	(0.239)	(0.164)	(0.161)	(0.207)	(0.112)	(0.199)
Charitable/	0.095***	0.072	0.284*	−0.037	0.569*	−0.058	0.005
humanitarian	(0.020)	(0.230)	(0.135)	(0.306)	(0.231)	(0.103)	(0.162)
Consumer	0.061*	0.254	0.704*	−0.201	−0.984**	0.037	0.019
	(0.029)	(0.198)	(0.335)	(0.364)	(0.328)	(0.158)	(0.288)
Controls							
Female	−0.003	−0.115	0.042	0.274	0.039	0.115	−0.038
	(0.021)	(0.130)	(0.145)	(0.176)	(0.142)	(0.138)	(0.194)
Age	0.015***	0.005	−0.014**	0.005	−0.008	0.016***	0.015**
	(0.001)	(0.005)	(0.005)	(0.006)	(0.006)	(0.004)	(0.006)
Education	0.095***	0.071*	0.166***	0.167**	0.010*	0.288***	0.239***
	(0.005)	(0.032)	(0.038)	(0.055)	(0.050)	(0.058)	(0.047)
Income	0.041***	−0.011	0.053	0.011	−0.008	0.025	−0.080
	(0.005)	(0.037)	(0.045)	(0.030)	(0.042)	(0.039)	(0.050)
Life satisfaction	0.114***	0.098***	0.088*	0.189***	0.169***	0.142***	0.134*
	(0.005)	(0.029)	(0.039)	(0.049)	(0.039)	(0.043)	(0.057)
Postmaterialist	−0.157***	−0.072	0.118	0.074	0.088	0.122*	0.256**
	(0.009)	(0.060)	(0.070)	(0.072)	(0.071)	(0.054)	(0.080)
Constant	−3.519***	−0.841*	−2.600***)	3.558***	−2.646***	−4.249***	−4.671***
	(0.059)	(0.381)	(0.462	(0.609)	(0.603)	(0.484)	(0.595)
Total (N)	51338	1046	1204	692	1154	1043	828

Standard errors in parenthesis

*p < 0.05, ** p < 0.001, ***p < 0.001

Source: Authors' calculations using data from the World Values Survey 2008.

Table 14. Logit models predicting the effect of organization membership on political trust

Variable	Model 1 Total	Model 2 China	Model 3 Taiwan	Model 4 Japan	Model 5 South Korea	Model 6 US	Model 7 France
Organization Membership							
Church/religious	0.095***	0.055	0.134	0.374*	0.040	0.355***	0.234
	(0.012)	(0.399)	(0.111)	(0.191)	(0.084)	(0.085)	(0.171)
Sports/recreation	−0.002	−0.232	−0.077	0.119	0.201*	−0.040	−0.051
	(0.014)	(0.239)	(0.107)	(0.113)	(0.091)	(0.092)	(0.104)
Art, music, or	−0.025	−0.494*	0.044	−0.022	−0.131	0.025	0.027
educational	(0.016)	(0.238)	(0.152)	(0.147)	(0.111)	(0.104)	(0.132)
Labor unions	−0.015	0.207	−0.115	−0.064	0.002	−0.342**	−0.387*
	(0.018)	(0.297)	(0.151)	(0.226)	(0.219)	(0.132)	(0.189)
Political party	0.237***	0.900*	−0.015	−0.046	−0.186	−0.041	−0.323
	(0.020)	(0.432)	(0.193)	(0.271)	(0.251)	(0.103)	(0.293)
Environmental	0.097***	0.343	−0.056	0.007	0.202	−0.099	−0.226
	(0.023)	(0.438)	(0.207)	(0.325)	(0.234)	(0.150)	(0.184)
Professional	−0.039*	−0.217	0.126	−0.200	−0.014	0.101	0.111
	(0.019)	(0.471)	(0.135)	(0.180)	(0.191)	(0.115)	(0.170)
Charitable/	0.018	0.796	0.039	0.176	0.048	−0.021	0.085
humanitarian	(0.018)	(0.571)	(0.128)	(0.314)	(0.218)	(0.105)	(0.140)
Consumer	0.010	−0.271	−0.020	−0.163	−0.079	−0.194	0.218
	(0.027)	(0.358)	(0.333)	(0.389)	(0.253)	(0.168)	(0.240)
Controls							
Female	0.042*	0.391	−0.249	0.059	0.554***	0.043	0.077
	(0.018)	(0.263)	(0.130)	(0.189)	(0.132)	(0.140)	(0.164)
Age	−0.003***	0.002	0.007	0.017*	0.008	−0.006	0.007
	(0.001)	(0.011)	(0.005)	(0.007)	(0.006)	(0.004)	(0.005)
Education	−0.068***	−0.173**	−0.062	0.081	0.011	−0.090	0.065
	(0.004)	(0.062)	(0.032)	(0.057)	(0.043)	(0.058)	(0.041)
Income	0.024***	0.009	0.004	−0.039	0.071	0.039	−0.018
	(0.004)	(0.073)	(0.038)	(0.033)	(0.038)	(0.039)	(0.043)
Life satisfaction	0.092***	0.168**	0.110***	0.188***	0.118***	0.162***	0.127***
	(0.004)	(0.054)	(0.033)	(0.054)	(0.034)	(0.043)	(0.046)
Postmaterialist	−0.166***	−0.093	0.120	−0.205**	0.003	−0.336***	−0.079
	(0.008)	(0.112)	(0.063)	(0.077)	(0.064)	(0.057)	(0.066)
Political interest	0.237***	0.566***	0.194*	0.260*	0.252*	0.158	0.274**
	(0.010)	(0.135)	(0.075)	(0.130)	(0.084)	(0.089)	(0.093)
Constant	−0.939***	0.485	−1.879***	−3.710***	−2.604***	−1.154*	−2.711***
	(0.051)	(0.773)	(0.410)	(0.670)	(0.553)	(0.473)	(0.480)
Total (N)	51338	1046	1204	692	1154	1043	828

Standard errors in parenthesis
*p < 0.05, ** p < 0.001, ***p < 0.001
Source: Authors' calculations using data from the World Values Survey 2008.

organizations breeds people's trust in that government. In other words, it is the contrasting features of these two types of organizations that lead to their different implications for social trust and political trust. Still other unmeasured factors may shift some of these patterns in ways that complicate specific results.

Table 14 shows our second logistic regression results. Model 1 is the same as the second model in table 12 and includes all the countries surveyed in the WVS. Models 2–7 are the "membership of organization on social trust" multivariate regression models for each of the six countries in this book.

We showed earlier that different types of membership have different implications for social and political trust. Table 13 demonstrates that even the same type of organization *has very different impact on trust across different countries.* For instance, religious organizations have negative influence on people's trust in others in general terms (model 1); however, a positive association holds in France between social trust and religious organizations (model 7). Similarly, political parties are negatively associated with social trust generally (model 1) and in South Korea (model 5); while in China, members of political parties have more social trust than nonmembers (model 2). Consumer organizations increase social trust in Taiwan (model 3) but decrease trust in South Korea (model 5). The effects of control variables, such as education level and life satisfaction, on social trust are found significant and consistent across countries.

The final set of models (table 14) estimates the effect of membership of different types of organizations on trust in government across the six countries. Membership in religious organizations is positively related to political trust in both Japan (model 4) and the United States (model 6), but not in other countries. Membership in sports or recreation organizations is associated with higher levels of trust in the government in Korea (model 5). Chinese citizens who are members of art, music, or educational associations tend to have less trust in government, but political party members have more trust in their government (model 2). Similarly, control variables, such as life satisfaction, political interest, and postmaterialist values, have consistent impact on political trust across countries.

This analysis provides substantial support for our general hypothesis that *different types* of voluntary associations have very different implications for trust, and that social and political trust are two distinct phenomena, associated with different sources. Several of our other findings about demographic characteristics and some basic attitudes/values are consistent with past work, which adds confidence in the cumulative patterns that have emerged in many studies on trust. Yet our distinct addition of types of organizations clearly adds to past work. These results fit with a general theme in other chapters, that many patterns of social organizations are contextually specific, and historically conditioned. We should try to think more about how contexts work, specifically, rather than searching for universal patterns and reporting "inconsistent" results within a deeply abstract ideal. To help codify these sorts of specific patterns between associations and trust demands more attention to the specific types of organizations.

Conclusion

Global Themes

Throughout this book, we have assessed experiences from around the world that provide a range of options to policymakers, point to some good ideas, and include links to further information. Some options are attractive and simple; others are complex and have multiple consequences that no one is certain about. We seek to be open and frank about the state of knowledge, which is always partial. We have shown that different cultural, economic, and political backgrounds have created very different third sectors in different countries (especially differences in the degree of state involvement with nonprofits). At the same time, globalization and worldwide technological innovations have spurred global convergence on some trends, like the rise of environmental concerns.

Additionally, we have uncovered other broad patterns. In the West, for example (the United States and France, in this book), we see third sectors emerging primarily in opposition to institutionalized forces, either the government (the United States), or the state and church (France). Only later in the sector's development did civic groups begin to overtly cooperate with government agencies, creating a less contentious and more collaborative set of relationships. Conversely, in much of Asia we see the development of social organizations in conjunction with strong central states (think of China), that have, in recent years, undertaken some of the political functions, such as advocacy and occasionally dissent, that characterize nonprofit sectors in other parts of the world. Both models can be successful, though they face different challenges.

A major finding of this work is that the third sector can offer powerfully positive solutions for political and social life, including *service, innovation, advocacy, expressiveness, and community building.* The degree to which these outcomes occur, of course, depends on political and cultural context, combined with specific policies in the third sector area. As political leaders globally seek to show more responsiveness to citizens, it is often more efficient to deal with civil organizations than individual citizens. Here follow some concrete examples of trends and specific points that provide options, which policymakers may wish to consider.

Theme One: State Interaction

The question of third sector interaction with the state is perhaps one of the most critical of this book. And indeed, we have documented a range of relationships. We return here to our formulations of nonprofit relationships and institutional logics: clientelism, paternalism, bureaucracy, activism, and professionalization. As we noted in chapter 1, the issue is not to ask if one institutional logic is the correct interpretation throughout the world, but rather to examine them all for insights into associative life and the third sector generally at different times and different places.

We have found that relationships with the state run the spectrum. Contemporarily, all the third sectors examined here have at least some degree of complementarity with the national governments of their countries, apparent in institutional logics of bureaucracy and professionalization. In Asian countries, there has been more recent movement toward independence from the state (an institutional logic of activism), while in the West, there has been increased movement toward complementary relations.

The US third sector developed early in the country's history and stamped the country's political development at the outset. In the United States, with its history of weak government, the third sector is seen as playing an essential role in providing services—supplementing those that the state provided—as well as in organizing and generating political diversity (at times adversarially), and engendering social capital.

In Asia, the developmental pattern was almost the opposite. Japan has a strong statist tradition, but natural disasters in the country hastened the development of charitable giving, and thus an increased tolerance of third sector organizations because they were seen to supplement state shortcomings in delivery of aid. The current registration system for NPOs in Japan remains strict and requires ministerial authorization, limiting the overall number of legally registered civic organizations. Civic organizations in Korea also served as government collaborators, creating jobs for the public at times of economic and social downturns. Though there is no general law for social

Table 15. Response to the question: Having encountered something unfair, which department would you want to turn to?

	Frequency	Percentage
Supervisor	173	14.61%
Local government	582	49.16%
Court	190	16.05%
Union, Communist youth group, etc. social groups	25	2.11%
Nongovernmental organization	40	3.38%
Other	171	14.44%
Missing	3	0.25%
Total	1,184	100%

Source: China General Social Survey 2006.

organizations in Korea, organizations need ministerial authorization to be officially registered. The Korean state remains wary of NPOs and offers only a narrow margin of fundraising to prevent them from becoming too financially independent from the government. Taiwanese civic organizations also faced strong state involvement at the onset, but with the opening up of the regulations, third sector organizations were able to increase citizen participation, becoming membership-based organizations that have more autonomy in their funding structure. Japan, Korea, and China pose strict regulations on the registration of social organizations, a practice that may inhibit third sector growth, and further limit development of horizontal third sector coordination and communication. All three of these countries could be characterized as somewhat lacking in international nonprofit coordination efforts. In Korea, however, with the development of information technology, coalitions among third sector organizations have become increasingly common.

In China, high state involvement in the third sector has influenced the extent to which individuals participate in social organization activities. That is to say, the public anticipates leadership by the government as a problem solver in China—so when the public is faced with choices in addressing grievances or problems, they more often choose government channels over nongovernmental organizations. Chinese citizens responding to the China General Social Survey strongly prefer going to their local government over nongovernmental organizations (see table 15).

With third sector participation higher in the United States, civic organizations can promote social cohesion and interactions among individuals, acting as a mediator in a country with a long history of suspicion toward the central state. Historically, some scholars of civil society in China have treated it as a "counter-elite structure"; however, Clark and others have made a strong argument in favor of a New Political Culture in China, which sees associational life and civil society as less revolutionary per se and more related to ideas of participation, consumption, and service delivery that are unique to this political context (see chapter 7 of this volume).

In France, on the other hand, the third sector (uniquely labeled the "social economy" in French) was not created as an aggregate consequence of private groups attempting to solve social problems, as in the United States, nor as system of third-party governance organizations, as in many places in Asia. Rather, the French third sector formed as a consequence of an ideological struggle between the Catholic Church and Republicanism over the rights of the individual. The French third sector has been marked by a strong statist presence in which the institutional logic of bureaucracy was most prominent. Developing under a strong state, third sector organizations in France collaborated with the government in solving socioeconomic problems, and gradually, the state's attitude toward these organizations shifted from hostility to tolerance to eventual cooperation, moving closer to patterns like those in countries such as Japan and China.

France's experience, and those of the Asian countries considered in this book, help to debunk the common myth that contemporary third sectors are essentially antistate. As we have shown, the relationships with governments are complex—they depend on the country and its religious and cultural history, but also the type, function, and funding of the organizations themselves.

In recent decades we see a partial convergence on the matters of community cohesion and citizen participation. Financial support from the government has increased in the United States since the 1960s, but this has led to the bureaucratization of many nonprofit organizations, wherein organizations may take on the "color" of the state and lose the autonomy that can make their inputs valuable. Many other countries grapple with this challenge, and it is a significant one: there are real benefits to government and community collaboration, and the balance of integration and autonomy can be difficult. Third sector autonomy remains a constant issue; autonomy depends on levels of government funding, on legal setups, and on the (formal or informal) political relationship between the organization and government.

Theme Two: Participation

Alexis de Tocqueville's observations on the function of small civic groups in the United States set the theoretical expectation that such groups are largely responsible for the high degrees of civic participation in the United States. A great deal of work, both theoretical and empirical, has addressed this claim in the past thirty years.

With the publication of Putnam's (2000) *Bowling Alone*, policymakers and scholars began to ask themselves about the fate of democracy in an era of declining participation in traditional civic groups. It became a bestseller, as it detailed decline in classic civic groups of the sort Tocqueville studied—neighborhood associations, service groups like Lions and Boy Scouts, and so forth. But we have stressed how it underplayed the role of the Internet, social media, the arts, and other new forms of social engagement that are particularly important with younger citizens in many countries. These new patterns we have termed "New New Social Movements," NNSMs, to underscore their lack of classic organizational character—membership, dues, officers, and so on. Further, much civic organization has incorporated activities that engage the participants and audience in an explicitly emotional manner. For instance, they use makeup, costuming, dancing, or other symbols designed to attract paparazzi that can capture the drama for others via TV or the Internet. Preparations for these demonstrations are a focal point for recruitment of new participants, although often there is no organization; it is more a diffuse movement of people who come together as they feel engaged to participate. They increasingly involve music, art, dancing in part as these seem to build more heat among the participants and communicate powerfully to others via mass media. They help create what we have analyzed as "scenes," which energize associations. Clark et al. (2014) and Silver and Clark (2016) go further, suggesting that consumption and participation in "scenes" can in some cases augment and even substitute for organized participation.

Scenes join people in a physical space via activities often focused on consumption issues and lifestyle: peace rallies, immigrant protests, coffee house conversations. Street scenes can embody the spontaneous activism of many third sector activists, but scenes do not require any organization. They may be violent or peaceful, as in candlelight protests in Korea. Scenes as activist settings thus overlap with the NNSMs discussed in the introduction. Emotional engagement heightened by music and dance, combined with physical presence at a powerful scene, captures the activist part of our institutional logic of activism. Indeed, some third sector activists feel tempted to drop out of their movements to avoid institutional clientelism, bureaucracy, paternalism, and professionalism. Some do, such as an Indonesian/Australian woman, who lived in New Orleans during Hurricane Katrina, quit her job, and formed a nursing volunteer organization to help in Katrina; then she continued this work in Indonesia (National Public Radio and Ruskie 2015:2).

That she was featured on NPR and found followers illustrates that this is not a unique case, but a widespread ideal in some circles.

Questionnaire surveys and growing memberships of social organizations in all six of our countries suggest the extent of new concerns, as do studies of the New Political Culture. These patterns emerge in direct reaction not so much against third sector organizations as against governments and corporations that are seen as "out of touch" with new citizen concerns. As traditional bureaucratic jobs are seen as alienating and political rewards as corrupting by many young persons, some leaders have sought to respond by encouraging third sector organizations, intended to be counters to large protests and political discontent. Social media are the electronic extension of physical scenes, which have become major vehicles for activism as the numbers of participants can escalate hugely and rapidly if ignited by critical events. These themes are analyzed in seven volumes on scenes (Scenes Project n.d.; see T. Clark et al. 2014; Silver and Clark 2016; Navarro 2012; Sawyer 2011).

Youthful activism is heightened by declining social controls by families and jobs, as young people participate in more nonfamily scenes, marry later, and change jobs more often. In the United States, young persons change jobs about once a year and more often choose to work for temporary employment agencies for years than commit to one job (this dynamic has also been heightened by the economic instability beginning with the so-called Great Recession beginning in 2008). Many live with their parents longer, as in other countries, particularly if unemployment benefits are not available. These factors combine to create a sort of reserve army of potential activists for third sector organizations. We have little systematic data on these trends as many such persons are missed by the normal census and related information systems. They have still been documented powerfully in a few selected studies such as one by Adrian Favell (2008) on thousands of French women who have moved to England for a decade or more and refuse to marry or take permanent jobs. Yet the gendered change seems strongest in Asia, heighted by China's one-child policy and preference for males (*Economist* 2011, 2015). Almost one-third of Japanese women in their thirties are unmarried; this trend is also visible in young Korean women who refuse to marry farmers and who leave small towns to go to Seoul. The farmers have married foreign women in such numbers that third sector associations in Korea have sprung up to help them learn about Korean life.

The main point here is that the third sector interacts with other social dynamics, including scenes, dynamics of urbanization, and demography. For instance, new patterns of politics are emerging across the world as human life comes to be organized increasingly around cities—a process of metropolitanization that Sellers et al. (2013b) analyze extensively in cross-national comparative work. Their results suggest that, across the board, voter turnout falls with the population size or population density of a municipality. Occupational diversity—that is, many different types of people living and working together—similarly has a negative effect on voter turnout, and economically homogeneous communities turn out to vote more. They found that residential stability raised election turnout in the United States but suppressed it in France, and that those effects were typically more powerful at a local rather than national level. Electoral competition—in some places a dynamic that is strongly and explicitly cultivated by third sector organizations—likewise has diverse effects on participation. For example, it has a positive effect in the United States but negative in France. Taken together, the results of the country studies provide compelling evidence that metropolitanization is an important source of variations in national and local political participation (Sellers et al. 2013a). Probing the distinctive French case, DellaPosta and Clark (2014:91) found that in French local and national elections, communes with more third sector organizations did not have higher voter turnout, but that in European Union elections, voters in these same communes turned out in larger numbers if there were more local third sector groups. The EU elections featured more parties and candidates stressing lifestyle, environment, and related issues than did traditional political parties in French elections. In this sense some younger French voters, like Asians, are reacting against traditional hierarchies and finding new third sector activities that are sympathetic.

These are some concrete illustrations of how third sector organizations—the density of civic life, the types of organizations, and the like—interact with these new dynamics of urban scenes and processes of urbanization and metropolitanization more generally.

Theme Three: Legitimacy

Our third cross-national point is that third sector organizations have been (and are routinely still) used as tools of state legitimation the world over. These organizations have at times been able to counter the demands for responsiveness (via participation) that citizens make of their political leaders. This cycle of demand making from the bottom and responsiveness from the top (often mediated by social organizations) creates the patterns of conflicts and continual adaptation that are common to the third sector globally today. Two institutional logics figure heavily into these questions of legitimacy: bureaucracy and professionalization. Bureaucracy represents the complicated state-civic relationship that circumscribes many third sectors, while professionalization has been used to help keep both state control and clientelism at bay by establishing norms, training, and practices around social organizations. While both provide structure beyond protest, both risk excluding average citizens and undermining their trust in the state (see chapter 8).

Nations can undergo significant change, cycling through periods of expansion and restriction of the legal status and role of the nonprofit sector in service provision, but in many cases the third sector still serves a legitimating function. In comparing Japan and France, we see a distinction, for instance, between state actions that are truly for the public's benefit and state actions that seek to look as though they are for the public's benefit (Moore 2001). The distinction turns on a new criterion activist citizens apply to civic and political leaders: authenticity.

Using case studies and historical work, Moore found that the French were more willing to reach out to nonprofit entities to solve fiscal problems in the 1980s than during the Revolution or the social movements of the late 1960s; that is, in the 1960s, problems with legitimacy seemed to drive the French state toward noncooperation with associations, seeing them as disruptive. Later on, the French state seemed to embrace a strategy of collaboration that increased the perceptions of government legitimacy through some third sector organizations. Echoing other scholars (see Florini 2000), Moore suggests that legal status generally confers some inherent legitimacy; in the case of France, that legitimacy was important in preventing the state from unilaterally disbanding third sector organizations (especially political organizations) in 1971 during a time of political upheaval. The general point here is simply that while the third sector can serve a number of extremely constructive social functions, it can also be used to uphold existing power structures and disguise genuine state crises.

In Japan, by contrast, the 1998 Nonprofit Law came about precisely *because of* widespread citizen disillusionment on issues that were broader than economic concerns—another sort of crisis of legitimacy, and the law may have helped the state regain some of the legitimacy that it had lost. Japanese citizens were concerned that too many environmental concessions were being made to the development of business; these preoccupations led to a distrust of the government and lack of confidence in its stewardship abilities. Thus, public support and investment in third sector organizations grew, and state legitimacy was somewhat restored during this process. Our case study in the chapter on Japan showed specifics.

Similarly, the United States has used nonprofit organizations to fill the gap between the state's capacity and citizens' need, thus compensating for a weak system of government service provision. While in the case of the United States the third sector may not have "transmitted" legitimacy so specifically as some suggested occurred in the Japan case, with a well-developed tax structure and a high degree of autonomy, the US third sector gives the appearance of a competent, legally and socially sanctioned institutional go-between for citizens and the services they lack. Corporate leaders have similarly increased responsiveness to their staffs, such that some (especially US firms) offer a leave of absence for a year or more if new staff want to work for third sector organizations; corporations also collect money, match staff financial contributions, and channel volunteers to third sector groups for causes supported by their staffs.

One major driver of change in the third sector is the enhancement of citizens as a source of legitimacy and related global pressures toward democracy. Small organized groups in the early twenty-first century have even been able to unseat long established regimes after a few days of public demonstrations—for instance, in Cairo and Kiev between 2011 and 2014. Combined with decreased citizen support and trust in government in many countries (see chapter 8), this generates pressure for government leaders to build new links to citizens as part of legitimacy, service provision, and democratic input. Such nongovernment dominated activity is especially important for those services with heavy social inputs and coproduction (where people serve themselves in part), such as elderly care or youth and cultural organizations.

This entire pattern of organizations as legitimators, mediated by a newfound independence from entrenched political parties and government agencies, illustrates patterns we find generally in the New Political Culture. These patterns of government adaptation were central in over fifty books from the Fiscal Austerity and Urban Innovation Project and later work on scenes (FAUI Project n.d.; Clark et al. 2014).

Whereas civil society and associations emerged outside government in the United States and much of the West, this was far less so in Asia. Civil service in Asia began as a practice of moralism and responsibility to nation, obedience to authority, and a traditional belief in the responsibility to serve and aid (Estifania 2004:127S). As an extension of paternalistic authority, civic service has been more actively managed by the state in Korea, Japan, Taiwan, and China.

Third sector organizations can clearly play an important role in legitimating the state. But aside from that, the sector can offer powerfully positive solutions for political and social life, including *service, innovation, advocacy, expressiveness, and community building*. The degree to which these outcomes occur, of course, depends on political and cultural context, combined with specific policies in the third sector area. As political leaders globally seek to show more responsiveness to citizens, it is often more efficient to deal with civil organizations than individual citizens

Theme Four: Institutional Logics

As we have shown, the third sector is a rich and varied space; in each country it bears the stamp of the history and culture that created it. The clearest example is one of our central leitmotifs: the fractious, dissenting tenor of the US third sector is foundationally distinct from the close partnerships of associations with Asian and other governments.

And yet there are similarities. We have traced the five institutional logics in nonprofit sectors around the globe to understand their common patterns. As we noted in chapter 1, the institutional logics illustrate how socially constructed belief systems capture people's cognition and behavior in distinctive environments. They are important organizational characteristics, defining the "desirable" norms and values and mediating meaning within an organization. The five institutional logics include:

- *Clientelism*, the trade of votes and partisan support for public decisions with divisible benefits, like jobs and contracts. Clientelism advances particular interests over the general interest. Political clientelism and patronage are cultural phenomena: a reflection within the political sphere of a certain way of understanding interpersonal relationships between those with power and those without it.
- *Paternalism*, or behavior that limits the autonomy or decision-making power of individuals or entities for their own good. It is a relationship in which one entity's choice is insufficiently voluntary to be genuinely considered the entity's own (family foundations in the United States, for instance, can at times be very paternalistic—the control rests in the hands of the donors with little room for dialogue or collaboration). Paternalism, unlike clientelism, is not a relationship meant to produce material or power benefits for a certain group; rather, it is an approach that emphasizes what critics view as a condescending nature of interactions between the powerful and the powerless.
- *Bureaucracy*, in which the national state incarnates centralized bureaucratic power. The central state in many places traditionally resisted the "private" initiatives of the third sector, as it often sought monopolistic control of fundamental social policies. An institutional logic of bureaucracy continues within the third sector, especially as large organizations like the Red Cross and CARE negotiate power sharing and responsibilities with local or national governments around the world.

- *Activism*, primarily seen among the grassroots organizations and volunteers impatient with clientelism, paternalism, and bureaucratic constraints and who are more open to using contentious practices to further their goals. Those operating under this kind of institutional logic often call on the language and tactics of social movements to make sense of their own participation.
- *Professionalization*, which involves transforming a job into a skilled profession, typically implying the establishment of accepted qualifications, professional norms, industry standards, professional bodies, and training programs. It signals a technical, systematic knowledge as well as the presence of professional norms within any given occupation.

The presence, absence, and combination of these five institutional logics create tensions, synergies, and unevenness that we have seen in different proportions in individual organizations and patterns across third sectors in the countries that we have examined. The various approaches are likened to often competing efforts to build and maintain legitimacy and organizational coherence, especially to nudge larger, older organizations and also the state to change. The continuing tensions among these five institutional logics are a key part of the ongoing transformation of the third sector globally. The interactions among them challenge entire approaches and sometimes spill over into challenges of entire political systems. Some analyses, for instance, find that increasing levels of professionalization among social movement organizations in the United States have dramatically changed the nature of social change itself, making it more institutionalized and less confrontational (see McAdam et al. 2005).

The five institutional logics are thus a central original framework of the book. We see increasing evidence of professionalization in third sectors throughout the countries examined here. In five of the six cases, third sectors emerged in countries with strong statist traditions and central governments. In the United States, the distinctive weak state created different dynamics. However, it is striking that *all six countries now operate within a relatively clear and established institutional logic of professionalization*. This is new. The third sector was so new and fragmented in many locations that it has been rapidly changing. This is due, as we have argued, to a combination of dynamics: globalization, commodification, increasing emphasis on transparency, neoliberal decentralization of governance functions, democratic challenges, and efforts to institutionalize dissent.

For instance, a major theme of the US nonprofit sector, particularly as it has expanded in recent decades, is the dramatic and increasing presence of the idea of civic management as an activity necessitating professional qualifications—a dynamic conflicting often with the logic of activism. Organizations that are successful *as organizations* have a disincentive to be confrontational (Minkoff 1999; Rucht 1999), and therefore, the rapid emergence of professional third sector management (in the United States especially) may have the effect of diluting some of the sector's contentiousness, compared especially to the turbulent 1960s. For instance, large organizations that receive funding from large foundations may be less inclined toward contention or toward taking radical positions on an issue for fear of angering their funders. More broadly, those who make a living doing social change work have less of an incentive to "work themselves out of a job" because their livelihoods depend, even indirectly, on the persistence of a social problem. In the midst of the social tumult that rocked the 1960s in the West, the French nonprofit sector showed evidence of institutional logics of solidarity and activism. Contemporarily, and similar to the United States, we see the emergence of the institutional logic of professionalization. In China, third sector organizations developed as service providing arms and collaborators of the government, requiring high levels of professionalization almost from the onset, to satisfy the demands of those relationships.

The global trend toward professionalization does merit a word of caution, however: institutionalized, professionalized third sectors are less well equipped to foment radical social change than are more flexible ones. When central governments fund third sectors, they do a number of constructive things, including institutionalizing civic life and ensuring its perpetuation. However, professionalization can also depoliticize. Decentralization of government functions and concurrent professionalization and marketization of nonprofit organizations are not inherently "bad"; our conflicting institutional logics suggest that this dynamic does, however, artificially inflate our understanding of nonprofits' critical and emancipatory potential, given that most of them are working under a structure that incentivizes conformism. Scholars and practitioners alike must remain alert to the field-wide incentives of those organizations tasked with social change and what they are capable of under this political and economic context.

The major instances of activism that swept the globe between 2010 and 2015—including student protests in France, the massive popular demonstrations in Egypt, Ukraine, France, Turkey, Spain, Hong Kong, and the United States—were all undertaken by groups that were temporarily or informally organized. They represent some of the most powerful demands for social change in half a century, remarkable because they were facilitated with very little formal organization, but with a heavy reliance on new technologies (notably Twitter, Facebook, and text messaging) and featuring themes of anti-authoritarianism and identity. Yet if such institutional logics constrained certain organizations in street demonstrations, they have sometimes been swept away by the activism of multiple conflicting individuals and little groups of participants.

Conclusion

It should be clear from this book that the lesson for political leaders the world over is similar: citizens can be challenged and focused on issues of public concern by engaging with third sector groups. *The participation of general citizens in organizations can build legitimacy and transform feelings of individual and family into broader civic pride.* It can *expand the horizons of self-interest* beyond the narrowly personal to those of the society to others, including society as a whole. This was dramatically illustrated in China, where as more persons migrate to cities, new issues emerge. The problems classically identified with urbanization are air pollution, smoke, traffic, crime, social control of theft, drugs, drunkenness, gambling, family conflicts, runaway children, and more. These problems grow more visible and challenging as the extended family weakens: the grandmother or elderly woman who would watch out of her window in a village might have solved them in an earlier era. The third sector worker can provide a new version of the elderly woman watching out of the window, but he or she may now also wear a stethoscope, offer the latest prescription drugs, and advise on what to eat and how to use hand cleaner to prevent spread of infection. He or she may inoculate against certain diseases and remind us that we should clean up after our dog, which has not observed proper sidewalk etiquette. At a national and global level, these new policies, like prescription drugs, are hugely costly and have major institutional and thus political implications.

Additionally, one finds increasing diversification, subtlety, and nuance among individuals and social sectors in terms of the types of services that citizens demand. These changing demands accompany increased education, income, travel, and media awareness, combined with blogs and the Internet—examples that create problems as well as solutions more visible globally. It is much harder for established civil servants and government agencies to react to these changes than it is for smaller, more nimble third sector organizations or private sector firms. These organizations—as part of their job—are continually seeking out and monitoring to improve the quality of their services and goods they provide to highly volatile and rapidly changing consumer demands. This "consumer feedback" is classically discussed in blogs as well as in many news magazines focused on lifestyle and how these issues are addressed or lived out by people around the world. Some of the most popular television talk shows in many countries of the world include unusually creative, opinionated, but also very empathetic hosts like Oprah Winfrey in Chicago or Pinky, star of *Buenos días Argentina* (Pinky went on to high elective office in Argentina). These and others provide commentary, recommend books, and invite speakers to talk about their personal examples in ways that are up-to-the-minute in seeking to go beyond what is classically available from the more established sources.

The third sector is important because it links people. It is important because it empowers them. It contains an unimaginable richness of experience, perspective, skill, and commitment, among those who make a living from it, those who constitute it, and those whom it serves. It is perhaps the largest repository of altruism and egalitarianism in the United States, and increasingly in other countries, as it coheres people around their moral visions. It has a critically important function of linking governments to people, though the mechanisms by which this occurs vary by country and region. Its task—representation of the underrepresented, voice for the voiceless, richness and creativity in the face of simple majorities and grinding politics-as-usual—is necessary to the healthy and constructive advancement of the human endeavor. Around the world, we find dramatic differences in how the third sector works, but we have assembled some lessons here for readers from every country.

References

Adams, Rebecca, Kristi Cahoon, and Ann C. Hodges. 2005. "Starting a Nonprofit: What You Need to Know." Richmond, VA: University of Richmond School of Law. Retrieved February 6, 2016 (http://HTML Citewww.arts.virginia.gov/resources/pdf/HowToFormANonprofit_1st_ed.pdf).

A.D.S.E.A. (Association Départementale de La Sauvegarde de l'Enfance et de l'Adolescence) 77. 2011. "Une association d'action éducative et sociale." Retrieved February 13, 2011 (http://www.adsea77.fr/).

Alagappa, Muthiah. 2004. Civil Society and Political Change in Asia: Expanding and Contracting Democratic Space. Stanford, CA: Stanford University Press.

Alexander, Jeffrey C. 1997. "The Paradoxes of Civil Society." International Sociology 12(2): 115–33.

———. 2006. The Civil Sphere. New York: Oxford University Press.

Alford, Robert R., and Roger Friedland. 1985. Powers of Theory: Capitalism, the State, and Democracy. Cambridge, UK: Cambridge University Press.

Almond, Gabriel A., and Sidney Verba. 1963. The Civic Culture: Political Attitudes and Democracy in Five Nations. Princeton, NJ: Princeton University Press.

———. 1989. The Civic Culture: Political Attitudes and Democracy in Five Nations. Newbury Park, CA: SAGE.

Amemia, Takako. 1998. "The Nonprofit Sector: Legal Background." In The Nonprofit Sector in Japan. Manchester, UK: Manchester University Press.

Amenomori, Takayoshi. 1997. "Defining the Nonprofit Sector: Japan." In Defining the Nonprofit Sector: A Cross-National Analysis, edited by Lester M. Salamon and Helmut K. Anheier, 188–214. Manchester, UK: Manchester University Press.

Amnesty International. 2008. Policing the Candlelight Protests in South Korea. London: Amnesty International.

Ansari, Ghaus, and P. Nas. 1983. Town-Talk: The Dynamics of Urban Anthropology. Leiden: Brill Archive.

Archambault, Edith. 1993. "Defining the Nonprofit Sector: France." Baltimore: Johns Hopkins University Institute for Policy Studies.

———. 1997. *The Nonprofit Sector in France*. Manchester, UK: Manchester University Press.

———. 2000. "Foundations in France." *ResearchGate* (2000.43). Retrieved July 18, 2016 (https://www.researchgate.net/publication/5070771_Foundations_in_France).

———. 2001. "Historical Roots of the Nonprofit Sector in France." *Nonprofit and Voluntary Sector Quarterly* 30(2): 204–20.

Arno, P. S. 1986. "The Nonprofit Sector's Response to the AIDS Epidemic: Community-Based Services in San Francisco." *American Journal of Public Health* 76(11): 1325–30.

Asia Foundation. 2001a. "Strengthening Philanthropy in the Asia Pacific: An Agenda for Action. Background Paper: Korea." Paper prepared for International Conference on Strengthening Philanthropy in the Asia Pacific, Asia Pacific Philanthropy Consortium, Bali, Indonesia.

———. 2001b. "Strengthening Philanthropy in the Asia Pacific: An Agenda For Action. Background Paper: Taiwan." Paper prepared for International Conference on Strengthening Philanthropy in the Asia Pacific, Asia Pacific Philanthropy Consortium, Bali, Indonesia.

Atoda, Naosumi, Takayoshi Amenomori, and Mio Ohta. 1998. "The Scale of the Japanese Nonprofit Sector." In *The Nonprofit Sector in Japan*, edited by Tadashi Yamamoto, 99–118. Manchester, UK: Manchester University Press.

Baer, Douglas, James Curtis, and Edward Grabb. 2001. "Has Voluntary Association Activity Declined? Cross-National Analyses for Fifteen Countries." *Canadian Review of Sociology/Revue canadienne de sociologie* 38(3): 249–74.

Baiocchi, Gianpaolo. 2006. "Inequality and Innovation: Decentralization as Opportunity Structure in Brazil." In *Decentralization and Local Governance in Developing Countries: A Comparative Perspective*, edited by Pranab Bardhan and Dilip Mookherjee, 53–80. Cambridge, MA: MIT Press.

Bakvis, Herman. 1981. *Catholic Power in the Netherlands*. Kingston, ON: McGill-Queen's University Press.

Banfield, Edward C. 1958. *The Moral Basis of a Backward Society*. Glencoe, IL: Free Press.

Barker, Colin, Alan Johnson, and Michael Lavalette. 2001. *Leadership and Social Movements*. Manchester, UK: Manchester University Press.

Barnett, Michael N., and Martha Finnemore. 1999. "The Politics, Power, and Pathologies of International Organizations." *International Organization* 53(4): 699–732.

Bekkers, René. 2012. "Trust and Volunteering: Selection or Causation? Evidence from a 4 Year Panel Study." *Political Behavior* 34(2): 225–47.

Belluck, Pam. 2012. "Cancer Group Halts Financing to Planned Parenthood." *New York Times*, January 31. Retrieved May 8, 2013 (http://www.nytimes.com/2012/02/01/us/cancer-group-halts-financing-to-planned-parenthood.html).

Berman, Sheri. 1997. "Civil Society and the Collapse of the Weimar Republic." *World Politics* 49(3): 401–29.

Bidet, Eric. 2002. "Explaining the Third Sector in South Korea." *VOLUNTAS: International Journal of Voluntary and Nonprofit Organizations* 13(2): 131–47.

Boas, Taylor C., and Jordan Gans-Morse. 2009. "Neoliberalism: From New Liberal Philosophy to Anti-Liberal Slogan." *Studies in Comparative International Development* 44(2): 137–61.

Borzaga, Carlo, and Jacques Defourny. 2004. *The Emergence of Social Enterprise.* London: Routledge.

Bothwell, Robert O. 2003. "The Challenges of Growing the NPO and Voluntary Sector in Japan." in *The Voluntary and Non-profit Sector in Japan: The Challenge of Change,* edited by Stephen P. Osborne, 121–49. London: Routledge.

Bowman, Woods, and Marion R. Fremont-Smith. 2006. "Nonprofits and State and Local Governments." in *Nonprofits and Government: Collaboration and Conflict.* Washington, DC: Urban Institute.

Brehm, John, and Wendy Rahn. 1997. "Individual-Level Evidence for the Causes and Consequences of Social Capital." *American Journal of Political Science* 41(3): 999–1023.

Brenner, Neil. 2001. "The Limits to Scale? Methodological Reflections on Scalar Structuration." *Progress in Human Geography* 25(4): 591–614.

———. 2009. "Open Questions on State Rescaling." *Cambridge Journal of Regions, Economy and Society* 2(1): 123–39.

Brenner, Neil, Jamie Peck, and Nik Theodore. 2010. "Variegated Neoliberalization: Geographies, Modalities, Pathways." *Global Networks* 10(2): 182–222.

Brinkley, Alan. 1996. "Liberty, Community, and the National Idea." *American Prospect* (29): 53–59.

Broadbent, Jeffrey. 1998. *Environmental Politics in Japan: Networks of Power and Protest.* Cambridge, UK: Cambridge University Press.

Brooke, James. 2002a. "Japan Premier Taking Heat over Firing of Minister." *New York Times,* January 31. Retrieved May 10, 2013 (http://www.nytimes.com/2002/01/31/world/japan-premier-taking-heat-over-firing-of-minister.html).

———. 2002b. "Japan's Foreign Minister Is Fired after Months of Feuding." *New York Times,* January 30. Retrieved May 10, 2013 (http://www.nytimes.com/2002/01/30/world/japan-s-foreign-minister-is-fired-after-months-of-feuding.html).

Brown, Mitchell, and Eric M. Uslaner. 2002. "Inequality, Trust, and Political Engagement." Paper prepared for Annual Meeting of the American Political Science Association, Boston, August 29–September 1. Retrieved March 9, 2016 (https://www.researchgate.net/profile/Eric_Uslaner/publication/242100160_Inequality_Trust_and_Political_Engagement/links/540b85910cf2f2b29a342c39.pdf).

Buffalo ReUse. N.d. Retrieved February 29, 2016 (http://www.buffaloreuse.org/).

Buffett, Peter. 2013. "The Charitable-Industrial Complex." *New York Times,* July 26. Retrieved August 7, 2013 (http://www.nytimes.com/2013/07/27/opinion/the-charitable-industrial-complex.html).

Burns, James MacGregor. 2012. *Leadership.* New York: Open Road Media.

Cain Miller, Claire. 2008. "Gay-Rights Activists Use Web to Organize Global Rally." *New York Times*, November 14. Retrieved October 26, 2010 (http://thecaucus.blogs .nytimes.com/2008/11/14/gay-rights-activists-use-web-to-organize-global-rally/).

Carter, Mary. 2011. "Interview: The Women's Intercultural Center." Telephone interview by Meghan Kallman. January 4.

Castree, Noel. 2008. "Neoliberalising Nature: The Logics of Deregulation and Re-regulation." *Environment and Planning A* 40(1): 131–52.

———. 2010. "Neoliberalism and the Biophysical Environment 1: What 'Neoliberalism' Is, and What Difference Nature Makes to It." *Geography Compass* 4(12): 1725–33.

Chamberlain, Heath B. 1993. "On the Search for Civil Society in China." *Modern China* 19(2): 199–215.

Chang, W. W., C. M. Huang, and Y. C. Kuo. 2013. "Design of Employee Training in Taiwanese Nonprofits." *Nonprofit and Voluntary Sector Quarterly*. Retrieved September 19, 2013 (http://nvs.sagepub.com/cgi/doi/10.1177/0899764013502878).

Children Are Us Foundation. 2011. "Children Are Us Foundation." Retrieved February 13, 2011 (http://www.c-are-us.org.tw/english/about).

China General Social Survey (China GSS). 2003, 2006. Retrieved March 11, 2016 (http://www.src.ust.hk/survey/GSS_e.html).

Choudhury, Enamul, and Shamima Ahmed. 2002. "The Shifting Meaning of Governance: Public Accountability of Third Sector Organizations in an Emergent Global Regime." *International Journal of Public Administration* 25(4): 561–88.

Chubb, Judith. 1982. Patronage, Power, and Poverty in Southern Italy: A Tale of Two Cities. Cambridge, UK: Cambridge University Press.

Chuqing, Zhou. 2013. "Dr. Zhao Responds to the Red Cross Trust Crisis: Public Trust Will Not Pick Up in a Short Time." *XinHuaNet*, March 7. Retrieved August 6, 2013 (http://news.xinhuanet.com/2013lh/2013–03/07/c_114924618.htm).

CINIC (China Internet Network Information Center). 2012. *Statistical Report on Internet Development in China*. Report no. 30. Beijing: China Internet Network Information Center.

CIRIEC (Centre Internationale de Recherches et de l' Information sur l' Économie Sociale et Coopérative). 2006. *Manual for Drawing Up the Satellite Accounts of Companies in the Social Economy: Cooperatives and Mutual Societies*. Liège, Belgium: Centre Internationale de Recherches et de l' Information sur l' Économie Sociale et Coopérative.

Clark, John. 1991. Democratizing Development: The Role of Voluntary Organizations. West Hartford, CT: Kumarian Press.

Clark, Terry Nichols, ed. 1994. *Urban Innovation: Creative Strategies for Turbulent Times*. Thousand Oaks, CA: SAGE.

———. 2004. *The City as an Entertainment Machine*. Bingley, UK: Emerald Group.

Clark, Terry Nicholas, et al. 2014. Can Tocqueville Karaoke? Global Contrasts of Citizen Participation, the Arts, and Development. Bingley, UK: Emerald Group.

Clark, Terry Nichols, and Vincent Hoffmann-Martinot. 1998. *The New Political Culture*. Boulder, CO: Westview Press.

Clark, Terry Nichols, and Seymour Martin Lipset. 2001. *The Breakdown of Class Politics: A Debate on Post-Industrial Stratification*. Washington, DC: Woodrow Wilson Center Press.

Clemens, Elisabeth S. 2006. "Lineages of the Rube Goldberg State: Building and Blurring Public Programs, 1900–1940." In *Rethinking Political Institutions: The Art of the State*, edited by Ian Shapiro, Stephen Skowronek, and Daniel Galvin, 187–215. New York: New York University Press.

Clinton, Courtney. 2010. "France: Social Economy Takes Centre Stage." *Vita,* October 28. Retrieved June 26, 2012 (http://www.vita.it/it/article/2010/10/28/social-economy-takes-centre-stage/105923/).

CNSA (Chinese Academy of Governance E-government Research Center). 2013. *Chinese Government Affairs Microblogs Evaluation Report 2012.* Beijing: Chinese Academy of Governance Publishing House.

Cohen, Lizabeth. 2003. A Consumers' Republic : The Politics of Mass Consumption in Postwar America. New York: Knopf.

Conger, Jay A., and Rabindra N. Kanungo. 1987. "Toward a Behavioral Theory of Charismatic Leadership in Organizational Settings." *Academy of Management Review* 12(4): 637–47.

———. 1998. Charismatic Leadership in Organizations. Thousand Oaks, CA: SAGE.

Cooley, Alexander, and James Ron. 2010. "The NGO Scramble: Organizational Insecurity and the Political Economy of Transnational Action." *International Security* 27(1): 5–39.

Cooney, K. 2010. "An Exploratory Study of Social Purpose Business Models in the United States." *Nonprofit and Voluntary Sector Quarterly* 40(1): 185–96. Retrieved October 22, 2010 (http://nvs.sagepub.com/content/early/2010/01/22/0899764009351591).

Cox, Robert Henry. 1993. The Development of the Dutch Welfare State: From Workers' Insurance to Universal Entitlement. Pittsburgh: University of Pittsburgh Press.

Creed, W. E. Douglas, Maureen A. Scully, and John R. Austin. 2002. "Clothes Make the Person? The Tailoring of Legitimating Accounts and the Social Construction of Identity." *Organization Science* 13(5): 475–96.

Crozier, Michel, Samuel P. Huntington, and Joji Watanuki. 1975. *The Crisis of Democracy: Report on the Governability of Democracies to the Trilateral Commission.* New York: New York University Press.

Curtis, James E., Douglas E. Baer, and Edward G. Grabb. 2001. "Nations of Joiners: Explaining Voluntary Association Membership in Democratic Societies." *American Sociological Review* 66(6): 783–805.

Dart, Raymond. 2004. "The Legitimacy of Social Enterprise." *Nonprofit Management and Leadership* 14(4): 411–24.

Defourny, Jacques. 2001. "Introduction: From Third Sector to Social Enterprise." In *The Emergence of Social Enterprise*, edited by Carlo Borzaga and Jacques Defourny, 1–28. London: Routledge. Retrieved July 31, 2012 (http://orbi.ulg.ac.be/handle/2268/90501).

Dehne, Anita, Peter Friedrich, Chang Woon Nam, and Rüdiger Parsche. 2008. "Taxation of Nonprofit Associations in an International Comparison." *Nonprofit and Voluntary Sector Quarterly* 37(4): 709–29.

DeHoog, Ruth Hoogland, and Lester M. Salamon. 2002. "Purchase-of-Service Contracting." In *Tools of Government: A Guide to the New Governance*, edited by Lester M. Salamon, 319–39. New York: Oxford University Press.

Delhey, Jan, and Kenneth Newton. 2003. "Who Trusts? The Origins of Social Trust in Seven Societies." *European Societies* 5(2): 93–137.

Della Porta, Donatella, and Mario Diani. 1999. *Social Movements: An Introduction.* Malden, MA: Blackwell.

DellaPosta, Daniel J., and Terry Nichols Clark, with Stephen Sawyer and Arkaida Dini. 2014. "Civic and Arts Activities Can Energize Politics, France and Europe." In *Can Tocqueville Karaoke?*, by Terry Nichols Clark et al., 93–115. Bingley, UK: Emerald Group. Retrieved March 17, 2016 (http://public.eblib.com/choice/public fullrecord.aspx?p=1766289).

DeMars, William Emile. 2005. NGOs and Transnational Networks: Wild Cards in World Politics. London: Pluto Press.

Deng, Guosheng. 2001. "Preliminary Analysis on Chinese NGO Survey." In *Zhong Guo NGO Yan Jiu: Yi Ge An Wei Zhong Xin [Case Study on China's NGOs].* Beijing: United Nations Centre of Regional Development and Tsinghua University NGO Research Centre.

Dichter, Thomas W. 1999. "Globalization and Its Effects on NGOs: Efflorescence or a Blurring of Roles and Relevance?" *Nonprofit and Voluntary Sector Quarterly* 28(4): 38–58.

———. 2003. Despite Good Intentions: Why Development Assistance to the Third World Has Failed. Amherst: University of Massachusetts Press.

DiMaggio, Paul J., and Walter W. Powell. 1983. "The Iron Cage Revisited: Institutional Isomorphism and Collective Rationality in Organizational Fields." *American Sociological Review* 48(2): 147–60.

Dobbin, Frank, and John R. Sutton. 1998. "The Strength of a Weak State: The Rights Revolution and the Rise of Human Resources Management Divisions." *American Journal of Sociology* 104(2): 441–76.

Duncan, Laura J. 2006. "Poverty and Income Effects on Voluntary Association Membership: A Cross-National Comparison." Diss., McMaster University. *Open Access Dissertations and Theses.* Retrieved September 30, 2013 (http://digitalcommons. mcmaster.ca/opendissertations/5603).

Easton, David. 1975. "A Re-assessment of the Concept of Political Support." *British Journal of Political Science* 5(4): 435–57.

Ebrahim, Alnoor. 2003. "Making Sense of Accountability: Conceptual Perspectives for Northern and Southern Nonprofits." *Nonprofit Management and Leadership* 14(2): 191–212.

———. 2005. "Accountability Myopia: Losing Sight of Organizational Learning." *Nonprofit and Voluntary Sector Quarterly* 34(1): 56–87.

Economist. 2008. "Ill Met by Candlelight." *Economist*, June 12. Retrieved July 4, 2013 (http://www.economist.com/node/11554714).

———. 2011. "Asia's Lonely Hearts." *Economist*, August 20. Retrieved August 31, 2015 (http://www.economist.com/node/21526350).

———. 2015. "Bare Branches, Redundant Males." *Economist*, April 18. Retrieved August 31, 2015 (http://www.economist.com/news/asia/21648715-distorted-sex-ratios-birth-generation-ago-are-changing-marriage-and-damaging-societies-asias).

Edele, Andreas. 2005. *Non-Governmental Organizations in China*. Geneva: Centre for Applied Studies in International Negotiations.

Eden Social Welfare Foundation. 2011. "Eden Social Welfare Foundation." Homepage. Retrieved February 13, 2011 (http://www.eden.org.tw/index.php).

EESC (European Economic and Social Committee). 2005. *The Social Economy in the European Union: France*. Brussels: European Economic and Social Committee.

Elazar, Daniel Judah. 1995. *The Covenant Tradition in Politics*. New Brunswick, NJ: Transaction.

———. 1997. Covenant and Constitutionalism: The Great Frontier and the Matrix of Federal Democracy. New Brunswick, NJ: Transaction.

———, ed. 2001. Commonwealth: The Other Road to Democracy—The Swiss Model of Democratic Self-Government. Lanham, MD: Lexington Books.

Estes, Richard J. 2000. "Charitable Foundations in East Asia: Emerging Partners in Development?" *Social Development Issues* 22(2/3): 3–14.

Estifania, Edna. 2004. "Civic Service in Asia and the Pacific." *Nonprofit and Voluntary Sector Quarterly* 33(4 suppl): 127S-47S.

Farm Fresh Rhode Island. 2011. "About Farm Fresh Rhode Island." Retrieved January 31, 2011 (http://www.farmfreshri.org/about/about.php).

FAUI (Fiscal Austerity and Urban Innovation) Project. FAUI Archives. Retrieved March 16, 2016 (http://faui.uchicago.edu/archive.html).

Favell, Adrian. 2008. Eurostars and Eurocities: Free Movement and Mobility in an Integrating Europe. Malden, MA: Wiley-Blackwell.

Feld, Scott L. 1981. "The Focused Organization of Social Ties." *American Journal of Sociology* 86(5): 1015–35.

Fligstein, Neil. 1987. "The Intraorganizational Power Struggle: Rise of Finance Personnel to Top Leadership in Large Corporations, 1919–1979." *American Sociological Review* 52(1): 44–58.

Florini, Ann M., ed. 2000. *The Third Force: The Rise of Transnational Civil Society*. Tokyo: Japan Center for International Exchange; Washington, DC: Carnegie Endowment for International Peace.

Foley, Michael W., and Bob Edwards. 1996. "The Paradox of Civil Society." *Journal of Democracy* 7(3): 38–52.

Foundation Center. 2010. *Foundation Yearbook*. 2010 ed. New York: Foundation Center.

Fox, Jonathan. 1994. "The Difficult Transition from Clientelism to Citizenship: Lessons from Mexico." *World Politics* 46(2): 151–84.

Friedland, Roger, and Robert K. Alford. 1991. "Bringing Society Back In: Symbols, Practices, and Institutional Contradictions." In *The New Institutionalism in Organizational Analysis*, edited by Walter W. Powell and Paul DiMaggio, 232–63. Chicago: University of Chicago Press.

Frumkin, Peter. 2005. *On Being Nonprofit: A Conceptual and Policy Primer*. Cambridge, MA: Harvard University Press.

Frumkin, Peter, and Mark T. Kim. 2001. "Strategic Positioning and the Financing of Nonprofit Organizations: Is Efficiency Rewarded in the Contributions Marketplace?" *Public Administration Review* 61(3): 266–75.

Fukuyama, Francis. 1996. *Trust: The Social Virtues and the Creation of Prosperity*. New York: Simon and Schuster.

———. 2001. "Social Capital, Civil Society and Development." *Third World Quarterly* 22(1): 7–20.

Gambetta, Diego. 1996. *The Sicilian Mafia: The Business of Private Protection*. Cambridge, MA: Harvard University Press.

Gladwell, Malcolm. 2010. "Small Change: Why the Revolution Will Not Be Tweeted." *New Yorker*, October 4. Retrieved April 18, 2012 (http://www.newyorker.com /reporting/2010/10/04/101004fa_fact_gladwell?currentPage=all).

Glanville, Jennifer L. 2001. "Does Organizational Diversity Promote Trust?" University of North Carolina Sociology Department Colloquium Series, April 18.

Gold, Thomas B. 1991. *Civil Society and Taiwan's Quest for Identity*. Berkeley: Center for Chinese Studies, University of California at Berkeley.

Gorski, Philip S. 2003. The Disciplinary Revolution: Calvinism and the Rise of the State in Early Modern Europe. Chicago: University of Chicago Press.

Granovetter, Mark S. 1973. "The Strength of Weak Ties." *American Journal of Sociology* 78(6): 1360–80.

Grodach, Carl., and Daniel Silver, eds. 2012. *The Politics of Urban Cultural Policy: Global Perspectives*. London: Routledge.

Gronbjerg, Kirsten A., Helen K. Liu, and Thomas H. Pollak. 2009. "Incorporated but Not IRS-Registered: Exploring the (Dark) Grey Fringes of the Nonprofit Universe." *Nonprofit and Voluntary Sector Quarterly* 39(5): 925–45.

Gronbjerg, Kirsten A., and Laurie Paarlberg. 2002. "Extent and Nature of Overlap between Listings of IRS Tax-Exempt Registration and Nonprofit Incorporation: The Case of Indiana." *Nonprofit and Voluntary Sector Quarterly* 31(4): 565–94.

Gross, Michael L. 1997. *Ethics and Activism: The Theory and Practice of Political Morality*. Cambridge, MA: Cambridge University Press.

Gugerty, Mary Kay, Mark Sidel, and Angela L. Bies. 2010. "Introduction to Minisymposium: Nonprofit Self-Regulation in Comparative Perspective—Themes and Debates." *Nonprofit and Voluntary Sector Quarterly*, August 2. Retrieved October 23, 2010 (http://nvs.sagepub.com/content/early/2010/07/30/0899764010372971.abstract).

Gusfield, Joseph R. 1966. "Functional Areas of Leadership in Social Movements." *Sociological Quarterly* 7(2): 137–56.

Habermas, Jürgen. 2001. *The Postnational Constellation: Political Essays.* Cambridge, MA: MIT Press.

Haddad, Mary Alice. 2007a. *Politics and Volunteering in Japan: A Global Perspective.* Cambridge, UK: Cambridge University Press.

———. 2007b. "Transformation of Japan's Civil Society Landscape." *Journal of East Asian Studies* 7(3): 413–37. Retrieved February 3, 2011 (http://findarticles.com/p/articles/mi_hb3241/is_3_7/ai_n29387760/).

Hahn, Sangjin, and Angus McCabe. 2006. "Welfare-to-Work and the Emerging Third Sector in South Korea: Korea's Third Way?" *International Journal of Social Welfare* 15(4): 314–20.

Hanks, Michael, and Bruce K. Eckland. 1978. "Adult Voluntary Associations and Adolescent Socialization." *Sociological Quarterly* 19(3): 481–90.

Hasegawa, Koichi, Chika Shinohara, and Jeffrey P. Broadbent. 2007. "The Effects of 'Social Expectation' on the Development of Civil Society in Japan." *Journal of Civil Society* 3(2): 179–203.

Healthy Families/Thriving Communities Collaborative Council. 2011. "Healthy Families/Thriving Communities Collaborative Council." Retrieved January 23, 2011 (http://www.hftcc.org/).

Heurlin, Christopher. 2009. "Governing Civil Society: The Political Logic of NGO-State Relations Under Dictatorship." *VOLUNTAS: International Journal of Voluntary and Nonprofit Organizations* 21(2): 220–39.

Hong, Caroline. 2004. "Mentally Disabled Focus of Education Campaign." *Taipei Times*, June 11. Retrieved February 13, 2011 (http://www.taipeitimes.com/News/taiwan/archives/2004/06/11/2003174580).

Hooghe, Marc. 2003. "Voluntary Associations and Democratic Attitudes: Value Congruence as a Causal Mechanism." In *Generating Social Capital: Civil Society and Institutions in Comparative Perspective*, edited by Marc Hooghe and Dietlind Stolle, 89–111. New York: Palgrave Macmillan.

Hopkins, Bruce. 2011. *The Law of Tax-Exempt Organizations.* 10th ed. Hoboken, NJ: John Wiley and Sons.

Howell, Jude, and Jenny Pearce. 2002. *Civil Society and Development: A Critical Exploration.* Boulder, CO: Lynne Rienner.

Hsiao, Hsin-Huang Michael. 1990. "Emerging Social Movements and the Rise of a Demanding Civil Society in Taiwan." *Australian Journal of Chinese Affairs* no. 24: 163–80.

———. 2003. "NGOs and Democratization in Taiwan: Their Interactive Roles in Building a Viable Civil Society." In *Civil Society in Asia*, edited by David C. Schak and Wayne Hudson, 180–91. Aldershot, UK: Ashgate.

Hsia, Renee Yuen-Jan, and Lynn T. White. 2002. "Working amid Corporatism and Confusion: Foreign NGOs in China." *Nonprofit and Voluntary Sector Quarterly* 31(3): 329–51.

Hustinx, Lesley, Femida Handy, and Ram A. Cnaan. 2012. "Student Volunteering in

China and Canada: Comparative Perspectives." *Canadian Journal of Sociology/Cahiers Canadiens de Sociologie* 37(1): 55–83.

Imada, Makato. 2003. "The Philanthropic Tradition and Fundraising for the Voluntary and Nonprofit Sector in Japan." In *The Voluntary and Non-profit Sector in Japan: The Challenge of Change*, edited by Stephen P. Osborne, 188–95. London: Routledge.

Inglehart, Ronald. 1990. *Culture Shift in Advanced Industrial Society*. Princeton, NJ: Princeton University Press.

———. 1997. Modernization and Postmodernization: Cultural, Economic, and Political Change in 43 Societies. Princeton, NJ: Princeton University Press.

Institut français d'opinion publique (French Public Opinion Institute). 2013. *Regards internationaux sur la situation économique et sur la mondialisation.* (http://www.ifop.com/media/poll/2160–1-study_file.pdf)

Jang, Wonho, Terry Clark, and Miree Byun. 2011. *Scenes Dynamics in Global Cities: Seoul, Tokyo, and Chicago*. Seoul: Seoul Development Institute.

Japan Foundation Center. 2012. "The Japan Foundation Center." Retrieved July 19, 2012 (http://www.jfc.or.jp/eibun/index.html).

Japan Times. 2002. "Koizumi Sacks Tanaka, Nogami; Suzuki Also Walks Following Row." *Japan Times*, January 31. Retrieved May 10, 2013 (http://archive.is/PGZM).

Jepperson, Ronald L., and John W. Meyer. 1991. "The Public Order and the Construction of Formal Organizations." In *The New Institutionalism in Organizational Analysis*, edited by Walter W. Powell and Paul DiMaggio, 204–31. Chicago: University of Chicago Press.

Jie, Chen. 2006. "The NGO Community in China." *China Perspectives* no. 68: 29–40.

Johns Hopkins Center for Civil Society Studies. 2004. (http://ccss.jhu.edu/wp-content/uploads/downloads/2013/02/Comparative-data-Tables_2004_FORMATTED_2.2013.pdf)

Jones de Almeida, Adjoa Florência. 2009. "The Revolution Will Not Be Funded." *Utne Reader*. Retrieved April 12, 2013 (http://www.utne.com/Politics/Revolution-Will-not-be-Funded-Nonprofit-Industrial-Complex.aspx).

Kahl, Sigrun. 2005. "The Religious Roots of Modern Poverty Policy: Catholic, Lutheran, and Reformed Protestant Traditions Compared." *European Journal of Sociology* 46(01): 91–126.

Kaipin, Kui. 2009. "Facilitating or Impeding—A Discourse on the Two-Sided Effects of Japan's NPO Law on the Growth of Civil Society." *China Nonprofit Review* 1(1): 79–98.

Kallman, Meghan Elizabeth. 2012. "Institutional Logics and Identity in Nonprofit Funding Relationships." Working paper, Brown University, Providence, RI.

———. 2013. "Get Your Schmooze On: Tensions, Perspectives, and Paradoxes in NGO Funding Relationships." *British Journal of Arts and Social Sciences* 13(1): 44–68.

———. 2015. "Material, Emotional, and Professional Dynamics: Idealism, Commitment and Self-Regulation in the Peace Corps." In *Materiality, Rules, and Regulation:*

New Trends in Management and Organization Studies, edited by G. F. Lanzara, F.-X. de Vaujany, N. Mitev, and A. Mukherjee, 73–99. London: Palgrave.

Kamiya, Setsuko. 2009. "Community Groups Provide Lifelines in Many Ways." *Japan Times Online*, September 15. Retrieved January 24, 2011 (http://search.japantimes.co.jp/cgi-bin/nn20090915i1.html).

Kang, Yoonhee. 2012. "Korean Civil Society and Trust-Building between South Korea and the United States." *Asia Policy* no. 13: 61–80.

Kankainen, Tomi. 2009. "Voluntary Associations and Trust in Finland." *Research on Finnish Society* 2: 5–17.

Khan, Huma. 2012. "Susan G. Komen Apologizes for Cutting Off Planned Parenthood Funding." *ABC News Blogs*, February 3. Retrieved May 8, 2013 (http://abcnews.go.com/blogs/politics/2012/02/susan-g-komen-apologizes-for-cutting-off-planned-parenthood-funding/).

Kim, Hyuk-Rae. 2000. "The State and Civil Society in Transition: The Role of Non-Governmental Organizations in South Korea." *Pacific Review* 13(4): 595–613.

Kim, Jack. 2008. "Anti-U.S. Beef Protest Draws 100,000 S. Koreans." *Reuters*, May 31. Retrieved July 4, 2013 (http://www.reuters.com/article/2008/05/31/us-korea-protest-idUSSEO21734120080531).

Kim, Ji-Young. 2005. "'Bowling Together' Isn't a Cure-All: The Relationship between Social Capital and Political Trust in South Korea." *International Political Science Review* 26(2): 193–213.

Kim, Pan S., and M. Jae Moon. 2003. "NGOs as Incubator of Participative Democracy in South Korea: Political, Voluntary, and Policy Participation." *International Journal of Public Administration* 26(5): 549–67.

Kim, Sungmoon. 2007. "A Post-Confucian Civil Society: Liberal Collectivism and Participatory Politics in South Korea." Diss., University of Maryland. ProQuest.

Kim, Sunhyuk, and Sŏn-hyŏk Kim. 2000. *The Politics of Democratization in Korea: The Role of Civil Society*. Pittsburgh: University of Pittsburgh Press.

Knack, Stephen, and Philip Keefer. 1997. "Does Social Capital Have an Economic Payoff? A Cross-Country Investigation." *Quarterly Journal of Economics* 112(4): 1251–88.

Korean Federation for Environmental Movement. 2011. "Korean Federation for Environmental Movement." Retrieved February 15, 2011 (http://english.kfem.or.kr/index.htm).

Ku, Chung-Hwa. 1999. "The Structural Transformation of Civic Association and the Development of NPOs in Taiwan." *Taiwan: A Radical Quarterly in Social Studies* no. 36: 123–45.

Kuan, Yu-Yuan, and Shu-Twu Wang. 2010. "The Impact of Public Authorities on the Development of Social Enterprises in Taiwan." *Journal of Public Affairs Review* 11(1).

La Cimade. 2011. "La Cimade." *La Cimade: L'humanité passe par l'autre*, 1–23. Retrieved February 13, 2011 (http://www.cimade.org/la_cimade/cimade/rubriques/116-comptes-et-rapports).

Laratta, Rosario. 2011. "Ethical Climate and Accountability in Nonprofit Organizations." *Public Management Review* 13(1): 43–63.

Levi, Margaret. 1998. "A State of Trust." In *Trust and Governance*, edited by Valerie Braithwaite and Margaret Levi, 77–101. New York: Russell Sage Foundation.

Ligue des Droits de l'Homme. 2011. "Groupes de Travail." Ligue des Droits de l'Homme. Retrieved February 16, 2011 (http://www.ldh-france.org/groupes-travail/).

Lindsay, Graeme, and Les Hems. 2004. "Sociétés Coopératives d'Intérêt Collectif: The Arrival of Social Enterprise within the French Social Economy." *Voluntas: International Journal of Voluntary and Nonprofit Organizations* 15(3): 265–86.

Lin, Paul. 2013. "Taiwanese Youth Bolstering Protest." *Taipei Times*, August 9. Retrieved September 19, 2013 (http://www.taipeitimes.com/News/editorials/archives/2013/08/09/2003569250).

Lin, Teh-Chang. 2005. "An Assessment of Civil Society in Taiwan: Transforming State-Society Relations: The Challenge, Dilemma, and Prospect of Civil Society in Taiwan." *CIVICUS Civil Society Index*. Project report. Taiwan: Center for International NGO Studies, National Sun Yat-sen University, Kaohsiung.

Liu, Xiaohua. 2002. *NGOs in China: An Overview*. National City, CA: International Community Foundation.

Ljubownikow, Sergej, and Jo Crotty. 2014. "Civil Society in a Transitional Context: The Response of Health and Educational NGOs to Legislative Changes in Russia's Industrialized Regions." *Nonprofit and Voluntary Sector Quarterly* 43(4): 759–76.

Lord, Peter B. 2010. "After Century-Long Decline, Rhode Island Farms Are Experiencing a Growth Spurt." *Providence Journal*, November 13. Retrieved January 31, 2011 (http://www.projo.com/news/content/Farms_rebounding_11-13-10_IEKSLPD_v37.3a48a5e.html).

Ma, Qiusha. 2002a. "Defining Chinese Nongovernmental Organizations." *VOLUNTAS: International Journal of Voluntary and Nonprofit Organizations* 13(2): 113–30.

———. 2002b. "The Governance of NGOs in China since 1978: How Much Autonomy?" *Nonprofit and Voluntary Sector Quarterly* 31(3): 305–28.

Magistad, Mary Kay. 2012. "How Weibo Is Changing China." *Yale Global Online*, August 9. Retrieved October 12, 2012 (http://yaleglobal.yale.edu/content/how-weibo-changing-china).

McAdam, Doug, Robert J. Sampson, Simon Weffer, and Heather MacIndoe. 2005. "'There Will Be Fighting in the Streets': The Distorting Lens of Social Movement Theory." *Mobilization: An International Quarterly* 10(1): 1–18.

McCarthy, John D., and Mayer N. Zald. 1977a. "Resource Mobilization and Social Movements: A Partial Theory." *American Journal of Sociology* 82(6): 1212–41.

———. 1977b. "The Trend of Social Movements in America: Professionalization and Resource Mobilization." Center for Research on Social Organization. CRSO Working Paper no. 164. (http://hdl.handle.net/2027.42/50939)

McCarthy, Kathleen D. 1982. Noblesse Oblige: Charity and Cultural Philanthropy in Chicago, 1849–1929. Chicago: University of Chicago Press.

Millhaupt, Curtis J. 2004. "Nonprofit Organizations as Investor Protection: Economic

Theory and Evidence from East Asia." *Yale Journal of International Law* 29(169): 169–207.

Ming, Wang, and Xu Yushan. 2010. "Foundations in China." *China Nonprofit Review* 2(1): 19–51.

Ministry of Civil Affairs of the People's Republic of China. 2010. "Statistics on Development of Civil Administration in China." (http://www.mca.gov.cn/article/zwgk/mzyw/201506/20150600832371.shtml)

Minkoff, Debra C. 1999. "Bending with the Wind: Strategic Change and Adaptation by Women's and Racial Minority Organizations." *American Journal of Sociology* 104(6): 1666–1703.

Mirowski, Philip, and Dieter Plehwe, eds. 2009. *The Road from Mont Pelerin: The Making of the Neoliberal Thought Collective.* Cambridge, MA: Harvard University Press.

Moore, Louella. 2001. "Legitimation Issues in the State-Nonprofit Relationship." *Nonprofit and Voluntary Sector Quarterly* 30(4): 707–19.

Morris, Aldon D., and Suzanne Staggenborg. 2007. "Leadership in Social Movements." In *The Blackwell Companion to Social Movements*, edited by David A. Snow, Sarah A. Soule, and Hanspeter Kriesi, 171–96. Malden, MA: Blackwell.

Moulaert, Frank, and Oana Ailenei. 2005. "Social Economy, Third Sector and Solidarity Relations: A Conceptual Synthesis from History to Present." *Urban Studies* 42(11): 2037–53.

Nanami, Akiko. 2007. "Showing Japan's Face or Creating Powerful Challengers? Are NGOs Really Partners to the Government in Japan's Foreign Aid?" Diss., University of Canterbury.

National Center for Charitable Statistics. 2011. "Core Files." Retrieved October 2, 2013 (http://nccs.urban.org/database/overview.cfm#core).

National Council of Nonprofits. 2013. "State Law Nonprofit Audit Requirements." Retrieved September 8, 2013 (http://www.councilofnonprofits.org/nonprofit-audit-guide/state-law-audit-requirements).

Navarro, Clemente J., ed. 2012. *Las dimensiones culturales de la ciudad: Creatividad, entretenimiento y difusión cultural en las ciudades españolas.* Madrid: Los Libros de la Catarata.

Newson, Marc, and Craig Deegan. 2002. "Global Expectations and Their Association with Corporate Social Disclosure Practices in Australia, Singapore, and South Korea." *International Journal of Accounting* 37(2): 183–213.

Newton, Kenneth. 1997. "Social Capital and Democracy." *American Behavioral Scientist* 40(5): 575–86.

———. 2001. "Trust, Social Capital, Civil Society, and Democracy." *International Political Science Review* 22(2): 201–14.

Newton, Kenneth, and Pippa Norris. 1999. "Confidence in Public Institutions: Faith, Culture or Performance." Paper prepared for Annual Meeting of the American Political Science Association, Atlanta, GA, September 1–5.

Norris, Pippa. 1999. Critical Citizens : Global Support for Democratic Government: Global Support for Democratic Government. Oxford: Oxford University Press.

Nyssens, Marthe, Sophie Adam, and Toby Johnson. 2006. Social Enterprise: At the Crossroads of Market, Public Policies and Civil Society. London: Routledge.

Olson, Mancur. 1982. The Rise and Decline of Nations: Economic Growth, Stagflation, and Social Rigidities. New Haven, CT: Yale University Press.

Osborne, Stephen P. 2003. The Voluntary and Non-profit Sector in Japan: The Challenge of Change. London: Routledge.

Osborne, Stephen P., Kate McLaughlin, and Taro Miyamoto. 2003. "Managing the Japanese Voluntary and Non-profit Sector: An Agenda for the Future." In The Nonprofit Sector in Japan: The Challenge of Change, edited by Stephen P. Osborne, 221–31. London: Routledge.

Ospina, Sonia, William Diaz, and James F. O'Sullivan. 2002. "Negotiating Accountability: Managerial Lessons from Identity-Based Nonprofit Organizations." Nonprofit and Voluntary Sector Quarterly 31(1): 5–31.

Paoli, Letizia. 2004. "Italian Organised Crime: Mafia Associations and Criminal Enterprises." Global Crime 6(1): 19–31.

Park, Chan-ung, and S. V. Subramanian. 2012. "Voluntary Association Membership and Social Cleavages: A Micro-Macro Link in Generalized Trust." Social Forces 90(4): 1183–1205.

Park, Tae-Kyu, Ku-Hyun Jung, S. Wojciech Sokolowski, and Lester M. Salamon. 2004. "South Korea." In Global Civil Society: Dimensions of the Nonprofit Sector, edited by Lester M. Salamon and S. Wojciech Sokolowski, 200–214. Bloomfield, CT: Kumarian Press.

Paxton, Pamela. 2002. "Social Capital and Democracy: An Interdependent Relationship." American Sociological Review 67(2): 254–77.

Paxton, Pamela. 2007. "Association Memberships and Generalized Trust: A Multilevel Model Across 31 Countries." Social Forces 86(1): 47–76.

Peck, Jamie, Nik Theodore, and Neil Brenner. 2010. "Postneoliberalism and Its Malcontents." Antipode 41: 94–116.

Pelchat, Marie-Claude. 2004. "Enterprising Asian NPOs: Social Entrepreneurship in Taiwan." Paper prepared for the Conference of Asian Foundations and Organizations, Asian Institute of Management, Makati City, Philippines.

Peng, Jianmei, and Youping Liu. 2012. Report of the Philanthropy Study on International NGOs (USA Section) in China. Zurich: China Charity Information Center.

Perry, Elizabeth J. 1994. "Introduction: Chinese Political Culture Revisited." In Popular Protest and Political Culture in Modern China, 2nd ed., edited by Jeffrey N. Wasserstrom and Elizabeth J. Perry, 1–14. Boulder, CO: Westview Press.

Piattoni, Simona. 2001. Clientelism, Interests, and Democratic Representation: The European Experience in Historical and Comparative Perspective. Cambridge, UK: Cambridge University Press.

Polletta, Francesca, and James M. Jasper. 2001. "Collective Identity and Social Movements." Annual Review of Sociology 27: 283–305.

Prize4Life website. N.d. Retrieved March 20, 2016 (http://www.prize4life.org).

Przeworski, Adam, and Henry Teune. [1970] 2001. *The Logic of Comparative Social Inquiry*. Malabar, FL: Krieger.

Putnam, Robert D. 1993. *Making Democracy Work: Civic Traditions in Modern Italy*. Princeton, NJ: Princeton University Press.

———. 1995. "Tuning In, Tuning Out: The Strange Disappearance of Social Capital in America." *Political Science and Politics* 28(4): 664–83.

———. 2000. Bowling Alone: The Collapse and Revival of American Community. New York: Simon & Schuster.

———. 2012. "The Prosperous Community: Social Capital and Public Life." In *Cross Currents: Cultures, Communities, Technologies*, by Kristine L. Blair, Jen Almjeld, and Robin M. Murphy, 249–58. Boston: Wadsworth, Cengage Learning.

Reimann, Kim D. 2006. "A View from the Top: International Politics, Norms, and the Worldwide Growth of NGOs." *International Studies Quarterly* 50: 45–67.

Republic of China. 2006. "Charity Donations Destined for Social Welfare Funds Implementation Regulations." May 17. *Laws & Regulations Database of the Republic of China*. Ministry of Health and Welfare. Retrieved February 13, 2011 (http://law .moj.gov.tw/Eng/LawClass/LawAll.aspx?PCode=D0050138).

Roeger, Katie L., Amy Blackwood, and Sarah L. Pettijohn. 2011. "The Nonprofit Sector in Brief: Public Charities, Giving, and Volunteering." Chicago: National Center for Charitable Statistics at the Urban Institute. (http://www.urban.org /UploadedPDF/412434-NonprofitAlmanacBrief2011.pdf)

———. 2012. *The Nonprofit Almanac 2012*. Washington, DC: Urban Institute Press.

Rosenberg, Morris. 1956. "Misanthropy and Political Ideology." *American Sociological Review* 21(6): 690–95.

Rothstein, Bo, and Dietlind Stolle. 2001. "Social Capital and Street-Level Bureaucracy: An Institutional Theory of Generalized Trust." Paper prepared for the Trust in Government Conference at the Center for the Study of Democratic Politics, Princeton University, November 30.

———. 2007. "The Quality of Government and Social Capital: A Theory of Political Institutions and Generalized Trust." QoG Working Paper Series 2007:2. Göteborg: Quality of Government Institute, Göteborg University.

Rucht, Dieter. 1999. "Linking Organization and Mobilization: Michels's Iron Law of Oligarchy Reconsidered." *Mobilization: An International Quarterly* 4(2): 151–69.

Rusbridger, Alan. 2015. "Climate Change: Why the Guardian Is Putting Threat to Earth Front and Centre." *Guardian*, March 6. (http://www.theguardian.com/environment /2015/mar/06/climate-change-guardian-threat-to-earth-alan-rusbridger)

Ruskie, Stasia Elizabeth. 2015. "'You Came to Not Normal Land': Nurses' Experience of the Environment of Disaster: A Phenomenological Investigation." PhD dissertation, University of Tennessee, 2. (http://trace.tennessee.edu/utk_graddiss/3604)

Saich, Tony. 2000. "Negotiating the State: The Development of Social Organizations in China." *China Quarterly* no. 161: 124–41.

Salamon, Lester M. 1995. Partners in Public Service: Government-Nonprofit Relations in the Modern Welfare State. Baltimore: Johns Hopkins University Press.

———, ed. 2002. *The State of Nonprofit America*. Washington, DC: Brookings Institution Press.

———. 2003. *The Resilient Sector: The State of Nonprofit America*. Washington, DC: Brookings Institution Press.

Salamon, Lester M., and Helmut K. Anheier. 1996. *The Emerging Nonprofit Sector: An Overview*. Manchester, UK: Manchester University Press.

———. 1997. *Defining the Nonprofit Sector: A Cross-National Analysis*. Manchester, UK: Manchester University Press.

Salamon, Lester, Megan A. Haddock, S. Wojciech Sokolowski, and Helen S. Tice. 2007. "Measuring Civil Society and Volunteering: Initial Findings from Implementation of the UN Handbook on Nonprofit Institutions." Working paper no. 23. Baltimore: Johns Hopkins Center for Civil Society Studies. (http://ccss.jhu.edu/wp-content/uploads/downloads/2011/08/Measuring-Civil-Society.pdf)

Salamon, Lester, Leslie C. Hems, and Kathryn Chinnock. 2000. "The Nonprofit Sector: For What and for Whom?" Working Papers of the Johns Hopkins Comparative Nonprofit Sector Project, no. 37. Baltimore: Johns Hopkins Center for Civil Society Studies.

Salamon, Lester M., and S. Wojciech Sokolowski. 2004. *Global Civil Society: Dimensions of the Nonprofit Sector*. Baltimore: Kumarian Press.

Salamon, Lester M., S. Wojciech Sokolowski, and Stephanie Geller. 2012. "Holding the Fort: Nonprofit Employment during a Decade of Turmoil." Nonprofit Employment Bulletin no. 39. Baltimore: Johns Hopkins University Center for Civil Society Studies.

Samsung Foundation. 2013. "The Samsung Foundation of Culture." Retrieved April 15, 2013 (http://www.samsungfoundation.org/html/eng/foundation/culture_foundation.asp).

San Francisco AIDS Foundation. 2011. "Home—San Francisco AIDS Foundation." Retrieved February 14, 2011 (http://www.sfaf.org/).

San Francisco AIDS Foundation. 2016. "Black Brothers Esteem." Retrieved February 29, 2016 (http://sfaf.org/client-services/black-brothers-esteem/).

Sang-hun, Choe. 2008. "Beef Protest Turns Violent in South Korea." *New York Times*, June 30. Retrieved July 4, 2013 (http://www.nytimes.com/2008/06/30/world/asia/30korea.html).

Santos, Boaventura de Sousa. 2002. *Toward a New Legal Common Sense: Law, Globalization, and Emancipation*. 2nd ed. London: Butterworths LexisNexis.

Sargent, John, and Richard Wiltshire, eds. 1993. *Geographical Studies and Japan*. London: Routledge.

Sawyer, Stephen, ed. 2011. *Une cartographie culturelle de Paris-Métropole*. Paris: Rapport a la Mairie de Paris.

Scenes Overview. N.d. Retrieved March 16, 3016 (http://www.tnc-newsletter.blogspot.ca/).

Scenes Project. N.d. "Scenescapes." Retrieved March 16, 2016 (http://scenescapes.weebly.com/).

Schofer, Evan, and Marion Fourcade-Gourinchas. 2001. "The Structural Contexts of Civic Engagement: Voluntary Association Membership in Comparative Perspective." *American Sociological Review* 66(6): 806–28.

Sellers, Jefferey M. 2002. *Governing from Below: Urban Regions and the Global Economy*. Cambridge, UK: Cambridge University Press.

Sellers, Jefferey M., Daniel Kübler, Melanie Walter-Rogg, and Robert Alan Walks. 2013a. "Conclusion: Metropolitan Political Behavior in Comparative Perspective." In *The Political Ecology of the Metropolis: Metropolitan Sources of Electoral Behaviour in Eleven Countries*, edited by Jefferey M. Sellers, Daniel Kübler, Melanie Walter-Rogg, and Robert Alan Walks. Colchester, UK: ECPR Press.

———, eds. 2013b. The Political Ecology of the Metropolis: Metropolitan Sources of Electoral Behaviour in Eleven Countries. Colchester, UK: ECPR Press.

Shanti Project. 2011. "Shanti.org." Retrieved February 14, 2011 (http://www.shanti.org/).

Shattuck, Roger. 1958. The Banquet Years; The Arts in France, 1885–1918: Alfred Jarry, Henri Rousseau, Erik Satie, Guillaume Apollinaire. New York: Harcourt, Brace.

Shieh, Shawn, and Amanda Brown-Inz. 2013. "Mapping China's Public Interest NGOs." In *Chinese NGO Directory: A Civil Society in the Making*. Beijing: China Development Brief.

Shieh, Shawn, and Signe Knutson. 2013. *The Roles and Challenges of International NGOs in China's Development*. Beijing: China Development Brief.

Shue, Vivienne. 1994. "State Power and Social Organization in China." In *State Power and Social Forces: Domination and Transformation in the Third World*, edited by Joel S. Migdal, Atul Kohli, and Vivienne Shue, 65–88. New York: Cambridge University Press.

Silva, Filipe Carreira da. 2010. *Mead and Modernity: Science, Selfhood, and Democratic Politics*. Lanham, MD: Lexington Books.

Silver, Daniel, and Terry Nichols Clark. 2016. *Scenescapes: How Qualities of Place Shape Social Life*. Chicago: University of Chicago Press.

Silver, Daniel, Terry Nichols Clark, and Chris Graziul. 2011. "Scenes, Innovation, and Urban Development." In *Handbook of Creative Cities*, edited by David Emanuel Andersson, Åke E. Andersson, and Charlotta Mellander, 229–58. Cheltenham, UK: Edward Elgar.

Smith, Steven Rathgeb. 2006. "Government Financing of Nonprofit Activity." in *Nonprofits and Government: Collaboration and Conflict*, edited by Elizabeth T. Boris and C. Eugene Steurele, 219–56. Washington, DC: Urban Institute Press.

Snow, David A. 2007. "Framing Processes, Ideology, and Discursive Fields." In *The Blackwell Companion to Social Movements* edited by David A. Snow, Sarah A. Soule, and Hanspeter Kriesi, 380–412. Malden, MA: Blackwell.

Sodei, Takako. 1993. "Tradition Impedes Empowerment in Japan." *Ageing International* 20(1): 22–26.

Soros, George. 2004. Underwriting Democracy: Encouraging Free Enterprise and Democratic Reform among the Soviets and in Eastern Europe. New York: PublicAffairs.

Spires, Anthony J. 2011. "Organizational Homophily in International Grantmaking: US-Based Foundations and Their Grantees in China." *Journal of Civil Society* 7(3): 305–31.

Steel, Brent S. 1996. "Thinking Globally and Acting Locally? Environmental Attitudes, Behaviour and Activism." *Journal of Environmental Management* 47(1): 27–36.

Stolle, Dietlind. 1998. "Bowling Together, Bowling Alone: The Development of Generalized Trust in Voluntary Associations." *Political Psychology* 19(3): 497–525.

Stolle, Dietlind, and Thomas R. Rochon. 1998. "Are All Associations Alike? Member Diversity, Associational Type, and the Creation of Social Capital." *American Behavioral Scientist* 42(1): 47–65.

Stride, Helen, and Malcolm Higgs. 2014. "An Investigation into the Relationship between Values and Commitment: A Study of Staff in the U.K. Charity Sector." *Nonprofit and Voluntary Sector Quarterly* 43(3): 455–79.

Suzuki, Yasushi. 2007. "Chonaikai." In *The Blackwell Encyclopedia of Sociology*, edited by George Ritzer. Oxford: Blackwell. (http://www.blackwellreference.com/public /uid=31/tocnode?id=g9781405124331_yr2015_chunk_g97814051243319_ss1–33)

Takao, Yasuo. 2009. "Aging and Political Participation in Japan: The Dankai Generation in a Political Swing." *Asian Survey* 49(5): 852–72.

Tang, Wenfang. 2009. "Interpersonal Trust and Democracy in China." Paper prepared for the Annual Meeting of the American Political Science Association, Philadelphia, December 16. (http://www.asianbarometer.org/publications/3c07a171c9b89 b9aad5c0c2e371b346f.pdf)

Teegan, Hildy, Jonathan P. Doh, and Sushil Vachani. 2004. "The Importance of Nongovernmental Organizations (NGOs) in Global Governance and Value Creation: An International Business Research Agenda." *Journal of International Business Studies* 35(6): 463–83.

Terao, Tadayoshi. 2002. "Taiwan: From Subjects of Oppression to the Instruments of 'Taiwanization.'" In *The State of NGOs: Perspective from Asia*, edited by Shinichi Shigetomi, 263–87. Singapore: Institute of Southeastern Studies.

———. 2007. "An Institutional Analysis of Environmental Pollution Disputes in Taiwan: Cases of 'Self-Relief.'" *Developing Economies* 40(3): 284–304.

Thompson, Derek. 2011. "Occupy the World: The '99 Percent' Movement Goes Global." *Atlantic*, October 15. Retrieved October 15, 2011 (http://www.theatlantic .com/business/archive/2011/10/occupy-the-world-the-99-percent-movement -goes-global/246757/).

Thornton, Jeremy. 2006. "Nonprofit Fund-Raising in Competitive Donor Markets." *Nonprofit and Voluntary Sector Quarterly* 35(2): 204–24.

Thornton, Patricia H., and William Ocasio. 1999. "Institutional Logics and the Historical Contingency of Power in Organizations: Executive Succession in the Higher Education Publishing Industry, 1958–1990." *American Journal of Sociology* 105(3): 801–43.

Tocqueville, Alexis de. [1835] 1969. *Democracy in America*. Reprint, Garden City, NY: Doubleday.

Trounstine, Jessica. 2008. *Political Monopolies in American Cities: The Rise and Fall of Bosses and Reformers.* Chicago: University of Chicago Press.

Tuan, Yang. 2011. *Annual Report on China's Philanthropy Development.* 2011. 北京市. 2011. Beijing: Social Sciences Academic Press.

Twu, Ruey-der. 2010. "The Growth and Transformation of the Nonprofit Sector in Taiwan." *Comment of Current Affairs* 11(1): 23–46.

Ullman, Claire F. 1998. *The Welfare State's Other Crisis: Explaining the New Partnership between Nonprofit Organizations and the State in France.* Bloomington: Indiana University Press.

US Congress. Joint Committee on Taxation. 2005. "Historical Development and Present Law of the Federal Tax Exemption for Charities and Other Tax-Exempt Organizations." Prepared for hearing on April 20, 2005.

US Department of Health and Human Services. 1993. "Family Preservation and Support Services Program Act of 1993—P.L. 103–66." Omnibus Budget Reconciliation Act of 1993. Retrieved January 23, 2011 (https://www.govtrack.us/congress/bills/103/hr2264/text/rh).

US Internal Revenue Service. 2008. "IRS Statistics of Income." 2008. *Charities & Other Tax-Exempt Organizations.* (http://www.irs.gov/pub/irs-soi/11esgiftsnap.pdf)

———. 2010. "Publication 557 (10/2010), Tax-Exempt Status for Your Organization." (http://www.irs.gov/publications/p557/index.html)

———. 2011. "Life Cycle of an Exempt Organization." Retrieved February 14, 2011 (http://www.irs.gov/charities/article/0,,id=169727,00.html).

———. 2013. "Application for Recognition of Exemption." Retrieved October 1, 2013 (http://www.irs.gov/Charities-&-Non-Profits/Application-for-Recognition-of-Exemption).

Uslaner, Eric M. 2000. "Producing and Consuming Trust." *Political Science Quarterly* 115(4): 569–90.

———. 2002. *The Moral Foundations of Trust.* New York: Cambridge University Press.

———. 2007. "Trust and Risk: Implications for Management." In *Trust in Cooperative Risk Management: Uncertainty and Scepticism in the Public Mind,* edited by Michael Siegrist, Timothy C. Earle, and Heinz Gutscher, 73–93. London: Earthscan.

———. 2008. "Trust as a Moral Value." In *The Handbook of Social Capital,* edited by Dario Castiglione, Jan W. Van Deth, and Guglielmo Wolleb, 101–21. Oxford: Oxford University Press.

Uslaner, Eric M., and Mitchell Brown. 2005. "Inequality, Trust, and Civic Engagement." *American Politics Research* 33(6): 868–94.

Venkataraman, Bina. 2011. "$1 Million Prize to Inventor of a Tracker for A.L.S." *New York Times,* February 3. Retrieved February 10, 2011 (http://www.nytimes.com/2011/02/08/health/08als.html?_r=1&scp=1&sq=prize4life&st=cse).

Verba, Sidney, and Norman Nie. 1972. *Participation in America: Political Democracy and Social Equality.* New York: Harper & Row.

Verbruggen, Sandra, Johan Christiaens, and Koen Milis. 2010. "Can Resource Dependence and Coercive Isomorphism Explain Nonprofit Organizations' Compliance with Reporting Standards?" *Nonprofit and Voluntary Sector Quarterly,* April 21. Retrieved October 22, 2010 (http://nvs.sagepub.com/content/early/2010/04/13/0899764009355061.abstract?rss=1&utm_source=twitterfeed&utm_medium=twitter).

Walzer, Michael. 1998. *Toward a Global Civil Society.* Providence, RI: Berghahn Books.

Wang, Fang. 1994. "The Political Economy of Authoritarian Clientelism in Taiwan." In *Democracy, Clientelism, and Civil Society,* edited by Luis Roniger and Ayse Gunes-Ayata, 181–206. Boulder, CO: Lynne Rienner.

Wang, Rachel. 2013. "Why No One Trusts Government Charities in China Anymore." *Atlantic,* March 13. (http://www.theatlantic.com/china/archive/2013/03/why-no-one-trusts-government-charities-in-china-anymore/273989/)

Wang, Shouguan, and Jianyu He. 2004. "Associational Revolution in China: Mapping the Landscapes." *Korea Observer* 35(3): 485–533. (http://www.cuhk.edu.hk/gpa/wang_files/NGO.pdf)

Warren, Mark E. 1996. "Deliberative Democracy and Authority." *American Political Science Review* 90(1): 46–60.

Weber, Max. 1947. *The Theory of Social and Economic Organization.* Translated by A. M. Henderson and Talcott Parsons. New York: Oxford University Press.

———. 1967. *Ancient Judaism.* Translated by Hans H. Gerth and Don Martindale. New York: Simon and Schuster.

———. 1968. *The Religion of China: Confucianism and Taoism.* Translated by Hans H. Gerth. Glencoe, IL: Free Press.

———. 2008. *The Protestant Ethic and the Spirit of Capitalism.* Digireads.com. La Vergne, TN: Ingram.

Wilensky, Harold L. 1964. "The Professionalization of Everyone?" *American Journal of Sociology* 70(2): 137–58.

Wilson, James Q. 1962. *The Amateur Democrat: Club Politics in Three Cities.* Chicago: University of Chicago Press.

Wirgau, Jessica, Kathryn Farley, and Courtney Jensen. 2010. "Is Business Discourse Colonizing Philanthropy? A Critical Discourse Analysis of (PRODUCT) RED." *Voluntas: International Journal of Voluntary and Nonprofit Organizations* 21(4): 611–30.

Wollebaek, Dag, and Per Selle. 2002. "Does Participation in Voluntary Associations Contribute to Social Capital? The Impact of Intensity, Scope, and Type." *Nonprofit and Voluntary Sector Quarterly* 31(1): 32–61.

Women's Intercultural Center. 2011. "Welcome to the Women's Intercultural Center." Retrieved January 23, 2011 (http://www.womensinterculturalcenter.org/).

Wong, Edward. 2011. "Online Scandal Underscores Chinese Distrust of Charities." *New York Times,* July 3. Retrieved August 6, 2013 (http://www.nytimes.com/2011/07/04/world/asia/04china.html).

World Relief Spokane. 2011. "Becoming a Volunteer Changed My Life." December 15. Retrieved February 29, 2016 (http://worldreliefspokane.org/how-becoming-a-volunteer-changed-my-life).

World Values Survey. 2008. World Values Survey Database. Retrieved March 14, 2016 (http://www.worldvaluessurvey.org/WVSDocumentationWV5.jsp).

Worms, Jean-Pierre. 2002. "France: Old and New Civic and Social Ties in France." In *Democracies in Flux: The Evolution of Social Capital in Contemporary Society*, edited by Robert D. Putnam, 137–188. Oxford: Oxford University Press. Retrieved September 26, 2013 (http://www.oxfordscholarship.com/view/10.1093/0195150899 .001.0001/acprof-9780195150896).

Yamamoto, Tadashi. 1998. *The Nonprofit Sector in Japan*. Manchester, UK: Manchester University Press.

Yang, Tuan. 2011. *Annual Report on China's Philanthropy Development*. Beijing: Social Sciences Academic Press.

YAYA, Inc. 2012. "YAYA: Young Aspirations/Young Artists." Retrieved October 26, 2010 (http://www.yayainc.com).

Ylvisaker, Paul N. 1987. "Foundations and Nonprofit Organizations." In *The Nonprofit Sector: A Research Handbook*, edited by Walter W. Powell, 360–79. New Haven, CT: Yale University Press.

Young, Dennis R. 2000. "Alternative Models of Government-Nonprofit Sector Relations: Theoretical and International Perspectives." *Nonprofit and Voluntary Sector Quarterly* 29(1): 149–72.

Zhang, Yang. 2010. "The Political Logic of Xiamen Anti-PX Movement in China." Paper presented to the East Asia Workshop, University of Chicago, Chicago.

Zheng, Jane. 2010. "The 'Entrepreneurial State' in 'Creative Industry Cluster' Development in Shanghai." *Journal of Urban Affairs* 32(2): 143–70.

Ziner, Karen Lee. 2010. "Days Later, a Turkey's Work Is Never Done." *Providence Journal*, November 28. Retrieved January 31, 2011 (http://www.projo.com/news /content/TURKEY_COMPOST_11-28-10_L5L612D_v23.388f06b.html).

Index

501(c)(3) status, 73

activism: associational life and, 191; in China, 169, 170, 187; corporatization of, 58, 217; decentralized/social media, 24–26, 218; in France, 105–7, 114, 121; identity and, 55, 225; institutional logic of, 15–16, 52–53, 55, 57, 214, 223–24; in Japan, 21, 130–32; morality and, 7, 12, 29; "scenes" as, 217; social movements and, 55; in South Korea, 141, 144, 146, 149, 151; in Taiwan, 155, 163; in the United States, 68, 86, 87, 102–4; youth and, 218
A.D.S.E.A., 118–20
advocacy, 1, 3, 6, 38, 53, 213, 221; food-related, 93; in France, 114, 118–23; in journalism, 35; in social services, 96–103; in South Korea, 144–50, 164
arts, 146, 162, 201, 217; income from, 81, 82; in nonprofit employment, 70; in policy, 32; professionalization and, 86–87; social services and, 66–67; in South Korea, 156
associationalism, 2, 114, 149, 195; Calvinism and, 8–9; civil society and, 37; nonprofits and, 68; political life and, 27; Tocqueville and, 5–7
authoritarianism: in China, 171, 173; clientelism and, 19; identity and, 225; in South Korea, 143, 149; in Taiwan, 155, 156, 158; trust and, 44

Banfield, Edward, 42, 45
Beef Protests, 149–51
bonding ties, 197–98, 204
bridging ties, 197–98, 204
Broadbent, Jeffrey, 131, 137–40
bureaucracy: in China, 176, 180; in France, 106, 107, 109, 117, 118; in government-civil society relationships, 38; institutional logic of, 12, 14, 15, 17, 219, 222; international NGOs and, 52, 54; in Japan, 124, 125, 130–32; in social enterprise, 60; in South Korea, 146, 148, 151, 169; and state interaction, 214; in the United States, 68

Calvinism, 7, 8, 28, 31, 45, 59
capitalism, 12, 28, 42, 109, 117, 118
CAREUS, 164–65
Catholicism: Calvinism and, 7, 8; in France, 105, 106, 110, 199, 216; post-Reformation, 35; Sisters of Mercy and, 87; trust and, 43
charity, 77, 108, 114; Calvinism and, 8; Charity Law, 183; clientelism and, 13; paternalism and, 14, 17; the third sector and, 34
Chicago, 13, 17, 25, 32
Children Are Us Foundation (CAREUS), 164–65
China, 2–3, 16, 23, 28, 39, 59, 157, 168–90
Chōnaikai, 132–34, 170–72
Church of England, 31
Cimade (Committee for the Inter-movement of Evacuees), 120–21

civic groups, 216, 217; in China, 187; *guanxi*, 41; in South Korea, 143, 151, 159, 163; state cooperation and, 213; trust and, 191; types of, 31–32; in the United States, 69, 109

clientelism: institutional logic of, 12, 13, 15, 18–21, 214, 220, 222; and "scenes," 217; in Taiwan, 155, 158, 163

Colombia, 32, 33, 49, 50, 51

Confuciansim, 141–43, 155

consumption patterns, 146, 149, 170, 186, 191, 216

cooperatives, 62, 64, 109–16, 143, 159

corporate responsibility, 63, 82, 95

crime, 8, 9, 31, 111

critical mass, 24–25

decentralization: in China, 175; in France, 107, 108, 111, 113, 117; legitimacy and, 2, 33, 34; neoliberalism and, 223, 224

democracy, 1–37, 191–93, 217, 221; in China, 173; in Italy, 43; in Japan, 138; in South Korea, 146, 149; in Taiwan, 155

Departmental Association for the Protection of Children and Adolescents (A.D.S.E.A.), 118–20

distrust, 193, 196–211. *See also* trust

donations: in China, 176, 179, 181–82; in France, 116; in Japan, 126, 130; Planned Parenthood and, 19–20; social enterprise and, 64–65; in South Korea, 149; in Taiwan, 160–62; in the United States, 73, 81

Eden Social Welfare Foundation, 165–68

education, 70–72, 88, 114, 148, 157, 200; activism and, 16; New Political Culture and, 46–49; nonprofit, 28–29; political orientation and, 10

educational foundations, 158

elections, 42, 122, 191, 219

emotional investment, 97, 98, 194

emotions, 27, 32, 217

England, 8, 31, 32, 218

environmental movement, 16, 22, 23, 30, 199–201; in China, 187–90; in Japan, 137–40; in South Korea, 151–54

evaluation, 53–59, 76–86

Farm Fresh Rhode Island, 93–95

federations, 187

feminism, 16, 23, 29, 107, 114

financial crisis, 31, 112

foundations: corporate, 129; in China, 177, 179, 181; family, 14, 222; in France, 109, 116; institutional logics and, 51–57; in Japan, 126–30; in nonprofit workforce, 50; professionalization and, 14–20; in South Korea, 145, 147–48; in Taiwan, 159–61; tax exemption and, 34; in the United States, 69, 73, 79, 82

framing, 23, 55

Germany, 22, 23, 33, 62, 197

globalization, 2, 10, 11, 52, 157, 186, 203

GONGOs (government-organized NGOs), 158, 169, 171–74, 179–82, 189

grassroots organizing, 1, 89, 99, 179–82, 207, 223; activism and, 15; foundations and, 55; Japanese NPOs and, 125

guanxi, 41, 156, 170, 171

Habermas, Jürgen, 1, 5, 37

Healthy Families/Thriving Communities Collaborative Council, 95–98

HIV/AIDS, 98–103

human rights, 16, 23, 52, 106, 126, 146

Human Rights League, The, 121–23

institutional logics, 1–37, 222–23

Internet, organizing via, 24–26. *See also* social media

Italy, 9, 42, 43, 49

KMT (Kuomintang/Chinese Nationalist Party), 155, 156, 158, 161, 168

Korean Federation for Environmental Movements (KFEM), 151–54

Latin America, 9, 32, 33, 46, 87, 170

legitimacy, 2, 3, 82, 85, 219; associations and, 27; evaluation and, 76; in foundations, 55, 57; institutional logics and, 12; political, 33, 38

Luther, Martin, 7

Lutheranism, 7

moralism, 12, 23, 29, 35, 47, 221

music, 32, 104, 164, 199–201, 204–11; in demonstrations, 27, 217

mutual societies, 109, 113, 114–15

neoliberalism, 9–11, 46, 58, 61

New Political Culture, 9–11, 45–47, 112, 157, 216; in China, 185–88

New Social Movements, 22–28, 108, 111–14, 126, 157, 217
newspapers, 121, 130, 145, 189

online organizing, 24–26. *See also* social media
organizations, 40–45

participation, 191–95, 207, 215; associations and, 27, 31; in China, 183–85, 188; decline of, 86; democratic, 2, 5; evaluation and, 53; in Japan, 137, 146; organizations and, 40, 43–46; social economy and, 111–15; in Taiwan, 157
paternalism, institutional logic of, 12–15, 19, 54, 60, 117, 215, 222–23
Planned Parenthood, 19
political opportunity structure, 22, 23, 156
political parties, 199, 207, 211, 219, 221; in Europe, 22–23, 33; in France, 117; in Japan, 140, 146; moralism and, 30
postmaterialist values, 22, 204–11
Prize4Life, 91–93
professionalization: in China, 169, 180; evaluation and, 52–55; foundations and, 16–18, 26; in France, 102, 106; institutional logic of, 12, 214, 219; in Japan, 131, 135; social enterprise and, 60; in South Korea, 141, 146; in Taiwan, 156, 162; in the United States, 76–88
Protestantism, 6–7
public interest, 41, 54, 110, 127, 145
Putnam, Robert, 12, 31, 40, 42–45, 86, 191–204

Red Cross, 120, 159, 171, 182, 201
reform and opening, 172, 173
religious organizations, 82, 199–204, 211

San Francisco AIDS Foundation, 98–102
"scenes," 27, 217, 218
Schooner *SoundWaters*, 103–4
Shanti Project, 98–102

social capital, 34, 37–68, 187, 192–201
social economy, 64, 105, 109, 111–17
social enterprise, 60–66, 162, 165, 166
socialism, 22–23, 28, 107–8, 110, 112, 171, 187
social media, 16, 26, 41, 86, 190, 218; Weibo, 183, 185–87. *See also* online organizing
social movements, 217, 220, 223; activism and, 15–19; in France, 108, 111, 114; institutionalization of, 22–28; institutional logics and, 55; in Japan, 126; in Taiwan, 156, 157. *See also* New Social Movements
social services: in France, 113; in Japan, 126, 137; neoliberalism and, 9; nonprofit, 28; in South Korea, 146–49; in the United States, 71–72, 82, 87, 94–103; in the workforce, 50
SoundWaters, 103–4
state interaction, 214–16
statism, 106, 109, 110, 118
Switzerland, 7–9, 31, 199, 200

tax exemption, 34–35, 69, 72, 73, 79, 127
theater, 32, 78, 164
Tocqueville, Alexis de, 1–6, 40–43, 68, 103, 187, 216
trust: dis-, 193, 196–211; generalized, 2, 40, 41, 193, 195, 196; political and social, 192–211

unions, 22: civil society and, 37; in France, 111, 114, 117, 122; in Japan, 137; South Korea, 148, 192; and trust, 199–209

voluntary organizations, 40–41, 72, 75, 176, 192–96, 203
voting, 21, 43, 115, 191, 219, 222

Weibo, 183, 185–87. *See also* social media
Women's Intercultural Center, 87–90

Xiamen, 184, 188–90

Zedong, Mao, 172

MEGHAN ELIZABETH KALLMAN is a Postdoctoral Research Fellow at the Institute at Brown for Environment and Society, Brown University.

TERRY NICHOLS CLARK is a professor of sociology at the University of Chicago and the coauthor of *The Breakdown of Class Politics: A Debate on Post-Industrial Stratification.*

The University of Illinois Press
is a founding member of the
Association of American University Presses.

———————————————————————

University of Illinois Press
1325 South Oak Street
Champaign, IL 61820-6903
www.press.uillinois.edu